The Vagrant

GW01403332

George Gibbs

Alpha Editions

This edition published in 2024

ISBN : 9789362092069

Design and Setting By
Alpha Editions
www.alphaedis.com
Email - info@alphaedis.com

Contents

PROLOGUE

At the piano a man sat playing the "Revolutionary Étude" of Chopin. The room was magnificent in its proportions, its furnishings were massive, its paneled oak walls were hung with portraits of men and women in the costumes of a bygone day. Through the lofty windows, the casements of which were open to the evening sky there was a vista of forest and meadow-land stretching interminably to the setting sun. The mosquelike cupola of a village church, a few versts distant, glimmered like a pearl in the dusky setting of wooded hills, and close by it, here and there, tiny spirals of opalescent smoke marked the dwellings of Zukovo village.

But the man at the piano was detached, a being apart from this scene of quiet, absorbed in his piano, which gave forth the turbulence which had been in the soul of the great composer. The expression upon the dark face of the young musician was rapt and eager, until he crashed the chords to their triumphant conclusion when he sank back in his chair with a gasp, his head bent forward upon his breast, his dark gaze fixed upon the keys which still echoed with the tumult.

It was at this moment that a door at the side of the room was opened and a white-haired man in purple livery entered and stood in silence regarding rather wistfully the man at the piano, who raised his head abruptly like one startled from a dream.

"What is it, Vasili?" asked the musician.

The servant approached softly a few steps.

"I did not wish to intrude, Highness, but——"

As the old servant hesitated, the young man shrugged and rose, disclosing a tall, straight figure, clad in a dark blue blouse, loose trousers and brown boots liberally bespattered with mud. The glow of the sun which shot across his face as he came forward into the light, showed swarthy features, level brows, a straight nose, a well turned chin, a small mustache and a generous mouth which revealed a capacity for humor. He was quite calm now, and the tones of his voice were almost boyish in their confidence and gayety.

"Well, what is it, Vasili?" he repeated. "You have the air of one with much on your conscience. Out with it. Has Sacha been fighting with you again?"

"No, Master, not Sacha," said the old man clearing his throat nervously, "it is something worse—much worse than Sacha."

"Impossible!" said the other with a laugh as he took up a cigarette from the table. "Nothing could be worse than a Russian cook when she gets into a rage——"

"But it is, Master—something worse—much worse——"

"Really! You alarm me." The Grand Duke threw himself into an armchair and inhaled luxuriously of his cigarette. And then with a shrug, "Well?"

The old man came a pace or two nearer muttering hoarsely, "They've broken out in the village again," he gasped.

The Grand Duke's brow contracted suddenly.

"H-m. When did this happen?"

"Last night. And this morning they burned the stables of Prince Galitzin and looted the castle."

The young man sprang to his feet.

"You are sure of this?"

"Yes, Master. The word was brought by Serge Andriev less than ten minutes ago."

He took a few rapid paces up and down the room, stopping by the open window and staring out.

"Fools!" he muttered to himself. Then turning to the old servitor, "But, Vasili—why is it that I have heard nothing of this? To-day Conrad, the forester, said nothing to me. And the day before yesterday in the village the people swept off their caps to me—as in the old days. I could have sworn everything would be peaceful at Zukovo—at least, for the present———" he added as though in an afterthought.

"I pray God that may be true," muttered Vasili uncertainly. And then with unction, "In their hearts, they still love you, Highness. They are children—your children, their hearts still full of reverence for the Grand Duke Peter Nicholaevitch in whom runs the same blood as that which ran in the sacred being of the Little Father—but their brains! They are drunk with the poison poured into their minds by the Committeemen from Moscow."

"Ah," eagerly, "they returned?"

"Last night," replied the old man wagging his head. "And your people forgot all that you had said to them—all that they owe to you. They are mad," he finished despairingly, "mad!"

The Grand Duke had folded his arms and was staring out of the window toward the white dome of the church now dyed red like a globule of blood in the sunset.

The old man watched him for a moment, all the fealty of his many years of service in his gaze and attitude.

"I do not like the look of things, Highness. What does it matter how good their hearts are if their brains are bad?"

"I must go and talk with them, Vasili," said the Grand Duke quietly.

The old man took a step forward.

"If I might make so free——"

"Speak——"

"Not to-night, Master——"

"Why not?"

"It will be dangerous. Last night their voices were raised even against you."

"Me! Why? Have I not done everything I could to help them? I am their friend—because I believe in their cause: and they will get their rights too but not by burning and looting——"

"And murder, Master. Two of Prince Galitzin's foresters were killed."

The Grand Duke turned. "That's bad. Murder in Zukovo!" He flicked his extinguished cigarette out of the window and made a gesture with his hand.

"Go, Vasili. I want to think. I will ring if I need you."

"You will not go to Zukovo to-night?"

"I don't know."

And with another gesture he waved the servant away.

When Vasili had gone, the Grand Duke sat, his legs across the chair by the window, his arms folded along its back while his dark eyes peered out, beyond the hills and forests, beyond the reddened dome of the village church into the past where his magnificent father Nicholas Petrovitch held feudal sway over all the land within his vision and his father's fathers from the time of his own great namesake held all Russia in the hollow of their hands.

The Grand Duke's eyes were hard and bright above the slightly prominent cheek bones, the vestiges of his Oriental origin, but there was something of his English mother too in the contours of his chin and lips, which tempered the hardness of his expression. The lines at his brows were not the savage marks of anger, or the vengefulness that had characterized the pitiless blood which ran in his veins, but rather were they lines of disappointment, of perplexity at the problem that confronted him, and pity for his people who did not know where to turn for guidance. He still believed them to be his people, a heritage from his lordly parent, his children, who were responsible to him and to whom he was responsible. It was a habit of thought, inalienable, the product of the ages. But it was the calm philosophy of his English mother that had first given him his real sense of obligation to them, her teachings, even before the war began, that had shown him how terrible were the problems that confronted his future.

His service in the Army had opened his eyes still wider and when Russia had deserted her allies he had returned to Zukovo to begin the work of reconstruction in the ways his awakened conscience had dictated. He had visited their homes, offered them counsel, given them such money as he could spare, and had, he thought, become their friend as well as their hereditary guardian. All had gone well at first. They had listened to him, accepted his advice and his money and renewed their fealty under the new order of things, vowing that whatever happened elsewhere in Russia, blood and agony and starvation should not visit Zukovo.

But the news that Vasili brought was disquieting. It meant that the minds of his people were again disturbed. And the fact that Prince Galitzin had always been hated made the problems the Grand Duke faced none the less difficult. For his people had burned, pillaged and killed. They had betrayed him. And he had learned in the Army what fire and the smell of blood could do....

With a quick nod of resolution he rose. He would go to them. He knew their leaders. They would listen to him. They must *listen....*

He closed the piano carefully, putting away the loose sheets of music, picked up his cap and heavy riding crop from the divan, on his way to the door, pausing, his hand on the bell-rope as a thought brought a deeper frown to his brow.... Why had Conrad Grabar, his chief forester, said nothing to-day? He must *have known—for news such as this travels from leaf to leaf through the forest. Conrad! And yet he would have sworn by the faithfulness of his old friend and hunting companion. Perhaps Conrad had not known....*

The Grand Duke pulled the bell-rope, then went to the window again and stood as though listening for the voices of the woods. Silence. The sun had sunk, a dull red ball, and the dusk was falling swiftly. The aspens below his window quivered slightly, throwing their white leaves upwards as though in pain. The stately pines that he loved, mute, solemn, changeless, filled the air with balsam, but they gave no answer to his problem. It was difficult to believe that, there, in the restless souls of men war could rage. And yet....

He peered out more intently. Beyond the pine forest, a murky cloud was rising. A storm? Hardly. For the sun had set in a clear sky. But there was a cloud surely, growing in darkness and intensity. He could see it more clearly now, billowing upward in grim portent.

The Grand Duke started and then stared again. The cloud was of smoke. Through the woods, tiny lights were sparkling, picked out with ominous brilliancy against the velvet dusk. Peter Nicholaevitch leaned far out of the window, straining his ears to listen. And now he seemed to hear the crackle of flames, the distant sound of hoarse voices, shouting and singing.

And while he still listened, aware that a great crisis had come into his life, there was a commotion just below him, the sound of voices close at hand and he saw a man come running from the woods, approaching the gateway of the Castle.

He recognized him by the gray beard and thickset figure. It was Boris Rylov, the Huntsman, and as he ran he shouted to some one in the courtyard below. The Grand Duke made out the words:

"They're burning the Hunting Lodge—where is the Master——?"

Peter Nicholaevitch waited at the window no longer, but ran out of the room and down the flight of stairs into the great hall below. For he knew what had happened now. The Red Terror had come to Zukovo.

He went out to the garden terrace, crossing quickly to the courtyard where he met the frightened group of servants that had assembled.

Boris, the Huntsman, much out of breath was waving his arms excitedly toward the cloud of smoke rising above the pine trees, now tinged a dirty orange color from beneath.

"They came from all directions, Master," he gasped, "like the black flies upon a dead horse—hundreds—thousands of them from the village and all the country round. I talked with the first that came, Anton Lensky, Gleb Saltykov, Michael Kuprin and Conrad Grabar——"

"Conrad——!" gasped the Grand Duke.

"Yes, Highness," muttered Boris, his head bowed, "Conrad Grabar. They tried to restrain me. Michael Kuprin I struck upon the head with a stick—and then I fled—to warn your Highness—that they mean to come hither."

The face of the Grand Duke, a trifle pale under its tan, was set in stern lines, but there was no fear in his manner as he quickly questioned, his eyes eagerly scrutinizing the frightened men and women about him while he spoke to them with cool decision.

"Thanks, Friend Rylov—you have done me a service I shall not forget." Then to the others, "If there are any of you who fear to remain with me, you may go. I cannot believe that they will come to Zukovo Castle, but we will close the gate to the courtyard at once. I will talk with them from the terrace wall."

"Master! Highness!" broke in the Huntsman violently, "you do not understand. You cannot stay here. They are mad. They will kill you. It is for that they come——"

"Nevertheless—I mean to stay——"

"It is death——"

"Go thou, then, and Vasili, and Ivan. For before they burn Zukovo, I mean to talk with them——"

"It is madness——!"

"Come, Highness," broke in Leo Garshin, the head-groom, eagerly, "I will put the saddle upon Vera, and you can go out of the iron gate from the stable-yard into the forest. Nothing can catch you and you can reach the river——"

"No, Leo——" put in the Grand Duke kindly. "I shall stay."

The servants glanced at one another, appalled at the Master's attitude. Some of them, had already disappeared into the Castle but others, less timorous, had already rushed to close the courtyard gate.

"You say they are many, Friend Rylov?" he asked again.

"As the hairs of your head, Master—from Ivanovna, Jaroslav—everywhere—and women, Highness, more terrible than the men——"

"And the leaders——?"

"Dmitri Sidorov of the Zemstvo and Michael Kositzin and Anton Lensky. See, yonder! Where the road turns from the clearing—they come!"

The keen eyes of Boris saw further through the forest than those of most men but in a moment those of the Grand Duke Peter confirmed him. Figures were moving in the twilight, along the roads and bypaths.

To Peter Nicholaevitch they seemed like a great river which had flooded over its banks seeking new levels. Behind them the flames from the wooden hunting lodge roared upward painting a lurid sky. He saw that the flood came rapidly, and above the roar of the flames came the sound of voices singing the Russian version of the "Marseillaise." The Grand Duke stood at the terrace wall watching their approach. He knew that if they meant to attack the Castle the gate could not hold long, but he had hope that he might still be able to prevail upon them to listen to him. In a moment they saw him and began running forward toward the courtyard gate. He recognized individuals now—Anton Lensky, Michael Kuprin, with his head tied in a dirty handkerchief—and Conrad Grabar. The defection of his old instructor in wood-lore disturbed him. Conrad must have known what was to happen and he had said nothing. If Conrad had turned against him, what hope had he of prevailing against the others?

The singing died away and in its place, shouts and cries burst forth in a bedlam. "Open the gate!" "Let us in!"

The Grand Duke had heard that note in men's voices in the Carpathian passes, and he knew what it meant, but while his gaze sought out the fat figure of Michael Kositzin who was the leader of the uprising, he held up his hand for silence.

There was a roar of voices.

"Peter Nicholaevitch wishes to speak."

"It is our turn to speak now."

"Nasha pora prishlà," (*our time has come*).

"Let the little master speak."

"We know no little masters here!"

"No, nor old ones!"

"Smiert Bourjouiam" (*Death to the bourgeoisie*).

But as the young Grand Duke began to speak the voices of the most rabid of the peasants were hushed for a moment by the others.

"My friends and my children" he began, "one word before you do something that you will forever regret. I am your friend. I am young—of the new generation. I have kept abreast of the new thought of the time and I believe in the New Life that is for you and for us all. I have proved it to you by bringing the New Life to Zukovo by peaceful means, by friendliness and brotherhood while other parts of Russia near by are in agony and darkness." (Cries of "That is true.") "It was in my heart that I had brought the Revolution to Zukovo, a Revolution against the old order of things which can be no more, implanting in you the strong seeds of Peace and Brotherhood which would kill out the ugly weeds of violence and enmity."

Here a hoarse voice rang out: "Fire—only fire can clean." Then the reply of a woman, "Yes, Tovaristchi, it is the only way."

Peter Nicholaevitch tried to seek out the speakers with his gaze. One of them was Michael Kuprin whom when a child the Grand Duke had seen flogged in this very courtyard.

"There are sins of the past," he went on, raising his voice against the low murmur of the mob, "many sins against you, but one sin does not wash out another. Murder, rapine, vengeance will never bring peace to Zukovo. What you do to-day will be visited on you to-morrow. I pray that you will listen to me. I have fought for you and with you—with Gleb Saltykov and Anton Lensky, against the return of Absolutism in Russia. The old order of things is gone. Do not stain the new with crime in Zukovo. I beseech you to disperse—return to your homes and I will come to you to-morrow and if there are wrongs I will set them right. You have believed in me in the past. Believe in me now and all may yet be well in Zukovo. Go, my friends, before it is too late——"

The crowd wavered, murmuring. But just then a shot rang out and the cap of the Grand Duke twitched around on his head.

A roar went up from near the gate, "Nasha pora prishlà! Break in the gate!" cried the voices and there were those of women among them shouting "Tovaristchi! Forward!"

Over the heads of those in the front ranks, Peter Nicholaevitch saw some men bringing from the forest the heavy trunk of a felled pine tree. They meant to break down the gate. He knew that he had failed but still he stood upright facing them. Another shot, the bullet this time grazing his left arm. The sting of it angered him.

"Cowards!" he yelled, shaking his fist at them. "Cowards!"

A volley followed but no other bullets struck him. Behind him in the Castle doorway he heard the voice of Boris Rylov, calling to him hoarsely.

"Come, Master. For the love of God! There is yet time."

There was a crash of the heavy timbers at the gate.

"Come, Master——"

With a shrug Peter Nicholaevitch turned and walked across the terrace toward the Castle. "Bolvany!" he muttered. "I've finished with them."

Boris and Vasili stood just within the door, pleading with him to hurry, and together they made their way through the deserted kitchens and over past the vegetable gardens to the stables, where Leo Garshin awaited them, the saddles on several horses. Behind them they could now hear the triumphant cries as the courtyard gate crashed in.

"Hurry, Master!" cried Garshin eagerly.

"Where are the others?" asked the Grand Duke.

"Gone, Highness. They have fled."

Boris Rylov was peering out past an iron door into the forest.

"There is no one there?" asked Garshin.

"Not yet. They have forgotten."

"Come then, Highness."

But the Grand Duke saw that the aged Vasili was mounted first and then they rode out of the iron gate into a path which led directly into the forest. It was not until they were well clear of the buildings that a shout at one side announced that their mode of escape had been discovered. Men came running, firing pistols as they ran. Boris Rylov, bringing up the rear, reined in his horse and turning emptied a revolver at the nearest of their pursuers. One man fell and the others halted.

Until they found the other horses in the stables pursuit was fruitless.

Peter Nicholaevitch rode at the head of the little cavalcade, down the familiar aisles of the forest, his head bowed, a deep frown on his brows. It was Vasili who first noticed the blood dripping from his finger ends.

"Master," he gasped, "you are wounded."

"It is nothing," said the Grand Duke.

But Vasili bound the arm up with a handkerchief while Leo Garshin and Boris Rylov watched the path down which they had come. They could hear the crackling of the flames at the Hunting Lodge to the southward and the cries of the mob at the Castle, but there was no sign of pursuit. Perhaps they were satisfied to appease their madness with pillage and fire. Half an hour later Boris pointed backward. A new glow had risen, a redder, deeper glow.

"The Castle, Master——" wailed Vasili.

Peter Nicholaevitch drew rein at a cross-path, watched for a moment and then turned to his companions, for he had reached a decision.

"My good friends," he said gently, "our ways part here."

"Master! Highness!"

But he was resolute.

"I am going on alone. I will not involve you further in my misfortunes. You can do nothing for me—nor I anything for you except this. Vasili knows. In the vault below the wine-cellar, hidden away, are some objects of value. They will not find them. When they go away you will return. The visit will repay you. Divide what is there into equal parts—silver, plate and gold. As for me—forget me. Farewell!"

They saw that he meant what he said. He offered these few faithful servitors his hand and they kissed his fingers—a last act of fealty and devotion and in a moment they stood listening to the diminishing hoof-beats of Vera as the young master went out of their lives.

"May God preserve him," muttered Vasili.

"Amen," said Boris Rylov and Leo Garshin.

CHAPTER I
INTRODUCING PETER NICHOLS

The British refugee ship *Phrygia* was about to sail for Constantinople where her unfortunate passengers were to be transferred to other vessels sailing for Liverpool and New York. After some difficulties the refugee made his way aboard her and announced his identity to the captain. If he had expected to be received with the honor due to one of his rank and station he was quickly undeceived, for Captain Blashford, a man of rough manners, concealing a gentle heart, looked him over critically, examined his credentials (letters he had happened to have about him), and then smiled grimly.

"We've got room for one more—and that's about all."

"I have no money——" began the refugee.

"Oh, that's all right," shrugged the Captain, "you're not the only one. We've a cargo of twenty princes, thirty-two princesses, eighteen generals and enough counts and countesses to set up a new nation somewhere. Your 'Ighness is the only Duke that has reached us up to the present speakin' and if there are any others, they'll 'ave to be brisk for we're sailin' in twenty minutes."

The matter-of-fact tones with which the unemotional Britisher made this announcement restored the lost sense of humor of the Russian refugee, and he broke into a grim laugh.

"An embarrassment of riches," remarked the Grand Duke.

"Riches," grunted the Captain, "in a manner of speakin', yes. Money is not so plentiful. But jools! Good God! There must be half a ton of diamonds, rubies and emeralds aboard. All they're got left most of 'em, but complaints and narvousness. Give me a cargo of wheat and I'm your man," growled the Captain. "It stays put and doesn't complain," and then turning to Peter—"Ye're not expectin' any r'yal suite aboard the *Phrygia*, are ye?"

"No. A hammock for'rad will be good enough for me."

"That's the way I like to 'ear a man talk. Good God! As man to man, I arsk you,—with Counts throwin' cigarette butts around an' princesses cryin' all over my clean white decks an' all, what's a self-respectin' skipper to do? But I 'ave my orders to fetch the odd lot to Constantinople an' fetch 'em I will. Oh! They're odd—all right. Go below, sir, an' 'ave a look at 'em."

But Peter Nicholaevitch shook his head. He had been doing a deal of quiet thinking in those starry nights upon the Dnieper, and he had worked out his problem alone.

"No, thanks," he said quietly, "if you don't mind, I think I'd rather preserve my incognito."

"Incognito, is it? Oh, very well, suit yourself. And what will I be callin' your Highness?"

"Peter Nichols," said the Grand Duke with a smile, "it's as good as any other."

"Right you are, Peter Nichols. Lay for'rad and tell the bos'n to show you up to my cabin."

So Peter Nichols went forward, avoiding the cargo aft, until within a day's run of the Bosphorus when he found himself accosted by no less a person than Prince Galitzin who had strolled out to get the morning air. He tried to avoid the man but Galitzin planted himself firmly in his path, scrutinizing him eagerly.

"You too, Highness!" he said with an accent of grieved surprise.

The Grand Duke regarded him in a moment of silence.

"It must be evident to you, Prince Galitzin, that I have some object in remaining unknown."

"But, Your Highness, such a thing is unnecessary. Are we not all dedicated to the same misfortunes? Misery loves company."

"You mean that it makes you less miserable to discover that I share your fate?"

"Not precisely that. It is merely that if one holding your liberal views cannot escape the holocaust that has suddenly fallen there is little hope for the rest of us."

"No," said the Grand Duke shortly. "There is no hope, none at all, for us or for Russia."

"Where are you going?"

"To America."

"But, your Highness, that is impossible. We shall all have asylum in England until conditions change. You should go there with us. It will lend influence to our mission."

"No."

"Why?"

"I am leaving Russia for the present. She is outcast. For, not content with betraying others, she has betrayed herself."

"But what are you going to do?"

Peter Nicholaevitch smiled up at the sky and the fussy, fat, bejeweled sycophant before him listened to him in amazement.

"Prince Galitzin," said the Grand Duke amusedly, "I am going to do that which may bring the blush of shame to your brow or the sneer of pity to your lips. I am going to fulfill the destiny provided for every man with a pair of strong hands, and a willing spirit—I am going to work."

The Prince stepped back a pace, his watery eyes snapping in incomprehension.

"But your higher destiny—your great heritage as a Prince of the Royal blood of Holy Russia."

"There is no Holy Russia, my friend, until she is born again. Russia is worse than traitor, worse than liar, worse than murderer and thief. She is a fool."

"All will come right in time. We go to England to wait."

"I have other plans."

"Then you will not join us? Princess Anastasie, my daughter, is here. General Seminoff——"

"It is useless. I have made up my mind. Leave me, if you please."

Prince Galitzin disappeared quickly below to spread the information of his discovery among the disconsolate refugees and it was not long before it was known from one end of the *Phrygia* to the other that the fellow who called himself Peter Nichols was none other than the Grand Duke Peter Nicholaevitch, a cousin to his late Majesty Nicholas and a Prince of the Royal blood. Peter Nichols sought the Captain in his cabin, putting the whole case before him.

"H-m," chuckled the Captain, "Found ye out, did they? There's only a few of you left, that's why. Better stay 'ere in my cabin until we reach Constantinople. I'd be honored, 'Ighness, to say nothin' of savin' you a bit of bother."

"You're very kind."

"Not at all. Make yourself at 'ome. There's cigarettes on the locker and a nip of the Scotch to keep the chill out. Here's a light. You've been worryin' me some, 'Ighness. Fact is I didn't know just how big a bug you were until to-day when I arsked some questions. You'll forgive me, 'Ighness?"

"Peter Nichols," corrected the Grand Duke.

"No," insisted the Captain, "we'll give you yer title while we can. You know we British have a bit of a taste for r'yalty when we know it's the real thing. I don't take much stock in most of my cargo aft. And beggin' yer 'Ighness's pardon I never took much stock in Russia since she lay down on the job and left the Allies in the lurch——"

"Captain Blashford," said the Grand Duke quietly. "You can't hurt my feelings."

"But I do like you, 'Ighness, and I want to do all that I can to 'elp you when we get to anchor."

"Thanks."

"I take it that you don't want anybody ashore to know who ye are?"

"Exactly. Most of these refugees are going to England. I have reasons for not wishing to go with them."

"Where then do you propose to go?"

"To the United States," said the Grand Duke eagerly.

"Without money?"

"I'd have no money if I went to England unless I subsisted on the charity of my friends. My branch of the family is not rich. The war has made us poorer. Such securities as I have are in a vault in Kiev. It would be suicide for me to attempt to reclaim them now. I'm going to try to make my own way."

"Impossible!"

The Grand Duke laughed at the Englishman's expression.

"Why?"

"Yer 'ands, 'Ighness."

The Grand Duke shrugged and grinned.

"I'll risk it. I'm not without resources. Will you help me to a ship sailing for America?"

"Yes—but——"

"Oh, I'll work my passage over—if nobody bothers me."

"By George! I like your spirit. Give me your 'and, sir. I'll do what I can. If the *Bermudian* hasn't sailed from the Horn yet, I think I can manage it for ye."

"And keep me clear of the rest of your passengers?" added His Highness.

"Righto. They'll go on the *Semaphore*. You stay right 'ere and mum's the word." And Captain Blashford went out on deck leaving Peter Nichols to his cigarette and his meditations.

Many times had the Grand Duke Peter given thanks that the blood of his mother flowed strongly in his veins. He was more British than Russian and he could remember things that had happened since he had grown to adolescence which had made the half of him that was English revolt against the Russian system. It was perhaps his musical education rather than his University training or his travels in England and France that had turned him to the *Intelligentsia*. In the vast republic of art and letters he had imbibed the philosophy that was to threaten the very existence of his own clan. The spread of the revolution had not dismayed him, for he believed that in time the pendulum would swing back and bring a constitutional government to Russia. But in the weeks of struggle, privation, and passion a new Peter Nicholaevitch was born.

The failure of his plans in the sudden flood of anarchy which had swept over Zukovo, the treachery of those he had thought faithful and the attempt upon his life had changed his viewpoint. It takes a truly noble spirit to wish to kiss the finger that has pulled the trigger of a revolver, the bullet from which has gone through one's hat. From disappointment and dismay Peter Nicholaevitch had turned to anger. They hadn't played the game with him. It wasn't cricket. His resolution to sail for the United States was decided. To throw himself, an object of charity, upon the mercies of the Earl of Shetland, his mother's cousin, was not to be thought of.

To his peasants he had preached the gospel of labor, humility and peace, in that state of life to which they had been called. He had tried to exemplify it to them. He could do no less now, to himself. By teaching himself, he could perhaps fit himself to teach them. In England it would perhaps be difficult to remain incognito, and he had a pride in wishing to succeed alone and unaided. Only the United States, whose form of government more nearly approached the ideal he had for Russia, could offer him the opportunities to discover whether or not a prince could not also be a man.

To the Princess Anastasie he gave little thought. That their common exile and the chance encounter under such circumstances had aroused no return of an entente toward what had once been a half-sentimental attachment convinced him of how little it had meant to him. There were no royal prohibitions upon him now. To marry the Princess Anastasie and settle in

London, living upon the proceeds of her wealthy father's American and British securities, was of course the easiest solution of his difficulties. A life of ease, music, good sportsmanship, the comfort that only England knows.... She was comely too—blond, petite, and smoked her cigarette very prettily. Their marriage had once been discussed. She wanted it still, perhaps. Something of all this may have been somewhere in the back of Prince Galitzin's ambitious mind. The one course would be so easy, the other——

Peter Nicholaevitch rose and carefully flicked his cigarette through the open port. No. One does not pass twice through such moments of struggle and self-communion as he had had in those long nights of his escape along the Dnieper. He had chosen. Peter Nichols! The name amused him. If Captain Blashford was a man of his word to-night would be the end of the Grand Duke Peter Nicholaevitch, and the Princess Anastasie might find some more ardent suitor to her grace and beauty.

She did not seek him out. Perhaps the hint to Galitzin had been sufficient and the Grand Duke from his hiding place saw her pretty figure set ashore among the miscellany of martyred "r'yalty." He turned away from his port-hole with a catch of his breath as the last vestige of his old life passed from sight. And then quietly took up a fresh cigarette and awaited the Captain.

The details were easily arranged. Blashford was a man of resource and at night returned from a visit to the Captain of the *Bermudian* with word that all was well. He had been obliged to relate the facts but Captain Armitage could keep a secret and promised the refugee a job under his steward who was short-handed. And so the next morning, after shaving and dressing himself in borrowed clothes, Peter Nichols shook Captain Blashford warmly by the hand and went aboard his new ship.

Peter Nichols' new job was that of a waiter at the tables in the dining saloon. He was a very good waiter, supplying, from the wealth of a Continental experience, the deficiencies of other waiters he had known. He wore a black shell jacket and a white shirt front which remained innocent of gravy spots. The food was not very good nor very plentiful, but he served it with an air of such importance that it gained flavor and substance by the reflection of his deference. There were English officers bound for Malta, Frenchmen for Marseilles and Americans of the Red Cross without number bound for New York. Girls, too, clear-eyed, bronzed and hearty, who talked war and politics beneath his very nose, challenging his own theories. They noticed him too and whispered among themselves, but true to his ambition to do every task at the best of his bent, he preserved an immobile countenance and pocketed his fees, which would be useful ere long, with the grateful appreciation of one to whom shillings and franc pieces come as the gifts of God. Many were the attempts to draw him into a conversation, but where the queries could not be answered by a laconic "Yes, sir," or "No, sir," this paragon of waiters maintained a smiling silence.

"I'm sure he's a prince or something," he heard one young girl of a hospital unit say to a young medico of the outfit. "Did you ever see such a nose and brows in your life? And his hands———! You can never mistake hands. I would swear those hands had never done menial work for a thousand years."

All of which was quite true, but it made the waiter Peter uncomfortably careful. There were no women in the kitchen, but there was an amatory stewardess, fat and forty, upon whom the factitious technique of the saloon fell with singular insipidity. He fled from her. Peter, the waiter, was already a good democrat but he was not ready to spread his philosophy out so thin.

He slept forward, messed abaft the galley, enriched his vocabulary and broadened his point of view. There is no leveler like a ship's fo'c'sle, no better school of philosophy than that of men upon their "beam ends." There were many such—Poles, Slovaks, Roumanians, an Armenian or two, refugees, adventurers from America, old, young, dissolute, making a necessity of virtue under that successful oligarchy, the ship's bridge.

In the Americans Peter was interested with an Englishman's point of view. He had much to learn, and he invented a tale of his fortunes which let him into their confidences, especially into that of Jim Coast, waiter like himself, whose bunk adjoined his own. Jim Coast was a citizen of the world, inured to privation under many flags. He had been born in New Jersey, U. S. A., of decent people, had worked in the cranberry bogs, farmed in Pennsylvania, "punched" cattle in Wyoming, "prospected" in the Southwest, looted ranches in Mexico, fought against Diaz and again with the insurgents in Venezuela, worked on cattle-ships and so, by easy stages, had drifted across the breadth of Europe living by his wits at the expense of the credulous and the unwary. And now, for the first time in many years, he was going home—though just what that meant he did not know. He had missed great fortune twice—"by the skin of his teeth," as he picturesquely described it, once in a mine in Arizona and again in a land-deal in the Argentine. There were reasons why he hadn't dared to return to the United States before. He was a man with a grievance, but, however free in his confidences in other respects, gave the interested Peter no inkling as to what that grievance was.

No more curious acquaintanceship could possibly be imagined, but privation, like politics, makes strange bedfellows, and, from tolerance and amusement, Pete, as the other called him, found himself yielding, without stint, to the fantastic spell of Jim Coast's multifarious attractions. He seemed to have no doubts as to the possibility of making a living in America and referred darkly to possible "coups" that would net a fortune. He was an agreeable villain, not above mischief to gain his ends, and Peter, who cherished an ideal, made sure that, once safe ashore, it would be best if they parted company. But he didn't tell Jim Coast so, for the conversational benefits he derived from that gentleman's acquaintance were a liberal education.

We are admonished that they are blessed who just stand and wait, and Peter Nichols, three days out of New York harbor, found himself the possessor of forty dollars in tips from the voyage with sixty dollars coming to him as wages—not so bad for a first venture upon the high seas of industry. It was the first real money he had ever made in his life and he was proud of it, jingling it contentedly in his pockets and rubbing the bills luxuriously one against the other. But his plans required more than this, for he had read enough to know that in the United States one is often taken at one's own estimate, and that if he wasn't to find a job as a ditch-digger, he must make a good appearance. And so it was now time to make use of the one Grand Ducal possession remaining to him, a gold ring set with a gorgeous ruby that had once belonged to his father. This ring he had always worn and had removed from his finger at Ushan, in the fear that its magnificence might betray him. He had kept it carefully tied about his neck in a bag on a bit of string and had of course not even shown it to Jim Coast who might have deemed it an excuse to sever their strange friendship.

Through the Head Steward he managed a message to Captain Armitage and was bidden to the officer's cabin, where he explained the object of his visit, exhibited his treasure and estimated its value.

The Captain opened his eyes a bit wider as he gazed into the sanguine depths of the stone.

"If I didn't know something of your history, Nichols," he said with a wink, "I might think you'd been looting the strong box of the Sultan of Turkey. Pigeon's blood and as big as my thumb nail! You want to sell it?"

"I need capital."

"What do you want for it?"

"It's worth a thousand pounds of English money. Perhaps more, I don't know. I'll take what I can get."

"I see. You're afraid to negotiate the sale ashore?"

"Exactly. I'd be arrested."

"And you don't want explanations. H-m—leave it with me over night. I'll see the Purser. He'll know."

"Thanks."

The Captain offered the waiter in the shell-jacket the hospitality of his cabin, but Peter Nichols thanked him gratefully and withdrew.

The result of this arrangement was that the ruby ring changed owners. The Purser bought it for two thousand in cash. He knew a good thing when he saw it. But Peter Nichols was satisfied.

CHAPTER II
NEW YORK

The Duke-errant had prepared himself for the first glimpse of the battlements of lower New York, but as the *Bermudian* came up the bay that rosy spring afternoon, the western sun gilding the upper half of the castellated towers which rose from a sea of moving shadows, it seemed a dream city, the fortress of a fairy tale. His fingers tingled to express this frozen music, to relieve it from its spell of enchantment, and phrases of Debussy's "Cathédrale Engloutie" came welling up within him from almost forgotten depths.

"*Parbleu!* She's grown some, Pete, since I saw her last!"

This from his grotesque companion who was not moved by concord of sweet sounds. "They've buried the Trinity clean out of sight."

"The Trinity?" questioned Peter solemnly.

"Bless your heart——" laughed Coast, "I'd say so——But I mean, the church——And that must be the Woolworth Building yonder. Where's yer St. Paul's and Kremlin now? Some village,—what?"

"Gorgeous!" muttered Peter.

"Hell of a thing to tackle single-handed, though, eh, boh?"

Something of the same thought was passing through Peter's mind but he only smiled.

"I'll find a job," he said slowly.

"Waitin'!" sneered Coast. "Fine job that for a man with your learnin'. 'Hey, waiter! Some butter if you please,'" he satirized in mincing tones, "'this soup is cold—this beef is underdone. Oh, *cawn't* you give me some service here!' I say, don't you hear 'em—people that never saw a servant in their own home town. Pretty occupation for an old war horse like me or a globe-trotter like you. No. None for me. I'll fry my fish in a bigger pan. *Allons!* Pete. I like you. I'll like you more when you grow some older, but you've got a head above your ears that ain't all bone. I can use you. What d'ye say? We'll get ashore, some way, and then we'll show the U. S. A. a thing or two not written in the books."

"We'll go ashore together, Jim. Then we'll see."

"Righto! But I'll eat my hat if I can see you balancin' dishes in a Broadway Chop House."

Peter couldn't see that either, but he didn't tell Jim Coast so. Their hour on deck had struck, for a final meal was to be served and they went below to finish their duties. That night they were paid off and discharged.

The difficulties in the way of inspection and interrogation of Peter Nichols, the alien, were obviated by the simple expedient of his going ashore under cover of the darkness and not coming back to the ship—this at a hint from the sympathetic Armitage who gave the ex-waiter a handclasp and his money and wished him success.

Midnight found Peter and Jim Coast on Broadway in the neighborhood of Forty-second Street with Peter blinking comfortably up at the electric signs and marveling at everything. The more Coast drank the deeper was his cynicism but Peter grew mellow. This was a wonderful new world he was exploring and with two thousand dollars safely tucked on the inside of his waistcoat, he was ready to defy the tooth of adversity.

In the morning Peter Nichols came to a decision. And so over the coffee and eggs when Coast asked him what his plans were he told him he was going to look for a job.

Coast looked at him through the smoke of his cigar and spoke at last.

"I didn't think you'd be a quitter, Pete. The world owes us a livin'—you and me——Bah! It's easy if you'll use your headpiece. If the world won't give, I mean to take. The jobs are meant for little men."

"What are you going to do?"

"An enterprisin' man wouldn't ask such a question. Half the people in the world takes what the other half gives. You ought to know what half *I* belong to."

"I'm afraid I belong to the other half, Jim Coast," said Peter quietly.

"*Sacré—!*" sneered the other, rising suddenly. "Where you goin' to wait, Pete? At the Ritz or the Commodore? In a month you'll be waitin' on *me*. It'll be *Mister* Coast for you then, *mon garçon*, but you'll still be Pete." He shrugged and offered his hand. "Well, we won't quarrel but our ways split here."

"I'm sorry, Jim. Good-by."

He saw Coast slouch out into the street and disappear m the crowd moving toward Broadway. He waited for a while thinking deeply and then with a definite plan in his mind strolled forth. First he bought a second-hand suit case in Seventh Avenue, then found a store marked "Gentlemen's Outfitters" where he purchased ready-made clothing, a hat, shoes, underwear, linen and cravats, arraying himself with a sense of some satisfaction and packing in his suitcase what he couldn't wear, went forth, found a taxi and drove in state to a good hotel.

New York assimilates its immigrants with surprising rapidity. Through this narrow funnel they pour into the "melting pot," their racial characteristics already neutralized, their souls already inoculated with the spirit of individualism. Prepared as he was to accept with a good grace conditions as he found them, Peter Nichols was astonished at the ease with which he fitted into the niche that he had chosen. His room was on the eighteenth floor, to which and from which he was shot in an enameled lift operated by a Uhlan in a monkey-cap. He found that it required a rather nice adjustment of his muscles to spring forth at precisely the proper moment. There was a young lady who presided over the destinies of the particular shelf that he occupied in this enormous cupboard, a very pretty young lady, something between a French Duchess and a lady's maid. Her smile had a homelike quality though and it was worth risking the perilous catapulting up and down for the mere pleasure of handing her his room key. Having no valuables of course but his money which he carried in his pockets there was no danger from unprincipled persons had she been disposed to connive at dishonesty.

His bedroom was small but neat and his bathroom was neat but small, tiled in white enamel, containing every device that the heart of a clean man could desire. He discovered that by dropping a quarter into various apertures he could secure almost anything he required from tooth paste to razor blades. There was a telephone beside his bed which rang at inconvenient moments and a Bible upon the side table proclaimed the religious fervor of this extraordinary people. A newspaper was sent in to him every morning whether he rang for it or not, and every time he did ring, a lesser Uhlan brought a thermos bottle containing iced water. This perplexed him for a time but he was too much ashamed of his ignorance to question. You see, he was already acquiring the first ingredient of the American character—omniscience, for he found that in New York no one ever admits that he doesn't know everything.

But it was all very wonderful, pulsing with life, eloquent of achievement. He was in no haste. By living with some care, he found that the money from his ruby would last for several months. Meanwhile he was studying his situation and its possibilities. Summing up his own attainments he felt that he was qualified as a teacher of the piano or of the voice, as an instructor in languages, or if the worst came, as a waiter in a fashionable restaurant—perhaps even a head-waiter—which from the authority he observed in the demeanor of the lord of the hotel dining room seemed almost all the honor that a person in America might hope to gain. But, in order that no proper opportunity should slip by, he scanned the newspapers in the hope of finding something that he could do.

As the weeks passed he made the discovery that he was being immensely entertained. He was all English now. It was not in the least difficult to make acquaintances. Almost everybody spoke to everybody without the slightest feeling of restraint. He learned the meaning of the latest American slang but found difficulty in applying it, rejoiced in the syncopation of the jazz, America's original contribution to the musical art, and by the end of a month thought himself thoroughly acclimated.

But he still surprised inquiring glances male and female cast in his direction. There was something about his personality which, disguise it as he might under American-made garments and American-made manners, refused to be hidden. It was his charm added to his general good nature and adaptability which quickly made Peter Nichols some friends of the better sort. If he had been willing to drift downward he would have cast in his lot with Jim Coast. Instead, he followed decent inclinations and found himself at the end of six weeks a part of a group of young business men who took him home to dine with their wives and gave him the benefit of their friendly advice. To all of them he told the same story, that he was an Englishman who had worked in Russia with the Red Cross and that he had come to the United States to get a job.

It was a likely story and most of them swallowed it. But one clever girl whom he met out at dinner rather startled him by the accuracy of her intuitions.

"I have traveled a good deal, Mr. Nichols," she said quizzically, "but I've never yet met an Englishman like you."

"It is difficult for me to tell whether I am to consider that as flattery or disapproval," said Peter calmly.

"You talk like an Englishman, but you're entirely too much interested in everything to be true to type."

"Ah, really——"

"Englishmen are either bored or presumptuous. You're neither. And there's a tiny accent that I can't explain——"

"Don't try——"

"I must. We Americans believe in our impulses. My brother Dick says you're a man of mystery. I've solved it," she laughed, "I'm sure you're a Russian Grand Duke incognito."

Peter laughed and tried bravado.

"You are certainly all in the mustard," he blundered helplessly.

And she looked at him for a moment and then burst into laughter.

These associations were very pleasant, but, contrary to Peter's expectations, they didn't seem to be leading anywhere. The efforts that he made to find positions commensurate with his ambitions had ended in blind alleys. He was too well educated for some of them, not well enough educated for others.

More than two months had passed. He had moved to a boarding house in a decent locality, but of the two thousands dollars with which he had entered New York there now remained to him less than two hundred. He was beginning to believe that he had played the game and lost and that within a very few weeks he would be obliged to hide himself from these excellent new acquaintances and go back to his old job. Then the tide of his fortune suddenly turned.

Dick Sheldon, the brother of the girl who was "all in the mustard," aware of Peter's plight, had stumbled across the useful bit of information and brought it to Peter at the boarding house.

"Didn't you tell me that you'd once had something to do with forestry in Russia?" he asked.

Peter nodded. "I was once employed in the reafforestation of a large estate," he replied.

"Then I've found your job," said Sheldon heartily, clapping Peter on the back. "A friend of Sheldon, Senior's, Jonathan K. McGuire, has a big place down in the wilderness of Jersey—thousands of acres and he wants a man to take charge—sort of forestry expert and general superintendent, money no object. I reckon you could cop out three hundred a month as a starter."

"That looks good to me," said Peter, delighted that the argot fell so aptly from his lips. And then, "You're not spoofing, are you?"

"Devil a spoof. It's straight goods, Nichols. Will you take it?"

Peter had a vision of the greasy dishes he was to escape.

"Will I?" he exclaimed delightedly. "Can I get it?"

"Sure thing. McGuire is a millionaire, made a pot of money somewhere in the West—dabbles in the market. That's where Dad met him. Crusty old rascal. Daughter. Living down in Jersey now, alone with a lot of servants. Queer one. Maybe you'll like him—maybe not."

Peter clasped his friend by the hands.

"Moloch himself would look an angel of mercy to me now."

"Do you think you can make good?"

"Well, rather. Whom shall I see? And when?"

"I can fix it up with Dad, I reckon. You'd better come down to the office and see him about twelve."

Peter Sheldon, Senior, looked him over and asked him questions and the interview was quite satisfactory.

"I'll tell you the truth, as far as I know it," said Sheldon, Senior (which was more than Peter Nichols had done). "Jonathan K. McGuire is a strange character—keeps his business to himself——. How much he's worth nobody knows but himself and the Treasury Department. Does a good deal of buying and selling through this office. A hard man in a deal but reasonable in other things. I've had his acquaintance for five years, lunched with him, dined with him—visited this place in Jersey, but I give you my word, Mr. Nichols, I've never yet got the prick of a pin beneath that man's skin. You may not like him. Few people do. But there's no harm in taking a try at this job."

"I shall be delighted," said Nichols.

"I don't know whether you will or not," broke in Sheldon, Senior, frankly. "Something's happened lately. About three weeks ago Jonathan K. McGuire came into this office hurriedly, shut the door behind him, locked it—and sank into a chair, puffing hard, his face the color of putty. He wouldn't answer any questions and put me off, though I'd have gone out of my way to help him. But after a while he looked out of the window, phoned for his car and went again, saying he was going down into Jersey."

"He was sick, perhaps," ventured Peter.

"It was something worse than that, Mr. Nichols. He looked as though he had seen a ghost or heard a banshee. Then this comes," continued the broker, taking up a letter from the desk. "Asks for a forester, a good strong man. You're strong, Mr. Nichols? Er—and courageous? You're not addicted to 'nerves'? You see I'm telling you all these things so that you'll go down to Black Rock with your eyes open. He also asks me to engage other men as private police or gamekeepers, who will act under your direction. Queer, isn't it? Rather spooky, I'd say, but if you're game, we'll close the bargain now. Three hundred a month to start with and found. Is that satisfactory?"

"Perfectly," said Peter with a bow. "When do I begin?"

"At once if you like. Salary begins now. Fifty in advance for expenses."

"That's fair enough, Mr. Sheldon. If you will give me the directions, I will go to-day."

"To-morrow will be time enough." Sheldon, Senior, had turned to his desk and was writing upon a slip of paper. This he handed to Peter with a check.

"That will show you how to get there," he said as he rose, brusquely. "Glad to have met you. Good-day."

And Peter felt himself hand-shaken and pushed at the same time, reaching the outer office, mentally out of breath from the sudden, swift movement of his fortunes. Sheldon, Senior, had not meant to be abrupt. He was merely a business man relaxing for a moment to do a service for a friend. When Peter Nichols awoke to his obligations he sought out Sheldon, Junior, and thanked him with a sense of real gratitude and Sheldon, Junior, gave him a warm handclasp and Godspeed.

The Pennsylvania Station caused the new Superintendent of Jonathan K. McGuire to blink and gasp. He paused, suit case in hand, at the top of the double flight of stairs to survey the splendid proportions of the waiting room where the crowds seemed lost in its great spaces. In Europe such a building would be a cathedral. In America it was a railway station. And the thought was made more definite by the Gregorian chant of the train announcer which sounded aloft, its tones seeking concord among their own echoes.

This was the portal to the new life in which Peter was to work out his own salvation and the splendor of the immediate prospect uplifted him with a sense of his personal importance in the new scheme of things of which this was a part. He hadn't the slightest doubt that he would be able to succeed in the work for which he had been recommended, for apart from his music—which had taken so many of his hours—there was nothing that he knew more about or loved better than the trees. He had provided himself the afternoon before with two books by American authorities and other books and monographs were to be forwarded to his new address.

As he descended the stairs and reached the main floor of the station, his glance caught the gaze of a man staring at him intently. The man was slender and dark, dressed decently enough in a gray suit and soft hat and wore a small black mustache. All of these facts Peter took note of in the one glance, arrested by the strange stare of the other, which lingered while Peter glanced away and went on. Peter, who had an excellent memory for faces, was sure that he had never seen the man before, but after he had taken a few steps, it occurred to him that in the stranger's eyes he had noted the startled distention of surprise and recognition. And so he stopped and turned, but as he did so the fellow dropped his gaze suddenly, and turned and walked away. The incident was curious and rather interesting. If Peter had had more time he would have sought out the fellow and asked him why he was staring at him, but there were only a few moments to spare and he made his way out to the concourse where he found his gate and descended to his train. Here he ensconced himself comfortably in the smoking car, and was presently shot under the Hudson River (as he afterwards discovered) and out into the sunshine of the flats of New Jersey.

He rolled smoothly along through the manufacturing and agricultural districts, his keenly critical glances neglecting nothing of the waste and abundance on all sides. He saw, too, the unlovely evidences of poverty on the outskirts of the cities, which brought to his mind other communities in a far country whose physical evidences of prosperity were no worse, if no better, than these. Then there came a catch in his throat and a gasp which left him staring but seeing nothing. The feeling was not nostalgia, for that far country was no home for him now. At last he found himself muttering to himself in English, "My home—my home is here."

After a while the mood of depression, recurrent moments of which had come to him in New York with diminishing frequency, passed into one of contemplation, of calm, like those which had followed his nights of passion on the Dnieper, and at last he closed his eyes and dozed. Visions of courts and camps passed through his mind—of brilliant uniforms and jeweled decorations; of spacious polished halls, resplendent with ornate mirrors and crystal pendant chandeliers; of diamond coronets, of silks and satins and powdered flunkies. And then other visions of gray figures crouched in the mud; of rain coming out of the dark and of ominous lights over the profile of low hills; of shrieks; of shells and cries of terror; of his cousin, a tall, bearded man on a horse in a ravine waving an imperious arm; of confusion and moving thousands, the creak of sanitars, the groans of men calling upon mothers they would never see. And then with a leap backward over the years, the vision of a small man huddled against the wall of a courtyard being knouted until red stains appeared on his gray blouse and then mingled faintly in the mist and the rain until the small man sank to the full length of his imprisoned arms like one crucified....

Peter Nichols straightened and passed a hand across his damp forehead. Through the perspective of this modern civilization what had been passing before his vision seemed very vague, very distant, but he knew that it was not a dream....

All about him was life, progress, industry, hope—a nation in the making, proud of her brief history which had been built around an ideal. If he could bring this same ideal back to Russia! In his heart he thanked God for

America—imperfect though she was, and made a vow that in the task he had set for himself he should not be found wanting.

Twice he changed trains, the second time at a small junction amid an ugliness of clay-pits and brickyards and dust and heat. There were perhaps twenty people on the platform. He walked the length of the station and as he did so a man in a gray suit disappeared around the corner of the building. But Peter Nichols did not see him, and in a moment, seated in his new train in a wooden car which reminded him of some of the ancient rolling stock of the St. Petersburg and Moscow Railroad, he was taken haltingly and noisily along the last stage of his journey.

But he was aware of the familiar odor of the pine balsam in his nostrils, and as he rolled through dark coverts the scent of the growing things in the hidden places in the coolth and damp of the sandy loam. He saw, too, tea-colored streams idling among the sedges and charred wildernesses of trees appealing mutely with their blackened stumps like wounded creatures in pain, a bit of war-torn Galicia in the midst of peace. Miles and miles of dead forest land, forgotten and uncared for. There was need here for his services.

With a wheeze of steam and a loud crackling of woodwork and creaking of brakes the train came to a stop and the conductor shouted the name of the station. Rather stiffly the traveler descended with his bag and stood upon the small platform looking about him curiously. The baggage man tossed out a bundle of newspapers and a pouch of mail and the train moved off. Apparently Peter Nichols was the only passenger with Pickerel River as a destination.

And as the panting train went around a curve, at last disappearing, it seemed fairly reasonable to Peter Nichols that no one with the slightest chance of stopping off anywhere else would wish to get off here. The station was small, of but one room and a tiny office containing, as he could see, a telegraph instrument, a broken chair with a leather cushion, a shelf and a rack containing a few soiled slips of paper, but the office had no occupant and the door was locked. This perhaps explained the absence of the automobile which Mr. Sheldon had informed him would meet him in obedience to his telegram announcing the hour of his arrival. Neither within the building nor without was there any person or animate thing in sight, except some small birds fluttering and quarreling along the telegraph wires.

There was but one road, a sandy one, wearing marks of travel, which emerged from the scrub oak and pine and definitely concluded at the railroad track. This, then, was his direction, and after reassuring himself that there was no other means of egress, he took up his black suitcase and set forth into the wood, aware of a sense of beckoning adventure. The road wound in and out, up and down, over what at one time must have been the floor of the ocean, which could not be far distant. Had it not been for the weight of his bag Peter would have enjoyed the experience of this complete isolation, the fragrant silences broken only by the whisper of the leaves and the scurrying of tiny wild things among the dead tree branches. But he had no means of knowing how far he would have to travel or whether, indeed, there had not been some mistake on Sheldon, Senior's, part or his own. But the directions had been quite clear and the road must of course lead somewhere—to some village or settlement at least where he could get a lodging for the night.

And so he trudged on through the woods which already seemed to be partaking of some of the mystery which surrounded the person of Jonathan K. McGuire. The whole incident had been unusual and the more interesting because of the strange character of his employer and the evident fear he had of some latent evil which threatened him. But Peter Nichols had accepted his commission with a sense of profound relief at escaping the other fate that awaited him, with scarcely a thought of the dangers which his acceptance might entail. He was not easily frightened and had welcomed the new adventure, dismissing the fears of Jonathan K. McGuire as imaginary, the emanations of age or an uneasy conscience.

But as he went on, his bag became heavier and the perspiration poured down his face, so reaching a cross-path that seemed to show signs of recent travel he put the suitcase down and sat on it while he wiped his brow. The shadows were growing longer. He was beginning to believe that there was no such place as Black Rock, no such person as Jonathan K. McGuire and that Sheldon, Senior, and Sheldon, Junior, were engaged in a conspiracy against his peace of mind, when above the now familiar whisperings of the forest he heard a new sound. Faintly it came at first as though from a great distance, mingling with the murmur of the sighing wind in the pine trees, a voice singing. It seemed a child's voice—delicate, clear, true, as care-free as the note of a bird—unleashing its joy to the heavens.

Peter Nichols started up, listening more intently. The sounds were coming nearer but he couldn't tell from which direction, for every leaf seemed to be taking up the lovely melody which he could hear quite clearly now. It was an air with which he was unfamiliar, but he knew only that it was elemental in its simplicity and under these circumstances startlingly welcome. He waited another long moment, listening, found the direction from which the voice was coming, and presently noted the swaying of branches and the crackling of dry twigs in the path near by, from which, in a moment, a strange figure emerged.

At first he thought it was a boy, for it wore a pair of blue denim overalls and a wide-brimmed straw hat, from beneath which the birdlike notes were still emitted, but as the figure paused at the sight of him, the song suddenly ceased—he saw a tumbled mass of tawny hair and a pair of startled blue eyes staring at him.

"Hello," said the figure, after a moment, recovering its voice.

"Good-afternoon," said Peter Nichols, bowing from the waist in the most approved Continental manner. You see he, too, was a little startled by the apparition, which proclaimed itself beneath its strange garments in unmistakable terms to be both feminine and lovely.

CHAPTER III
THE OVERALL GIRL

They stood for a long moment regarding each other, both in curiosity; Peter because of the contrariety of the girl's face and garments, the girl because of Peter's bow, which was the most extraordinary thing that had ever happened in Burlington County. After a pause, a smile which seemed to have been hovering uncertainly around the corners of her lips broke into a frank grin, disclosing dimples and a row of white teeth, the front ones not quite together.

"Could you tell me," asked Peter very politely as he found his voice, "if this road leads to Black Rock?"

She was still scrutinizing him, her head, birdlike, upon one side.

"That depends on which way you're walkin'," she said.

She dropped her "g" with careless ease, but then Peter had noticed that many Americans and English people, some very nice ones, did that.

Peter glanced at the girl and then down the road in both directions.

"Oh, yes, of course," he said, not sure whether she was smiling at or with him. "I came from a station called Pickerel River and I wish to go to Black Rock."

"You're *sure* you want to go there?"

"Oh, yes."

"I guess that's because you've never been to Black Rock, Mister."

"No, I haven't."

The girl picked a shrub and nibbled at it daintily.

"You'd better turn and go right back." Her sentence finished in a shrug.

"What's the matter with Black Rock?" he asked curiously.

"It's just the little end of nothin'. That's all," she finished decisively.

The quaint expression interested him. "I must get there, nevertheless," he said; "is it far from here?"

"Depends on what you call far. Mile or so. Didn't the 'Lizzie' meet the six-thirty?"

Peter stared at her vacuously, for this was Greek.

"The 'Lizzie'?"

"The tin 'Lizzie'—Jim Hagerman's bus—carries the mail and papers. Sometimes he gives me a lift about here."

"No. There was no conveyance of any sort and I really expected one. I wish to get to Mr. Jonathan K. McGuire's."

"Oh!"

The girl had been examining Peter furtively, as though trying vainly to place him definitely in her mental collection of human bipeds. Now she stared at him with interest.

"Oh, you're goin' to McGuire's!"

Peter nodded. "If I can ever find the way."

"You're one of the new detectives?"

"Detective!" Peter laughed. "No. Not that I'm aware. I'm the new superintendent and forester."

"Oh!"

The girl was visibly impressed, but a tiny frown puckered her brow.

"What's a forester?" she asked.

"A fellow who looks after the forests."

"The forests don't need any lookin' after out here in the barrens. They just grow."

"I'm going to teach them to grow better."

The girl looked at him for a long moment of suspicion. She had taken off her hat and the ruddy sunlight behind her made a golden halo all about her head. Her hands he had noted were small, the fingers slender. Her nose was well shaped, her nostrils wide, the angle of her jaw firmly modeled and her slender figure beneath the absurd garments revealed both strength and grace. But he did not dare to stare at her too hard or to question her as to her garments. For all that Peter knew it might be the custom of Burlington County for women to wear blue denim trousers.

And her next question took him off his guard.

"You city folk don't think much of yourselves, do you?"

"I don't exactly understand what you mean," said Peter politely, marking the satirical note.

"To think you can make these trees grow better!" she sniffed.

"Oh, I'm just going to help them to help themselves."

"That's God's job, Master."

Peter smiled. She wouldn't have understood, he thought, so what was the use of explaining. There must have been a superior quality in Peter's smile, for the girl put on her hat and came down into the road.

"I'm goin' to Black Rock," she said stiffly, "follow me." And she went off with a quick stride down the road.

Peter Nichols took up his bag and started, with difficulty getting to a place beside her.

"If you don't mind," he said, "I'd much rather walk with you than behind you."

She shrugged a shoulder at him.

"Suit yourself," she said.

In this position, Peter made the discovery that her profile was quite as interesting as her full face, but she no longer smiled. Her reference to the Deity entirely eliminated Peter and the profession of forestry from the pale of useful things. He was sorry that she no longer smiled because he had decided to make friends at Black Rock and he didn't want to make a bad beginning.

"I hope you don't mind," said Peter at last, "if I tell you that you have one of the loveliest voices that I have ever heard."

He marked with pleasure the sudden flush of color that ran up under her delicately freckled tan. Her lips parted and she turned to him hesitating.

"You—you heard me!"

"I did. It was like the voice of an angel in Heaven."

"Angel! Oh! I'm sorry. I—I didn't know any one was there. I just sing on my way home from work."

"You've been working to-day?"

She nodded. "Yes—Farmerettin'."

"Farmer——?"

"Workin' in the vineyard at Gaskill's."

"Oh, I see. Do you like it?"

"No," she said dryly. "I just do it for my health. Don't I look sick?"

Peter wasn't used to having people make fun of him. Even as a waiter he had managed to preserve his dignity intact. But he smiled at her.

"I was wondering what had become of the men around here."

"They're so busy walkin' from one place to another to see where they can get the highest wages, that there's no time to work in between."

"I see," said Peter, now really amused. "And does Mr. Jonathan McGuire have difficulty in getting men to work for him?"

"Most of his hired help come from away—like you———But lately they haven't been stayin' long."

"Why?"

She slowed her pace a little and turned to look at him curiously.

"Do you mean that you don't know the kind of a job you've got?"

"Not much," admitted Peter. "In addition to looking after the preserve, I'm to watch after the men—and obey orders, I suppose."

"H-m. Preserve! Sorry, Mr. what's your name———"

"Peter Nichols———" put in Peter promptly.

"Well, Mr. Peter Nichols, all I have to say is that you're apt to have a hard time."

"Yes, I'm against it!" translated Peter confidently.

The girl stopped in the middle of the road, put her hands on her hips and laughed up at the purpling sky. Her laugh was much like her singing—if angels in Paradise laugh (and why shouldn't they?). Then while he wondered what was so amusing she looked at him again.

"*Up* against it, you mean. You're English, aren't you?"

"Er—yes—I am."

"I thought so. There was one of you in the glass factory. He always muffed the easy ones."

"Oh, you work in a glass factory?"

"Winters. Manufacturin' whiskey and beer bottles. Now we're goin' dry, they'll be makin' pop and nursin' bottles, I guess."

"Do you help in the factory?"

"Yes, and in the office. I can shorthand and type a little."

"You must be glad when a summer comes."

"I am. In winter I can't turn around without breakin' something. They dock you for that———"

"And that's why you sing when you can't break anythin'?"

"I suppose so. I like the open. It isn't right to be cooped up."

They were getting along beautifully and Peter was even beginning to forget the weight of his heavy bag. She was a quaint creature and quite as unconscious of him as though he hadn't existed. He was just somebody to talk to. Peter ventured.

"Er—would you mind telling me your name?"

She looked at him and laughed friendly.

"You must have swallowed a catechism, Mr. Nichols. But everybody in Black Rock knows everybody else—more'n they want to, I guess. There's no reason I shouldn't tell you. I don't mind your knowin'. My name is Beth Cameron."

"Beth———?"

"Yes, Bess—the minister had a lisp."

Peter didn't lack a sense of humor.

"Funny, isn't it?" she queried with a smile as he laughed, "bein' tied up for life to a name like that just because the parson couldn't talk straight."

"Beth," he repeated, "but I like it. It's like you. I hope you'll let me come to see you when I get settled."

"H-m," she said quizzically. "You don't believe in wastin' your time, do you?" And then, after a brief pause, "You know they call us Pineys back here in the barrens, but just the same we think a lot of ourselves and we're a little offish with city folks. You can't be too particular nowadays about the kind of people you go with."

Peter stared at her and grinned, his sense of the situation more keenly touched than she could be aware of.

"Particular, are you? I'm glad of that. All the more credit to me if you'll be my friend."

"I didn't say I was your friend."

"But you're going to be, aren't you? I know something about singing. I've studied music. Perhaps I could help you."

"You! You've studied? Lord of Love! You're not lyin', are you?"

He laughed. "No. I'm not lying. I was educated to be a musician."

She stared at him now with a new look in her eyes but said nothing. So Peter spoke again.

"Do you mean to say you've never thought of studying singing?"

"Oh, yes," she said slowly at last, "I've thought of it, just as I've thought of goin' in the movies and makin' a million dollars. Lots of good *thinkin'* does!"

"You've thought of the movies?"

"Yes, once. A girl went from the glass factory. She does extra ladies. She visited back here last winter. I didn't like what it did to her."

"Oh!" Peter was silent for a while, aware of the pellucid meaning of her "it." He was learning quite as much from what she didn't say as from what she did. But he evaded the line of thought suggested.

"You do get tired of Black Rock then?"

"I would if I had time. I'm pretty busy all day, and—see here—Mr.—er— Nichols. If I asked as many questions as you do, I'd know as much as Daniel Webster."

"I'm sorry," said Peter, "I beg your pardon."

They walked on in silence for a few moments, Peter puzzling his brain over the extraordinary creature that chance had thrown in his way. He could see that she was quite capable of looking out for herself and that if her smattering of sophistication had opened her eyes, it hadn't much harmed her.

He really wanted to ask her many more questions, but to tell the truth he was a little in awe of her dry humor which had a kind of primitive omniscience and of her laughter which he was now sure was more *at*, than with, him. But he had, in spite of her, peered for a moment into the hidden places of her mind and spirit.

It was this intrusion that she resented and he could hardly blame her, since they had met only eighteen minutes ago. She trotted along beside him as though quite unaware of the sudden silence or of the thoughts that might have been passing in his mind. It was Beth who broke the silence.

"Is your bag heavy?" she asked.

"Not at all," said Peter, mopping the perspiration from his forehead. "But aren't we nearly there?"

"Oh, yes. It's just a mile or so."

Peter dropped his bag.

"That's what you said it was, back there."

"Did I? Well, maybe it isn't so far as that now. Let me carry your bag a while."

Thus taunted, he rose, took the bag in his left hand and followed.

"City folks aren't much on doin' for themselves, are they? The taxi system is very poor down here yet."

Her face was expressionless, but he knew that she was laughing at him. He knew also that his bag weighed more than any army pack. It seemed too that she was walking much faster than she had done before—also that there was malicious humor in the smile she now turned on him.

"Seems a pity to have such a long walk—with nothin' at the end of it."

"I don't mind it in the least," gasped Peter. "And if you don't object to my asking you just one more question," he went on grimly, "I'd like you to tell me what is frightening Mr. Jonathan K. McGuire?"

"Oh, McGuire. I don't know. Nobody does. He's been here a couple of weeks now, cooped up in the big house. Never comes out. They say he sees ghosts and things."

"Ghosts!"

She nodded. "He's hired some of the men around here to keep watch for them and they say some detectives are coming. You'll help too, I guess."

"That should be easy."

"Maybe. I don't know. My aunt works there. She's housekeeper. It's spooky, she says, but she can't afford to quit."

"But they haven't *seen* anything?" asked Peter incredulously.

"No. Not yet. I guess it might relieve 'em some if they did. It's only the things you don't see that scare you."

"It sounds like a great deal of nonsense about nothing," muttered Peter.

"All right. Wait until you get there before you do much talkin'."

"I will, but I'm not afraid of ghosts." And then, as an afterthought, "Are you?"

"Not in daylight. But from what Aunt Tillie says, it must be something more than a ghost that's frightenin' Jonathan K. McGuire."

"What does she think it is?"

"She doesn't know. Mr. McGuire won't say. He won't allow anybody around the house without a pass. Oh, he's scared all right and he's got most of Black Rock scared too. He was never like this before."

"Are you scared?" asked Peter.

"No. I don't think I am really. But it's spooky, and I don't care much for shootin'."

"What makes you think there will be shooting?"

"On account of the guns and pistols. Whatever the thing is he's afraid of, he's not goin' to let it come near him if he can help it. Aunt Tillie says that what with loaded rifles, shotguns and pistols lyin' loose in every room in the house, it's as much as your life is worth to do a bit of dustin'. And the men—Shad Wells, Jesse Brown, they all carry automatics. First thing they know they'll be killin' somebody," she finished with conviction.

"Who is Shad Wells——?"

"My cousin, Shadrack E. Wells. He was triplets. The other two died."

"Shad," mused Peter.

"Sounds like a fish, doesn't it? But he isn't." And then more slowly, "Shad's all right. He's just a plain woodsman, but he doesn't know anything about making the trees grow," she put in with prim irony. "You'll be his boss, I guess. He won't care much about that."

"Why?"

"Because he's been runnin' things in a way. I hope you get along with him."

"So do I——"

"Because if you don't, Shad will eat you at one gobble."

"Oh!" said Peter with a smile. "But perhaps you exaggerate. Don't you think I might take two—er—gobbles?"

Beth looked him over, and then smiled encouragingly.

"Maybe," she said, "but your hands don't look over-strong."

Peter looked at his right hand curiously. It was not as brown as hers, but the fingers were long and sinewy.

"They are, though. When you practice five hours a day on the piano, your hands will do almost anything you want them to."

A silence which Peter improved by shifting his suitcase. The weight of it had ceased to be amusing. And he was about to ask her how much further Black Rock was when there was a commotion down the road ahead of them, as a dark object emerged from around the bend and amid a whirl of dust an automobile appeared.

"It's the 'Lizzie'," exclaimed Beth unemotionally.

And in a moment the taxi service of Black Rock was at Peter's disposal.

"Carburetor trouble," explained the soiled young man at the wheel briefly, without apology. And with a glance at Peter's bag—

"Are you the man for McGuire's on the six-thirty?"

Peter admitted that he was and the boy swung the door of the tonneau open.

"In here with me, Beth," he said to the girl invitingly.

In a moment, the small machine was whirled around and started in the direction from which it had come, bouncing Peter from side to side and enveloping him in dust. Jim Hagerman's "Lizzie" wasted no time, once it set about doing a thing, and in a few moments from the forest they emerged into a clearing where there were cows in a meadow, and a view of houses. At the second of these, a frame house with a portico covered with vines and a small yard with a geranium bed, all enclosed in a picket fence, the "Lizzie" suddenly stopped and Beth got down.

"Much obliged, Jim," he heard her say.

Almost before Peter had swept off his hat and the girl had nodded, the "Lizzie" was off again, through the village street, and so to a wooden bridge across a tea-colored stream, up a slight grade on the other side, where Jim Hagerman stopped his machine and pointed to a road.

"That's McGuire's—in the pines. They won't let me go no further."

"How much do I owe you?" asked Peter, getting down.

"It's paid for, Mister. Slam the door, will ye?" And in another moment Peter was left alone.

It was now after sunset, and the depths of the wood were bathed in shadow. Peter took the road indicated and in a moment reached two stone pillars where a man was standing. Beyond the man he had a glimpse of lawns, a well-kept driveway which curved toward the wood. The man at the gate was of about Peter's age but tall and angular, well tanned by exposure and gave an appearance of intelligence and capacity.

"I came to see Mr. McGuire," said Peter amiably.

"And what's your name?"

"Nichols. I'm the new forester from New York."

The young man at the gate smiled in a satirical way.

"Nichols. That was the name," he ruminated. And then with a shout to some one in the woods below, "Hey, Andy. Come take the gate."

All the while Peter felt the gaze of the young man going over him minutely and found himself wondering whether or not this was the person who was going to take him at a gobble.

It was. For when the other man came running Peter heard him call the gateman, "Shad."

"Are you Mr. Shad Wells?" asked Peter politely with the pleasant air of one who has made an agreeable discovery.

"That's my name. Who told you?"

"Miss Beth Cameron," replied Peter. "We came part of the way together."

"H-m! Come," he said laconically and led the way up the road toward the house. Peter didn't think he was very polite.

Had it not been for the precautions of his guide, Peter would have been willing quite easily to forget the tales that had been told him of Black Rock. The place was very prettily situated in the midst of a very fine growth of pines, spruce and maple. At one side ran the tea-colored stream, tumbling over an ancient dam to levels below, where it joined the old race below the ruin that had once been a mill. The McGuire house emerged in a moment from its woods and shrubbery, and stood revealed—a plain square Georgian dwelling of brick, to which had been added a long wing in a poor imitation of the same style and a garage and stables in no style at all on the slope beyond. It seemed a most prosaic place even in the gathering dusk and Peter seemed quite unable to visualize it as the center of a mystery such as had been described. And the laconic individual who had been born triplets was even less calculated to carry out such an illusion.

But just as they were crossing the lawn on the approach to the house, the earth beneath a clump of bushes vomited forth two men, like the fruit of the Dragon's Teeth, armed with rifles, who barred their way. Both men were grinning from ear to ear.

"All right, Jesse," said Shad with a laugh. "It's me and the new forester." He uttered the words with an undeniable accent of contempt.

The armed figures glanced at Peter and disappeared, and Peter and Mr. Shad Wells went up the steps of the house to a spacious portico. There was not a human being in sight and the heavy wooden blinds to the lower floor were tightly shut. Before his guide had even reached the door the sound of their footsteps had aroused some one within the house, the door was opened the length of its chain and a face appeared at the aperture.

"Who is it?" asked a male voice.

"Shad Wells and Mr. Nichols, the man from New York."

"Wait a minute," was the reply while the door was immediately shut again.

Peter glanced around him comparing this strange situation with another that he remembered, when a real terror had come, a tangible terror in the shape of a countryside gone mad with blood lust. He smiled toward the bush where the armed men lay concealed and toward the gate where the other armed man was standing. It was all so like a situation out of an *opéra bouffe* of Offenbach.

What he felt now in this strange situation was an intense curiosity to learn the meaning of it all, to meet the mysterious person around whom all these preparations centered. Peter had known fear many times, for fear was in the air for weeks along the Russian front, the fear of German shells, of poison gas, and of that worst poison of all—Russian treachery. But that fear was not like this fear, which was intimate, personal but intangible. He marked it in the scrutiny of the man who opened the door and of the aged woman who suddenly appeared beside him in the dim hallway and led him noiselessly up the stair to a lighted room upon the second floor. At the doorway the woman paused.

"Mr. Nichols, Mr. McGuire," she said, and Peter entered.

CHAPTER IV
THE JOB

The room was full of tobacco smoke, through which Peter dimly made out a table with an oil lamp, beside which were chairs, a sofa, and beyond, a steel safe between the windows. As Peter Nichols entered, a man advanced from a window at the side, the shutter of which was slightly ajar. It was evident that not content to leave his safety in the hands of those he had employed to preserve it, he had been watching too.

He was in his shirt sleeves, a man of medium height, compactly built, and well past the half century mark. The distinguishing features of his face were a short nose, a heavy thatch of brows, a square jaw which showed the need of the offices of a razor and his lips wore a short, square mustache somewhat stained by nicotine.

In point of eagerness the manner of his greeting of the newcomer left nothing to be desired. Peter's first impression was that Jonathan K. McGuire was quite able to look out for himself, which confirmed the impression that the inspection to which Peter had been subjected was nothing but a joke. But when his employer began speaking rather jerkily, Peter noticed that his hands were unsteady and that neither the muscles of his face nor of his body were under complete control. Normally, he would have seemed much as Sheldon, Senior, had described him—a hard-fisted man, a close bargainer who had won his way to his great wealth by the sheer force of a strong personality. There was little of softness in his face, little that was imaginative. This was not a man to be frightened at the Unseen or to see terrors that did not exist. Otherwise, to Peter he seemed commonplace to the last degree, of Irish extraction probably, the kind of person one meets daily on Broadway or on the Strand. In a fur coat he might have been taken for a banker; in tweeds, for a small tradesman; or in his shirt as Peter now saw him, the wristbands and collar somewhat soiled from perspiration, for a laboring man taking his rest after an arduous day. In other words, he was very much what his clothes would make of him, betraying his origins in a rather strident voice meant perhaps to conceal the true state of his mind.

"Glad to see you, Mr. Nichols. Thought you were never comin'," he jerked out.

"I walked most of the way from Pickerel River. Something went wrong, with the 'Lizzie.'"

"Oh—er—'Lizzie'. The flivver! I couldn't send my own car. I've got only one down here and I might need it."

"It doesn't matter in the least—since I'm here."

"Sit down, Mr. Nichols," went on McGuire indicating a chair. "You've been well recommended by Mr. Sheldon. I talked to him yesterday over long distance. He told you what I wanted?"

"Something. Not much," said Peter with a view to getting all the information possible. "You wanted a forester——?"

"Er—er—yes, that's it. A forester." And then he went on haltingly—"I've got about twenty thousand acres here—mostly scrub oak—pine and spruce. I've sold off a lot to the Government. A mess of it has been cut—there's been a lot of waste—and the fire season is coming around. That's the big job—the all-the-year job. You've had experience?"

"Yes—in Russia. I'm a trained woodsman."

"You're a good all-round man?"

"Exactly what——?" began Peter.

"You know how to look after yourself—to look after other men, to take charge of a considerable number of people in my employ?"

"Yes. I'm used to dealing with men."

"It's a big job, Mr. Nichols—a ticklish kind of a job for a furriner—one with some—er—unusual features—that may call for—er—a lot of tact. And—er—courage."

It seemed to Peter that Jonathan K. McGuire was talking almost at random, that the general topic of forestry was less near his heart to-night than the one that was uppermost in Peter's mind, the mystery that surrounded his employer and the agencies invoked to protect him. It seemed as if he were loath to speak of them, as if he were holding Peter off at arm's length, so to say, until he had fully made up his mind that this and no other man was the one he wanted, for all the while he was examining the visitor with burning, beady, gray eyes, as though trying to peer into his mind.

"I'm not afraid of a forester's job, no matter how big it is, if I have men enough," said Peter, still curious.

"And you're a pretty good man in a pinch, I mean——" he put in jerkily, "you're not easy scared—don't lose your nerve."

"I'll take my chances on that," replied Peter calmly. "I'm used to commanding men, in emergencies—if that's what you mean."

"Yes. That's what I mean. Er—you're an Englishman, Mr. Sheldon says."

"Er—yes," said Peter, "an Englishman," for this was the truth now more than ever before, and then repeated the story he had told in New York about his work in Russia. While Peter was talking, McGuire was pacing up and down the room with short nervous strides, nodding his head in understanding from time to time. When Peter paused he returned to his chair.

"You British are a pretty steady lot," said McGuire at last. "I think you'll do. I like the way you talk and I like your looks. Younger than I'd hoped maybe, but then you're strong—Mr. Sheldon says you're strong, Mr. Nichols."

"Oh, yes," said Peter, his curiosity now getting the better of him. "But it might be as well, Mr. McGuire, if you let me know just what, that is unusual, is to be required of me. I assume that you want me to take command of the men policing your grounds—and immediate property?"

"Er—yes. That will have to be put in shape at once—at once." He leaned suddenly forward in his chair, his hairy hands clutching at his knees, while he blurted out with a kind of relieved tension, "No one must come near the house at night. No one, you understand——"

"I understand, sir——" said Peter, waiting patiently for a revelation.

"There'll be no excuse if any one gets near the house without my permission," he snarled. And then almost sullenly again—"You understand?"

"Perfectly. That should not be difficult to——"

"It may be more difficult than you think," broke in McGuire, springing to his feet again, and jerking out his phrases with strange fury.

"Nothing is to be taken for granted. Nothing," he raged. Peter was silent for a moment, watching McGuire who had paced the length of the room and back.

"I understand, sir," he said at last. "But doesn't it seem to you that both I and the man under me could do our work with more intelligence if we knew just who or what is to be guarded against?" Mr. McGuire stopped beside him as though transfixed by the thought. Then his fingers clutched at the back of a chair to which he clung for a moment in silence, his brows beetling. And when he spoke all the breath of his body seemed concentrated in a hoarse whisper.

"You won't know that. You understand, I give the orders. You obey them. I am not a man who answers questions. Don't ask them."

"Oh, I beg your pardon. So long as this thing you fear is human——"

"Human! A ghost! Who said I was afraid? Sheldon? Let him think it. This is *my* business. There are many things of value in this house," and he glanced towards the safe. "I'm using the right of any man to protect what belongs to him."

"I see," said Peter.

The man's tension relaxed as he realized Peter's coolness.

"Call it a fancy if you like, Mr. Nichols———" he said with a shrug. "A man of my age may have fancies when he can afford to gratify 'em."

"That's your affair," said Peter easily. "I take it then that the systematic policing of the grounds is the first thing I am to consider."

"Exactly. The systematic policing of the grounds—the dividing of your men into shifts for day and night work—more at night than in the day. Three more men come to-morrow. They will all look to you for orders."

"And who is in charge now?"

"A man named Wells—a native—the foreman from one of the sawmills— but he—er—well, Mr. Nichols—I'm not satisfied. That's why I wanted a man from outside."

"I understand. And will you give the necessary orders to him?"

"Wells was up here to-day, I told him."

"How many men are on guard here at the house?"

"Ten and with the three coming—that makes thirteen———" McGuire halted—"thirteen—but you make the fourteenth," he added.

Peter nodded. "And you wish me to take charge at once?"

"At once. To-night. To-morrow you can look over the ground more carefully. You'll sleep in the old playhouse—the log cabin—down by the creek. They'll show you. It's connected with this house by 'phone. I'll talk to you again to-morrow; you'd better go down and get something to eat."

McGuire went to the door and called out "Tillie!"

And as a faint reply was heard, "Get Mr. Nichols some supper."

Peter rose and offered his hand.

"I'll try to justify your faith in me, sir. Much obliged."

"Good-night."

Peter went down the stairs with mingled feelings. If the words of Beth Cameron had created in his mind a notion that the mystery surrounding

Black Rock was supernatural in character, the interview with Jonathan K. McGuire had dispelled it. That McGuire was a very much frightened man was certain, but it seemed equally certain to Peter that what he feared was no ghost or banshee but the imminence of some human attack upon his person or possessions. Here was a practical man, who bore in every feature of his strongly-marked face the tokens of a successful struggle in a hard career, the beginnings of which could not have been any too fortunate. A westerner whose broad hands and twisted fingers spoke eloquently of manual labor, a man who still possessed to all appearances considerable physical strength—a prey to the fear of some night danger which was too ominous even to be talked about.

It was the quality of his terror that was disturbing. Peter was well acquainted with the physical aspects of fear—that is the fear of violence and death. That kind of fear made men restless and nervous, or silent and preoccupied; or like liquor it accentuated their weaknesses of fiber in sullenness or bravado. But it did not make them furtive. He could not believe that it was the mere danger of death or physical violence that obsessed his employer. That sort of danger perhaps there might be, but the fear that he had seen in McGuire's fanatical gray eyes was born of something more than these. Whatever it was that McGuire feared, it reached further within—a threat which would destroy not his body alone, but something more vital even than that—the very spirit that lived within him.

Of his career, Peter knew nothing more than Sheldon, Senior, had told him—a successful man who told nothing of his business except to the Treasury Department, a silent man, with a passion for making money. What could he fear? Whom? What specter out of the past could conjure up the visions he had seen dancing between McGuire's eyes and his own?

These questions it seemed were not to be answered and Peter, as he sat down at the supper table, put them resolutely from his mind and addressed himself to the excellent meal provided by the housekeeper. For the present, at least, fortune smiled upon him. The terrors of his employer could not long prevail against the healthy appetite of six-and-twenty.

But it was not long before Peter discovered that the atmosphere of the room upstairs pervaded the dining room, library and halls. There were a cook and housemaid he discovered, neither of them visible. The housekeeper, if attentive, was silent, and the man who had opened the front door, who seemed to be a kind of general factotum, as well as personal bodyguard to Mr. McGuire, crept furtively about the house in an unquiet manner which would have been disturbing to the digestion of one less timorous than Peter.

Before the meal was finished this man came into the room and laid a police whistle, a large new revolver and a box of cartridges beside Peter's dish of strawberries.

"These are for you, sir," he whispered sepulchrally. "Mr. McGuire asked me to give them to you—for to-night."

"Thanks," said Peter, "and you——"

"I'm Stryker, sir, Mr. McGuire's valet."

"Oh!"

Peter's accent of surprise came from his inability to reconcile Stryker with the soiled shirt and the three days' growth of beard on the man upstairs, which more than ever testified to the disorder of his mental condition.

And as Stryker went out and his footsteps were heard no more, the housekeeper emerged cautiously from the pantry.

"Is everything all right, Mr. Nichols?" she asked in a stage whisper.

"Right as rain. Delicious! I'm very much obliged to you."

"I mean—er—there ain't anythin' else ye'd like?"

"Nothing, thanks," said Peter, taking up the revolver and breaking it. He had cut the cover of the cartridge box and had slipped a cartridge into the weapon when he heard the voice of the woman at his ear.

"D'ye think there's any danger, sir?" she whispered, while she nervously eyed the weapon.

"I'm sure I don't know. Not to you, I'd say," he muttered, still putting the cartridges in the pistol. As an ex-military man, he was taking great delight in the perfect mechanism of his new weapon.

"What is it——? I mean, d'ye think——," she stammered, "did Mr. McGuire say—just what it is he's afraid of?"

"No," said Peter, "he didn't." And then with a grin, "Do you know?"

"No, sir. I wish t'God I did. Then there'd be somethin' to go by."

"I'm afraid I can't help you, Mrs.——"

"Tillie Bergen. I've been housekeeper here since the new wing was put on——"

"Oh, yes," said Peter, pausing over the last cartridge as the thought came to him. "Then you must be Beth Cameron's aunt?"

"Beth?" The woman's sober face wreathed in a lovely smile. "D'ye know Beth?"

"Since this afternoon. She showed me the way."

"Oh. Poor Beth."

"Poor!"

"Oh, we're all poor, Mr. Nichols. But Beth she's—different from the rest of us somehow."

"Yes, she *is* different," admitted Peter frankly.

Mrs. Bergen sighed deeply. "Ye don't know how different. And now that—all this trouble has come, I can't get home nights to her. And she can't come to see me without permission. How long d'ye think it will last, sir?"

"I don't know," said Peter, slipping the revolver and cartridges into his pockets. And then gallantly, "If I can offer you my services, I'd be glad to take you home at night——"

"It's against orders. And I wouldn't dare, Mr. Nichols. As it is I've got about as much as I can stand. If it wasn't for the money I wouldn't be stayin' in the house another hour."

"Perhaps things won't be so bad after a time. If anything is going to happen, it ought to be pretty soon."

She regarded him wistfully as he moved toward the door. "An' ye'll tell me, sir, if anything out o' the way happens."

"I hope nothing is going to happen, Mrs. Bergen," said Peter cheerfully.

Stryker appeared mysteriously from the darkness as Peter went out into the hall.

"The upstairs girl made up your bed down at the cabin, sir. The chauffeur took your bag over. You'll need these matches. If you'll wait, sir, I'll call Mr. Wells."

Peter wondered at the man in this most unconventional household, for Stryker, with all the prescience of a well-trained servant, had already decided that Peter belonged to a class accustomed to being waited on. Going to the door he blew one short blast on a police whistle, like Peter's, which he brought forth from his pocket.

"That will bring him, sir," he said. "If you'll go out on the portico, he'll join you in a moment."

Peter obeyed. The door was closed and fastened behind him and almost before he had taken his lungs full of the clean night air (for the house had been hot and stuffy), a shadow came slouching across the lawn in the moonlight. Peter joined the man at once and they walked around the house, while Peter questioned him as to the number of men and their disposition about the place. There were six, he found, including Wells, with six more to sleep in the stable, which was also used as a guardhouse. Peter made the rounds of the sentries. None of them seemed to be taking the matter any too seriously and one at least was sound asleep beneath some bushes. Peter foresaw difficulties. Under the leadership of Shad Wells the strategic points were not covered, and, had he wished, he could have found his way, by using the cover of shadow and shrubbery, to the portico without being observed. He pointed this out to Wells who, from a supercilious attitude, changed to one of defiance.

"You seem to think you know a lot, Mister?" he said. "I'd like to see ye try it."

Peter laughed.

"Very well. Take your posts and keep strict watch, but don't move. If I don't walk across the lawn from the house in half an hour I'll give you ten dollars. In return you can take a shot if you see me."

He thought the men needed the object lesson. Peter was an excellent "point." He disappeared into the woods behind him and making his way cautiously out, found a road, doubling to the other side of the garage along which he went on his hands and knees and crawling from shrub to shrub in the shadows reached the portico without detection. Here he lighted a fag and quietly strolled down to the spot where he had left Shad Wells, to whom he offered a cigarette by way of consolation. Wells took it grudgingly. But he took it, which was one point gained.

"Right smart, aren't ye?" said Shad.

"No," said Peter coolly. "Anybody could have done it,—in three ways. The other two ways are through the pine grove to the left and from the big sycamore by the stream."

"And how do you know all that?"

"I was in the Army," said Peter. "It's a business like anything else."

And he pointed out briefly where the five men should be stationed and why, and Shad, somewhat mollified by the cigarette, shrugged and agreed.

"We'll do sentry duty in the regular way," went on Peter cheerfully, "with a corporal of the guard and a countersign. I'll explain in detail to-morrow." And then to Shad, "I'll take command until midnight, when you'll go on with the other shift until four. I'll make it clear to the other men. The countersign is the word 'Purple.' You'd better go and turn in. I'll call you at twelve."

Peter watched the figure of the woodsman go ambling across the lawn in the direction of the garage and smiled. He also marked the vertical line of light which showed at a window on the second floor where another kept watch. The man called Jesse, the one who had been asleep beneath the bushes, and who, fully awake, had watched Peter's exhibition of scouting, now turned to Peter with a laugh.

"I guess you're right, Mister. S'long's we're paid. But I'd like to know just what this 'ere thing is the ol' man's skeered of."

"You know as much as I do. It will probably have two legs, two hands and a face and carry a gun. You'd better be sure you're not asleep when it comes. But if you care to know what I think, you can be pretty sure that it's coming— and before very long."

"To-night?"

"How do I know? Have a cigarette? You cover from the road to the big cedar tree; and keep your eyes open—especially in the shadows—and don't let anybody get you in the back."

And so making the rounds, instilling in their minds a sense of real emergency, Peter gave the men their new sentry posts and made friends. He had decided to stay up all night, but at twelve he called Shad Wells and went down to look over his cabin which was a quarter of a mile away from the house near Cedar Creek (or "Crick" in the vernacular). The key was in the cabin door so he unlocked it and went in, and after striking a match found a kerosene lamp which he lighted and then looked about him.

The building had only one room but it was of large dimensions and contained a wooden bed with four posts, evidently some one's heirloom, a bureau, washstand, two tables and an easy chair or two. Behind the bed was a miscellaneous lot of rubbish, including a crib, a rocking horse, a velocipede, beside some smaller toys. Whom had these things belonged to? A grandson of McGuire's? And was the daughter of McGuire like her father, unlovely, soiled and terror-stricken? His desultory mental queries suddenly stopped as he raised his eyes to the far corner of the room, for there, covered with an old shawl, he made out the lines of a piano. He opened the keyboard and struck a chord. It wasn't so bad—a little tuning—he could do it himself....

So this was his new home! He had not yet had the time or the opportunity to learn what new difficulties were to face him on the morrow, but the personal affairs of his employer had piqued his interest and for the present he had done everything possible to insure his safety for the night. To-morrow perhaps he would learn something more about the causes of this situation. He would have an opportunity too to look over the property and make a report as to its possibilities. To a man inured as Peter was to disappointments, what he had found was good. He had made up his mind to fit himself soldierlike into his new situation and he had to admit now that he liked the prospect. As though to compensate for past mischief, Fate had provided him with the one employment in the new land for which he was best suited by training and inclination. It was the one "job" in which, if he were permitted a fair amount of freedom of action and initiative, he was sure that he could "make good." The trees he could see were not the stately pines of Zukovo, but they were pines, and the breeze which floated in to him through the cabin door was laden with familiar odors.

The bed looked inviting, but he resolutely turned his back to it and unpacked his suitcase, taking off his tailor-made clothing and putting on the flannel shirt, corduroy trousers and heavy laced boots, all of which he had bought before leaving New York. Then he went to the doorway and stood looking out into the night.

The moonbeams had laid a patine of silver upon the floor of the small clearing before the door, and played softly among the shadows. So silent was the night that minute distant sounds were clearly audible—the stream seemed to be tinkling just at his elbow, while much farther away there was a low murmur of falling water at the tumbling dam, mingling with the sighs of vagrant airs among the crowns of the trees, the rustle and creak of dry branches, the whispering of leaf to leaf. Wakeful birds deceived by the moon piped softly and were silent. An owl called. And then for the briefest moment, except for the stream, utter silence.

Peter strode forth, bathed himself in the moonlight and drank deep of the airs of the forest. America! He had chosen! Her youth called to his. He wanted to forget everything that had gone before, the horrors through which he had passed, both physical and spiritual,—the dying struggles of the senile nation, born in intolerance, grown in ignorance and stupidity which, with a mad gesture, had cast him forth with a curse. He had doffed the empty prerogatives of blood and station and left them in the mire and blood. The soul of Russia was dead and he had thought that his own had died with hers, but from the dead thing a new soul might germinate as it had now germinated in him. He had been born again. *Novaya Jezn!* The New Life! He had found it.

He listened intently as though for its heartbeats, his face turned up toward the silent pines. For a long while he stood so and then went indoors and sat at the old piano playing softly.

CHAPTER V
NEW ELEMENTS

Some of the men on guard in the middle watch reported that they had heard what seemed to be the sounds of music very far away in the woods and were disturbed at the trick their ears had played upon them. But Peter didn't tell them the truth. If listening for the notes of a piano would keep them awake, listen they should. He slept until noon and then went to the house for orders.

Morning seemed to make a difference in the point of view. If the moon had made the night lovely, the sun brought with it the promise of every good thing. The walk through the woods to Black Rock House was a joy, very slightly alleviated by the poor condition of the trees under which Peter passed. It was primeval forest even here, with valuable trees stunted and poor ones vastly overgrown according to nature's law which provides for the survival of the fittest. This was the law too, which was to be applied to Peter. Would he grow straight and true in this foreign soil or gnarled and misshapen like the cedars and the maples that he saw? Yes. He would grow and straight ... straight.

Optimism seemed to be the order of the new day. At the house he found that his employer had put on a clean shirt and was freshly shaven. The windows of the room were opened wide to the sunlight which streamed into the room, revealing its darkest corners. McGuire himself seemed to have responded to the effulgence of the sun and the balmy air which swept across his table. His manner was now calm, his voice more measured.

When Peter came into the room, Mr. McGuire closed the heavy doors of the steel safe carefully and turned to greet him.

"Oh, glad to see you, Nichols," he said more cheerfully. "A quiet night, I understand."

"Yes," laughed Nichols, "except for the man who got through the guards and smoked a cigarette on your portico."

"What!" gasped McGuire.

"Don't be alarmed, sir. It was only myself. I wanted to show Shad Wells the defects of his police system."

"Oh! Ah! Ha, ha, yes, of course. Very good. And you weren't shot at?"

"Oh, no, sir—though I'd given them leave to pot me if they could. But I think you're adequately protected now."

"Good," said McGuire. "Have a cigar. I'm glad you've come. I wanted to talk to you."

And when they had lighted their cigars, "It's about this very guard. I—I'm afraid you'll have to keep your men under cover at least in the daytime."

"Under cover?"

"Well, you see," went on McGuire in some hesitation, "my daughter (he called it darter) Peggy is motoring down from New York to-day. I don't want her, but she's coming. I couldn't stop her. She doesn't know anything about this—er—this guarding the house. And I don't want her to know. She mustn't know. She'd ask questions. I don't want questions asked. I'll get her away as soon as I can, but she mustn't be put into any danger."

"I see," said Peter examining the ash of his cigar. "You don't want her to know anything about the impending attempts upon your life and property."

"Yes, that's it," said McGuire impatiently. "I don't want her to find out. Er—she couldn't understand. You know women, Nichols. They talk too much." He paused "It's—er—necessary that none of her friends in New York or mine should know of—er—any danger that threatens me. And of course—er—any danger that threatens me would—in a way—threaten her. You see?"

"I think so."

"I've put all weapons under cover. I don't want her to see 'em. So when she comes—which may be at any moment—nothing must be said about the men outside and what they're there for. In the daytime they must be given something to do about the place—trimming the lawns, pruning trees or weeding the driveway. Pay 'em what they ask, but don't let any of 'em go away. You'll explain this to the new men. As for yourself—er—of course you're my new superintendent and forester."

McGuire got up and paced the floor slowly looking at Peter out of the tail of his eye.

"I like you, Nichols. We'll get along. You've got courage and intelligence—and of course anybody can see you're a gentleman. You'll keep on taking your meals in the house——"

"If you'd like me to go elsewhere——"

"No. I see no reason why Peggy shouldn't like you. I hope she will. But she's very headstrong, has been since a kid. I suppose I humor her a bit—who wouldn't? I lost my oldest girl and her boy with the 'flu.' Her husband's still in France. And Peggy's got a will of her own, Peg has," he finished in a kind of admiring abstraction. "Got a society bee in her bonnet. Wants to go with all the swells. I'm backin' her, Nichols. She'll do it too before she's through," he finished proudly.

"I haven't a doubt of it," said Peter soberly, though very much amused at his employer's ingenuousness. Here then, was the weak spot in the armor of this relentless millionaire—his daughter. The older one and her child were dead. That accounted for the toys in the cabin. Peggy sounded interesting'—if nothing else, for her vitality.

"I'd better see about this at once, then. If she should come——"

Peter rose and was about to leave the room when there was a sound of an automobile horn and the sudden roar of an exhaust outside. He followed McGuire to the window and saw a low red runabout containing a girl and a male companion emerging from the trees. A man in the road was holding up his hands in signal for the machine to stop and had barely time to leap aside to avoid being run down. The car roared up to the portico, the breathless man, who was Shad Wells, pursuing. Peter was glad that he had had the good sense not to shoot. He turned to his employer, prepared for either anger or dismay and found that McGuire was merely grinning and chuckling softly as though to himself.

"Just like her!" he muttered, "some kid, that!"

Meanwhile Shad Wells, making a bad race of it was only halfway up the drive, when at a signal and shout from McGuire, he stopped running, stared, spat and returned to his post.

There was a commotion downstairs, the shooting of bolts, the sounds of voices and presently the quick patter of feminine footsteps which McGuire, now completely oblivious of Peter, went to meet.

"Well, daughter!"

"Hello, Pop!"

Peter caught a glimpse of a face and straggling brown hair, quickly engulfed in McGuire's arms.

"What on earth——" began McGuire.

"Thought we'd give you a little touch of high life, Pop. It was so hot in town. And the hotel's full of a convention of rough necks. I brought Freddy with me and Mildred and Jack are in the other car. We thought the rest might do us good."

The voice was nasal and pitched high, as though she were trying to make herself audible in a crowd. Peter was ready to revise his estimate that her face was pretty, for to him no woman was more beautiful than her own voice.

"But you can't stay here, Peg," went on McGuire, "not more than over night—with all these people. I'm very busy——"

"H-m. We'll see about that. I never saw the woods look prettier. We came by Lakewood and Brown's Mills and—Why who——?"

As she sidled into the room she suddenly espied Peter who was still standing by the window.

"Who——? Why—Oh, yes, this is my new superintendent and forester. Meet my daughter,—Mr. Nichols."

Peter bowed and expressed pleasure. Miss McGuire swept him with a quick glance that took in his flannel shirt, corduroy breeches and rough boots, nodded pertly and turned away.

Peter smiled. Like Beth Cameron this girl was very particular in choosing her acquaintances.

"I nearly killed a guy in the driveway," she went on, "who was he, Pop?"

"Er—one of the gardeners, I've told them to keep people off the place."

"Well. I'd like to see him keep *me* off! I suppose he'll be trying to hold up Mildred and Jack——"

She walked to the window passing close beside Peter, paying as little attention to his presence as if he had been, an article of furniture.

"Can't you get this man to go down," she said indicating Peter, "and tell them it's all right?"

"Of course," said Peter politely. "I'll go at once. And I'd like to arrange to look over part of the estate with Wells, Mr. McGuire," he added.

"All right, Nichols," said the old man with a frown. And then significantly— "But remember what I've told you. Make careful arrangements before you go."

"Yes, sir."

Peter went down the stairs, amused at his dismissal. On the veranda he found a young man sitting on some suitcases smoking a cigarette. This was Freddy, of course. He afterwards learned that his last name was Mordaunt, that he was a part of Peggy's ambitions, and that he had been invalided home from a camp and discharged from the military service. As Freddy turned, Peter bowed politely and passed on. Having catalogued him by his clothing, Freddy like Peggy had turned away, smoking his cigarette.

Peter thought that some Americans were born with bad manners, some achieved bad manners, and others had bad manners thrust upon them.

Impoliteness was nothing new to him, since he had been in America. It was indigenous. Personally, he didn't mind what sort of people he met, but he seemed to be aware that a new element had come to Black Rock which was to make disquietude for Jonathan K. McGuire and difficulty for himself. And yet too there was a modicum of safety, perhaps, in the presence of these new arrivals, for it had been clear from his employer's demeanor that the terrors of the night had passed with the coming of the day.

He commented on this to Shad Wells, who informed him that night was always the old man's bad time.

"Seems sort o' like he's skeered o' the dark. 'Tain't nateral. 'Fraid o' ghosts, they say," he laughed.

"Well," said Peter, "we've got our orders. And the thing he fears isn't a ghost. It's human."

"Sure?"

"Yes. And since he's more afraid after dark he has probably had his warning. But we're not to take any chances."

Having given his new orders to Jesse, who was to be in charge during their absence, they struck into the woods upon the other side of the Creek for the appraisal of a part of the strip known as the "Upper Reserve." From an attitude of suspicion and sneering contempt Peter's companion had changed to one of indifference. The unfailing good humor of the new superintendent had done something to prepare the ground for an endurable relation between them. Like Beth Cameron Shad had sneered at the word "forester." He was the average lumberman, only interested in the cutting down of trees for the market—the commercial aspect of the business—heedless of the future, indifferent to the dangers of deforestation. Peter tried to explain to him that forestry actually means using the forest as the farmer uses his land, cutting out the mature and overripe trees and giving the seedlings beneath more light that they may furnish the succeeding crop of timber. He knew that the man was intelligent enough, and explained as well as he could from such statistics as he could recall how soon the natural resources of the country would be exhausted under the existing indifference.

"Quite a bit of wood here, Mister—enough for my job," said Shad.

But after a while Peter began to make him understand and showed him what trees should be marked for cutting and why. They came to a burned patch of at least a hundred acres.

"Is there any organized system for fighting these fires?" Peter asked.

"System! Well, when there's a fire we go and try to put it out——" laughed Wells.

"How do the fires start?"

"Campers—hunters mos'ly—in the deer season. Railroads sometimes—at the upper end."

"And you keep no watch for smoke?"

"Where would we watch from?"

"Towers. They ought to be built—with telephone connection to headquarters."

"D'ye think the old man will stand for that?"

"He ought to. It's insurance."

"Oh!"

"It looks to me, Wells," said Peter after a pause, "that a good 'crown' fire and a high gale, would turn all this country to cinders—like this."

"It's never happened yet."

"It may happen. Then good-by to your jobs—and to Black Rock too perhaps."

"I guess Black Rock can stand it, if the old man can."

They walked around the charred clearing and mounted a high sand dune, from which they could see over a wide stretch of country. With a high wooden platform here the whole of the Upper Reserve could be watched. They sat for a while among the sandwort and smoked, while Peter described the work in the German forests that he had observed before the war. Shad had now reached the point of listening and asking questions as the thought was more and more borne into his mind that this new superintendent was not merely talking for talk's sake, but because he knew more about the woods than any man the native had ever talked with, and wanted Shad to know too. For Peter had an answer to all of his questions, and Shad, though envious of Peter's grammar—for he had reached an age to appreciate it—was secretly scornful of Peter's white hands and carefully tied black cravat.

This dune was at the end of the first day's "cruise" and Shad had risen preparatory to returning toward Black Rock when they both heard a sound,—away off to their right, borne down to them clearly on the breeze— the voice of a girl singing.

"Beth," said Shad with a kindling eye. And then carelessly spat, to conceal his emotions.

"What on earth can she be doing in here?" asked Peter.

"Only half a mile from the road. It's the short cut from Gaskill's."

"I see," from Peter.

"Do you reckon you can find your way back alone, Nichols?" said Shad, spitting again.

Peter grinned. "I reckon I can try," he said.

Shad pointed with his long arm in the general direction of Heaven. "That way!" he muttered and went into the scrub oak with indecent haste.

Peter sat looking with undisguised interest at the spot where he had disappeared, tracing him for a while through the moving foliage, listening to the crackling of the underbrush, as the sounds receded.

It was time to be turning homeward, but the hour was still inviting, the breeze balmy, the sun not too warm, so Peter lay back among the grasses in the sand smoking a fresh cigarette. Far overhead buzzards were wheeling. They recalled those other birds of prey that he had often watched, ready to swoop down along the lines of the almost defenseless Russians. Here all was so quiet. The world was a very beautiful place if men would only leave it so. The voice of the girl was silent now. Shad had probably joined her. Somehow, Peter hadn't been able to think of any relationship, other than the cousinly one, between Shad Wells and Beth. He had only known the girl for half an hour but as Aunt Tillie Bergen had said, her niece seemed different from the other natives that Peter had met. Her teeth were sound and white, suggesting habits of personal cleanliness; her conversation, though careless, showed at the very least, a grammar school training. And Shad—well, Shad was nothing but a "Piney."

Pity—with a voice like that—she ought to have had opportunities—this scornful little Beth. Peter closed his eyes and dozed. He expected to have no difficulty in finding his way home, for he had a pocket compass and the road could not be far distant. He liked this place. He would build a tower here, a hundred-foot tower, of timbers, and here a man should be stationed all day— to watch for wisps of smoke during the hunting season. Smoke ... Tower ... In a moment he snored gently.

"Halloo!" came a voice in his dream. "Halloo! Halloo!"

Peter started rubbing his eyes, aware of the smoking cigarette in the grasses beside him.

Stupid, that! To do the very thing he had been warning Shad Wells against. He smeared the smoking stub out in the sand and sat up yawning and stretching his arms.

"Halloo!" said the voice in his dream, almost at his ear. "Tryin' to set the woods afire?"

The question had the curious dropping intonation at its end. But the purport annoyed him.

Nothing that she could have said could have provoked him more! Behind her he saw the dark face of Shad Wells break into a grin.

"I fell asleep," said Peter, getting to his feet.

Beth laughed. "Lucky you weren't burnt to death. *Then* how would the trees get along?"

Peter's toe burrowed after the defunct cigarette.

"I know what I'm about," he muttered, aware of further loss of dignity.

"Oh, do you? Then which way were you thinkin' of goin' home?"

Peter glanced around, pointed vaguely, and Beth Cameron laughed.

"I guess you'd land in Egg Harbor, or thereabouts."

Her laugh was infectious and Peter at last echoed it.

"You's better be goin' along with us. Shad asked me to come and get you, didn't you, Shad?"

Peter glanced at the woodsman's black scowl and grinned, recalling his desertion and precipitate disappearance into the bushes.

"I'm sure I'm very much obliged to you both," said Peter diplomatically. "But I think I can find my way in."

"Not if you start for Hammonton or Absecon, you can't. I've known people to spend the night in the woods a quarter of a mile from home."

"I shouldn't mind that."

"But Shad would. He'd feel a great responsibility if you didn't turn up for the ghost-hunt. Wouldn't you, Shad?"

Shad wagged his head indeterminately, and spat. "Come on," he said sullenly, and turned, leading the way out to the northward, followed by Beth with an inviting smile. She still wore her denim overalls which were much too long for her and her dusty brown boots seemed like a child's. Between moments of avoiding roots and branches, Peter watched her strong young figure as it followed their leader. Yesterday, he had thought her small; to-day she seemed to have increased in stature—so uncertain is the masculine judgment upon any aspect of a woman. But his notions in regard to her grace and loveliness were only confirmed. There was no concealing them under her absurd garments. Her flanks were long and lithe, like a boy's, but there was something feminine in the way she moved, a combination of ease and strength made manifest, which could only come of well-made limbs carefully jointed. Every little while she flashed a glance over her shoulder at him, exchanging a word, even politely holding back a branch until he caught it, or else when he was least expecting it, letting it fly into his face. From time to time Shad Wells would turn to look at them and Peter could see that he wasn't as happy as he might have been. But Beth was very much enjoying herself.

They had emerged at last into the road and walked toward Black Rock, Beth in the center and Peter and Shad on either side.

"I've been thinkin' about what you said yesterday," said Beth to Peter.

"About——?"

"Singin' like an angel in Heaven," she said promptly aware of Shad's bridling glance.

"Oh, well," repeated Peter, "you do—you know."

"It was very nice of you—and you a musician."

"Musician!" growled Shad. "He ain't a musician."

"Oh, yes, he is, and he says I've a voice like an angel. *You* never said that, Shad Wells."

"No. Nor I won't," he snapped surlily.

Peter would have been more amused if he hadn't thought that Shad Wells was unhappy.

He needed the man's allegiance and he had no wish to make an enemy of him.

"Musician!" Shad growled. "Then it was you the men heard last night."

"I found a piano in the cabin. I was trying it," said Peter. Shad said nothing in reply but he put every shade of scorn into the way in which he spat into the road.

"A piano——!" Beth gasped. "Where? What cabin?"

"The playhouse—where I live," said Peter politely.

"Oh."

There was a silence on the part of both of his companions, awkwardly long.

So Peter made an effort to relieve the tension, commenting on the new arrivals at Black Rock House.

At the mention of Peggy's name Beth showed fresh excitement.

"Miss McGuire! Here? When——?"

"This morning. Do you know her?"

"No. But I've seen her. I think she's just lovely."

"Why?"

"She wears such beautiful clothes and—and hats and veils."

Peter laughed. "And that's your definition of loveliness."

"Why, yes," she said in wonder. "Last year all the girls were copyin' her, puttin' little puffs of hair over their ears—I tried it, but it looked funny. Is she going to be here long? Has she got a 'beau' with her? She always had. It's a wonder she doesn't run over somebody, the way she drives."

"She nearly got me this mornin'," growled Shad.

"I wish she would—if you're going to look like a meat-ax, Shad Wells."

There was no reconciling them now, and when Beth's home was reached, all three of them went different ways. What a rogue she was! And poor Shad Wells who was to have taken Peter at a gobble, seemed a very poor sort of a creature in Beth's hands.

She amused Peter greatly, but she annoyed him a little too, ruffled up the shreds of his princely dignity, not yet entirely inured to the trials of social regeneration. And Shad's blind adoration was merely a vehicle for her amusement. It would have been very much better if she hadn't used Peter's compliment as a bait for Shad. Peter had come to the point of liking the rough foreman even if he was a new kind of human animal from anything in Peter's experience.

And so was Beth. A new kind of animal—something between a harrier and a skylark, but wholesome and human too, a denim dryad, the spirit of health, joy and beauty, a creature good to look at, in spite of her envy of the fashionable Miss Peggy McGuire with her modish hats, cerise veils and ear puffs, her red roadsters and her beaux. Poverty sat well upon Beth and the frank blue eyes and resolute chin gave notice that whatever was to happen to her future she was honorable and unafraid.

But if there was something very winning about her, there was something pathetic too. Her beauty was so unconscious of her ridiculous clothing, and yet Peter had come to think of it as a part of her, wondering indeed what she would look like in feminine apparel, in which he could not imagine her, for the other girls of Black Rock had not so far blessed his vision. Aunt Tillie Bergen had told him, over his late breakfast, of the difficulties that she and Beth had had to keep their little place going and how Beth, after being laid off for the summer at the factory, had insisted upon working in the Gaskill's vineyard to help out with the household. There ought to be something for Beth Cameron, better than this—something less difficult—more ennobling.

Thinking of these things Peter made his way back to the cabin. Nothing of a disturbing nature had happened around Black Rock House, except the arrival of the remainder of McGuire's unwelcome house party, which had taken to wandering aimlessly through the woods, much to the disgust of Jesse Brown, who, lost in the choice between "dudes" and desperadoes, had given up any attempt to follow Peter's careful injunctions in regard to McGuire. It was still early and the supper hour was seven, so Peter unpacked his small trunk which had arrived in his absence and then, carefully shutting door and windows, sat at the piano and played quietly at first, a "Reverie" of Tschaikowsky, a "Berceuse" of César Cui, the "Valse Triste" of Jean Sibelius and then forgetting himself—launched forth into Chopin's C Minor Étude. His fingers were stiff for lack of practice and the piano was far from perfect, but in twenty minutes he had forgotten the present, lost in memories. He had played this for Anastasie Galitzin. He saw the glint of the shaded piano lamp upon her golden head, recalled her favorite perfume.... Silver nights upon the castle terrace.... Golden walks through the autumn forest....

Suddenly a bell rang loudly at Peter's side, it seemed. Then while he wondered, it rang again. Of course—the telephone. He found the instrument in the corner and put the receiver to his ear. It was McGuire's voice.

"That you, Nichols?" it asked in an agitated staccato.

"Yes, sir."

"Well, it's getting dark, what have you done about to-night?"

"Same as last night," said Peter smiling, "only more careful."

"Well, I want things changed," the gruff voice rose. "The whole d—n house is open. I can't shut it with these people here. Your men will have to move in closer—but keep under cover. Can you arrange it?"

"Yes, I think so."

"I'll want you here—with me—you understand. You were coming to supper?"

"Yes, sir."

"Well—er—I've told my daughter and so—would you mind putting on a dress suit——? Er—if you have one—a Tuxedo will do."

"Yes, sir," said Peter. "That's all right."

"Oh—er—thanks. You'll be up soon?"

"Yes."

"Good-by."

With a grin, Peter hung up the receiver, recalling the soiled, perspiring, unquiet figure of his employer last night. But it seemed as though McGuire were almost as much in awe of his daughter as of the danger that threatened, for, in the McGuire household, Miss Peggy, it appeared, was paramount.

Peter's bathroom was Cedar Creek. In his robe, he ran down the dusky path for a quick plunge. Then, refreshed and invigorated, he lighted his lamp and dressed leisurely. He had come to his cravat, to which he was wont to pay more than a casual attention, when he was aware of a feeling of discomfort— of unease. In the mirror something moved, a shadow, at the corner of the window. He waited a moment, still fingering his cravat, and then sure that his eyes had made no mistake, turned quickly and, revolver in hand, rushed outside. Just as he did so a man with a startled face disappeared around the corner of the cabin. Peter rushed after him, shouting and turned the edge just in time to see his shape leap into the bushes.

"Who goes there?" shouted Peter crisply. "Halt, or I'll fire."

But the only reply was a furious crashing in the undergrowth. Peter fired twice at the sound, then followed in, still calling.

No sound. Under the conditions a chase was hopeless, so Peter paused listening. And then after a few moments a more distant crackling advised him that his visitor had gotten well away. And so after a while he returned to the cabin and with his weapon beside him finished his interrupted toilet.

But his brows were in a tangle. The mystery surrounding him seemed suddenly to have deepened. For the face that he had seen at the window was that of the stranger who had stared at him so curiously—the man of the soft hat and dark mustache—who had seemed so startled at seeing him in the Pennsylvania Station when he was leaving New York.

CHAPTER VI
THE HOUSE OF TERROR

Who—what was this stranger who seemed so interested in his whereabouts? Peter was sure that he had made no mistake. It was an unusual face, swarthy, with high cheek bones, dark eyes, a short nose with prominent nostrils. Perhaps it would not have been so firmly impressed on his memory except for the curious look of startled recognition that Peter had surprised on it at the station in New York. This had puzzled him for some moments in the train but had been speedily lost in the interest of his journey. The man had followed him to Black Rock. But why? What did he want of Peter and why should he skulk around the cabin and risk the danger of Peter's bullets? It seemed obvious that he was here for some dishonest purpose, but what dishonest purpose could have any interest in Peter? If robbery, why hadn't the man chosen the time while Peter was away in the woods? Peter grinned to himself. If the man had any private sources of information as to Peter's personal assets, he would have known that they consisted of a two-dollar watch and a small sum in money. If the dishonest purpose were murder or injury, why hadn't he attacked Peter while he was bathing, naked and quite defenseless, in the creek?

There seemed to be definite answers to all of these questions, but none to the fact of the man's presence, to the fact of his look of recognition, or to the fact of his wish to be unobserved. Was he a part of the same conspiracy which threatened McGuire? Or was this a little private conspiracy arranged for Peter alone? And if so, why? So far as Peter knew he hadn't an enemy in America, and even if he had made one, it was hardly conceivable that any one should go to such lengths to approach an issue and then deliberately avoid it.

But there seemed no doubt that something was up and that, later, more would be heard from this curious incident. It seemed equally certain that had the stranger meant to shoot Peter he could easily have done so in perfect safety to himself through the window, while Peter was fastening his cravat. Reloading his revolver and slipping it into his pocket, Peter locked the cabin carefully, and after listening to the sounds of the woods for awhile, made his way up the path to Black Rock House.

He had decided to say nothing about the incident which, so far as he could see, concerned only himself, and so when the men on guard questioned him about the shots that they had heard he told them that he had been firing at a mark. This was quite true, even if the mark had been invisible. Shad Wells was off duty until midnight so Peter went the rounds, calling the men to the guardhouse and telling them of the change in the orders. They were to wait until the company upon the portico went indoors and then, with Jesse in command, they were to take new stations in trees and clumps of bushes which Peter designated much nearer the house. The men eyed his dinner jacket with some curiosity and not a little awe, and Peter informed them that it was the old man's order and that he, Peter, was going to keep watch from inside the house, but that a blast from a whistle would fetch him out. He also warned them that it was McGuire's wish that none of the visitors should be aware of the watchmen and that therefore there should be no false alarms.

Curiously enough Peter found McGuire in a state very nearly bordering on calm. He had had a drink. He had not heard the shots Peter had fired nor apparently had any of the regular occupants of the house. The visitors had possibly disregarded them. From the pantry came a sound with which Peter was familiar, for Stryker was shaking the cocktails. And when the ladies came downstairs the two men on the portico came in and Peter was presented to the others of the party, Miss Delaplane, Mr. Gittings and Mr. Mordaunt. The daughter of the house examined Peter's clothing and then, having apparently revised her estimate of him, became almost cordial, bidding him sit next Miss Delaplane at table.

Mildred Delaplane was tall, handsome, dark and aquiline, and made a foil for Peggy's blond prettiness. Peter thought her a step above Peggy in the cultural sense, and only learned afterward that as she was not very well off, Peggy was using her as a rung in the social ladder. Mordaunt, Peter didn't fancy, but Gittings, who was jovial and bald, managed to inject some life into the party, which, despite the effect of the cocktails, seemed rather weary and listless.

McGuire sat rigidly at the head of the table, forcing smiles and glancing uneasily at doors and windows. Peter was worried too, not as to himself, but as to any possible connection that there might be between the man with the dark mustache and the affairs of Jonathan McGuire. Mildred Delaplane, who had traveled in Europe in antebellum days, found much that was interesting in Peter's fragmentary reminiscences. She knew music too, and in an unguarded moment Peter admitted that he had studied. It was difficult to lie to women, he had found.

And so, after dinner, that information having transpired, he was immediately led to the piano-stool by his hostess, who was frequently biased in her social judgments by Mildred Delaplane. Peter played Cyril Scott's "Song from the East," and then, sure of Miss Delaplane's interest, an Étude of Scriabine, an old favorite of his which seemed to express the mood of the moment.

And all the while he was aware of Jonathan McGuire, seated squarely in the middle of the sofa which commanded all the windows and doors, with one hand at his pocket, scowling and alert by turns, for, though the night had fallen slowly, it was now pitch black outside. Peter knew that McGuire was thinking he hadn't hired his superintendent as a musician to entertain his daughter's guests, but that he was powerless to interfere. Nor did he wish to excite the reprobation of his daughter by going up and locking himself in his room. Peggy, having finished her cigarette with Freddy on the portico, had come in again and was now leaning over the piano, her gaze fixed, like Mildred's, upon Peter's mobile fingers.

"You're really too wonderful a superintendent to be quite true," said Peggy when Peter had finished. "But *do* give us a 'rag.'"

Peter shook his head. "I'm sorry, but I can't do ragtime."

"Quit your kidding! I want to dance."

"I'm not—er—kidding," said Peter, laughing. "I can't play it at all—not at all."

Peggy gave him a look, shrugged and walked to the door.

"Fred-die-e!" she called.

Peter rose from the piano-stool and crossed to McGuire. The man's cigar was unsmoked and tiny beads of sweat stood out on his forehead.

"I don't think you need worry, sir," whispered Peter. "The men are all around the house, but if you say, I'll go out for another look around."

"No matter. I'll stick it out for a while."

"You're better off here than anywhere, I should say. No one would dare——"

Here Freddy at the piano struck up "Mary" and further conversation was drowned in commotion. Mildred Delaplane was preëmpted by Mr. Gittings and Peggy came whirling alone toward Peter, arms extended, the passion for the dance outweighing other prejudices.

Peter took a turn, but four years of war had done little to improve his steps.

"I'm afraid all my dancing is in my fingers," he muttered.

Suddenly, as Freddy Mordaunt paused, Peggy stopped and lowered her arms.

"Good Lord!" she gasped. "What's the matter with Pop?"

McGuire had risen unsteadily and was peering out into the darkness through the window opposite him, his face pallid, his lips drawn into a thin line. Peggy ran to him and caught him by the arm.

"What is it, Pop? Are you sick?"

"N-no matter. Just a bit upset. If you don't mind, daughter, I think I'll be going up."

"Can I do anything?"

"No. Stay here and enjoy yourselves. Just tell Stryker, will you, Nichols, and then come up to my room."

Peggy was regarding him anxiously as he made his way to the door and intercepted Peter as he went to look for the valet.

"What is it, Mr. Nichols?" she asked. "He may be sick, but it seems to me——" she paused, and then, "Did you see his eyes as he looked out of the window?"

"Indigestion," said Peter coolly.

"You'll see after him, won't you? And if he wants me, just call over."

"I'm sure he won't want you. A few home remedies——"

And Peter went through the door. Stryker had appeared mysteriously from somewhere and had already preceded his master up the stair. When Peter reached the landing, McGuire was standing alone in the dark, leaning against the wall, his gaze on the lighted bedroom which, the valet was carefully examining.

"What is it, sir?" asked Peter coolly. "You thought you saw something?"

"Yes—out there—on the side portico——"

"You must be mistaken—unless it was one of the watchmen——"

"No, no. I saw——"

"What, sir?"

"No matter. Do you think Peggy noticed?"

"Just that you didn't seem quite yourself——"

"But not that I seemed—er——"

"Alarmed? I said you weren't well."

Peter took the frightened man's arm and helped him into his room.

"I'm not, Nichols," he groaned. "I'm not myself."

"I wouldn't worry, sir. I'd say it was physically impossible for any one to approach the house without permission. But I'll go down and have another look around."

"Do, Nichols. But come back up here. I'll want to talk to you."

So Peter went down. And, evading inquiries in the hallway, made his way out through the hall and pantry. Here a surprise awaited him, for as he opened the door there was a skurry of light footsteps and in a moment he was in the pantry face to face with Beth Cameron, who seemed much dismayed at being discovered.

"What on earth are you doing here?" he asked in amazement.

She glanced at his white shirt front and then laughed.

"I came to help Aunt Tillie dish up."

"You!" He didn't know why he should have been so amazed at finding her occupying a menial position in this household. She didn't seem to belong to the back stairs! And yet there she was in a plain blue gingham dress which made her seem much taller, and a large apron, her tawny hair casting agreeable shadows around her blue eyes, which he noticed seemed much darker by night than by day.

She noticed the inflection of his voice and laughed.

"Why not? I thought Aunt Tillie would need me—and besides I wanted to peek a little."

"Ah, I see. You wanted to see Miss Peggy's new frock through the keyhole?"

"Yes—and the other one. Aren't they pretty?"

"I suppose so."

"I listened, too. I couldn't help it."

"Eavesdropping!"

She nodded. "Oh, Mr. Nichols, but you do play the piano beautifully!"

"But not like an angel in Heaven," said Peter with a smile.

"Almost—if angels play. You make me forget——" she paused.

"What——?"

"That's there's anything in the world except beauty."

In the drawing-room Freddy, having found himself, had swept into a song of the cabarets, to which there was a "close harmony" chorus.

"There's that——," he muttered, jerking a thumb in the direction from which he had come.

But she shook her head. "No," she said. "That's different."

"How—different?"

"Wrong—false—un—unworthy——"

As she groped for and found the word he stared at her in astonishment. And in her eyes back of the joy that seemed to be always dancing in them he saw the shadows of a sober thought.

"But don't you like dance music?" he asked.

"Yes, I do, but it's only for the feet. Your music is for—for *here*." And with a quick graceful gesture she clasped her hands upon her breast.

"I'm glad you think so, because that's where it comes from."

At this point Peter remembered his mission, which Beth's appearance had driven from his mind.

"I'll play for you sometime," he said.

He went past her and out to the servants' dining-room. As he entered with Beth at his heels, Mrs. Bergen, the housekeeper, turned in from the open door to the kitchen garden, clinging to the jamb, her lips mumbling, as though she were continuing a conversation. But her round face, usually the color and texture of a well ripened peach, was the color of putty, and seemed suddenly to have grown old and haggard. Her eyes through her metal-rimmed spectacles seemed twice their size and stared at Peter as though they saw through him and beyond. She faltered at the door-jamb and then with an effort reached a chair, into which she sank gasping.

Beth was kneeling at her side in a moment, looking up anxiously into her startled eyes.

"Why, what is it, Aunt Tillie?" she whispered quickly. "What it is? Tell me."

The coincidence was too startling. Could the same Thing that had frightened McGuire have frightened the housekeeper too? Peter rushed past her and out of the open door. It was dark outside and for a moment he could see nothing. Then objects one by one asserted themselves, the orderly rows of vegetable plants in the garden, the wood-box by the door, the shrubbery at the end of the portico, the blue spruce tree opposite, the loom of the dark and noncommittal garage. He knew that one of his men was in the trees opposite the side porch and another around the corner of the kitchen, in the hedge, but he did not want to raise a hue and cry unless it was necessary. What was this Thing that created terror at sight? He peered this way and that, aware of an intense excitement, in one hand his revolver and in the other his police whistle. But he saw no object move, and the silence was absolute. In a moment—disappointed—he hurried back to the servants' dining-room.

Mrs. Bergen sat dazed in her chair, while Beth, who had brought her a glass of water, was making her drink of it.

"Tell me, what is it?" Beth was insisting.

"Nothing—nothing," murmured the woman.

"But there is——"

"No, dearie——"

"Are you sick?"

"I don't feel right. Maybe—the heat——"

"But your eyes look queer——"

"Do they——?" The housekeeper tried to smile.

"Yes. Like they had seen——"

A little startled as she remembered the mystery of the house, Beth cast her glance into the darkness outside the open door.

"You *are*—frightened!" she said.

"No, no——"

"What was it you saw, Mrs. Bergen," asked Peter gently.

He was just at her side and at the sound of his voice she half arose, but recognizing Peter she sank back in her chair.

Peter repeated his question, but she shook her head.

"Won't you tell us? What was it you saw? A man——?"

Her eyes sought Beth's and a look of tenderness came into them, banishing the vision. But she lied when she answered Peter's question.

"I saw nothin', Mr. Nichols—I think I'll go up——"

She took another swallow of the water and rose. And with her strength came a greater obduracy.

"I saw nothin'——" she repeated again, as she saw that he was still looking at her. "Nothin' at all."

Peter and Beth exchanged glances and Beth, putting her hand under the housekeeper's arm, helped the woman to the back stairs.

Peter stood for a moment in the middle of the kitchen floor, his gaze on the door through which the woman had vanished. Aunt Tillie too! She had seen some one, some Thing—the same some one or Thing that McGuire had seen. But granting that their eyes had not deceived them, granting that each had seen Something, what, unless it were supernatural, could have frightened McGuire and Aunt Tillie too? Even if the old woman had been timid about staying in the house, she had made it clear to Peter that she was entirely unaware of the kind of danger that threatened her employer. Peter had believed her then. He saw no reason to disbelieve her now. She had known as little as Peter about the cause for McGuire's alarm. And here he had found her staring with the same unseeing eyes into the darkness, with the same symptoms of nervous shock as McGuire had shown. What enemy of McGuire's could frighten Aunt Tillie into prostration and seal her lips to speech? Why wouldn't she have dared to tell Peter what she had seen? What was this secret and how could she share it with McGuire when twenty-four hours ago she had been in complete ignorance of the mystery? Why wouldn't she talk? Was the vision too intimate? Or too horrible?

Peter was imaginative, for he had been steeped from boyhood in the superstitions of his people. But the war had taught him that devils had legs and carried weapons. He had seen more horrible sights than most men of his years, in daylight, at dawn, or silvered with moonlight. He thought he had exhausted the possibilities for terror. But he found himself grudgingly admitting that he was at the least a little nervous—at the most, on the verge of alarm. But he put his whistle in his mouth, drew his revolver again and went forth.

First he sought out the man in the spruce tree. It was Andy. He had seen no one but the people on the porch and in the windows. It was very dark but he took an oath that no one had approached the house from his side.

"You saw no one talking with Mrs. Bergen by the kitchen door?"

"No. I can't see th' kitchen door from here."

Peter verified. A syringa bush was just in line.

"Then you haven't moved?" asked Peter.

"No. I was afraid they'd see me."

"They've seen something——"

"You mean——?"

"I don't know. But look sharp. If anything comes out this way, take a shot at it."

"You think there's something——"

"Yes—but don't move. And keep your eyes open!"

Peter went off to the man in the hedge behind the kitchen—Jesse Brown.

"See anything?" asked Peter.

"Nope. Nobody but the chauffeur."

"The chauffeur?"

"He went up to th' house a while back."

"Oh—how long ago?"

"Twenty minutes."

"I see." And then, "You didn't see any one come away from the kitchen door?"

"No. He's thar yet, I reckon."

Peter ran out to the garage to verify this statement. By the light of a lantern the chauffeur in his rubber boots was washing the two cars.

"Have you been up to the house lately?"

"Why, no," said the man, in surprise.

"You're sure?" asked Peter excitedly.

"Sure——"

"Then come with me. There's something on."

The man dropped his sponge and followed Peter, who had run back quickly to the house.

It was now after eleven. From the drawing-room came the distracting sounds from the tortured piano, but there was no one on the portico. So Peter, with Jesse, Andy and the chauffeur made a careful round of the house, examining every bush, every tree, within a circle of a hundred yards, exhausting every possibility for concealment. When they reached the kitchen door again, Peter rubbed his head and gave it up. A screech owl somewhere off in the woods jeered at him. All the men, except Jesse, were plainly skeptical. But he sent them back to their posts and, still pondering the situation, went into the house.

It was extraordinary how the visitor, whoever he was, could have gotten away without having been observed, for though the night was black the eyes of the men outside were accustomed to it and the lights from the windows sent a glimmer into the obscurity. Of one thing Peter was now certain, that the prowler was no ghost or banshee, but a man, and that he had gone as mysteriously as he had come.

Peter knew that his employer would be anxious until he returned to him, but he hadn't quite decided to tell McGuire of the housekeeper's share in the adventure. He had a desire to verify his belief that Mrs. Bergen was frightened by the visitor for a reason of her own which had nothing to do with Jonathan McGuire. Any woman alarmed by a possible burglar or other miscreant would have come running and crying for help. Mrs. Bergen had been doggedly silent, as though, rather than utter her thoughts, she would have bitten out her tongue. It was curious. She had seemed to be talking as though to herself at the door, and then, at the sound of footsteps in the kitchen behind her, had turned and fallen limp in the nearest chair. The look in her face, as in McGuire's, was that of terror, but there was something of bewilderment in both of them too, like that of a solitary sniper in the first shock of a shrapnel wound, a look of anguish that seemed to have no outlet, save in speech, which was denied.

To tell McGuire what had happened in the kitchen meant to alarm him further. Peter decided for the present to keep the matter from him, giving the housekeeper the opportunity of telling the truth on the morrow if she wished.

He crossed the kitchen and servants' dining-room and just at the foot of the back stairs met Mrs. Bergen and Beth coming down. So he retraced his steps into the kitchen, curious as to the meaning of her reappearance.

At least she had recovered the use of her tongue.

"I couldn't go to bed, just yet, Mr. Nichols," she said in reply to Peter's question. "I just couldn't."

Peter gazed at her steadily. This woman held a clew to the mystery. She glanced at him uncertainly but she had recovered her self-possession, and her replies to his questions, if anything, were more obstinate than before.

"I saw nothin', Mr. Nichols—nothin'. I was just a bit upset. I'm all right now. An' I want Beth to go home. That's why I came down."

"But, Aunt Tillie, if you're not well, I'm going to stay——"

"No. Ye can't stay here. I want ye to go." And then, turning excitedly to Peter, "Can't ye let somebody see her home, Mr. Nichols?"

"Of course," said Peter. "But I don't think she's in any danger."

"No, but she can't stay here. She just can't."

Beth put her arm around the old woman's shoulder.

"I'm not afraid."

Aunt Tillie was already untying Beth's apron.

"I know ye're not, dearie. But ye can't stay here. I don't want ye to. I don't want ye to."

"But if you're afraid of something——"

"Who said I was afraid?" she asked, glaring at Peter defiantly. "I'm not. I just had a spell—all this excitement an' extra work—an' everything."

She lied. Peter knew it, but he saw no object to be gained in keeping Beth in Black Rock House, so he went out cautiously and brought the chauffeur, to whom he entrusted the safety of the girl. He would have felt more comfortable if he could have escorted her himself, but he knew that his duty was at the house and that whoever the mysterious person was it was not Beth that he wanted.

But what was Mrs. Bergen's reason for wishing to get rid of her?

As Beth went out of the door he whispered in her ear, "Say nothing of this—to any one."

She nodded gravely and followed the man who had preceded her.

When the door closed behind Beth and the chauffeur, Peter turned quickly and faced the housekeeper.

"Now," he said severely, "tell me the truth."

She stared at him with a falling jaw in a moment of alarm—then closed her lips firmly. And, as she refused to reply,

"Do you want me to tell Mr. McGuire that you were talking to a stranger at the kitchen door?"

She trembled and sinking in a chair buried her face in her hands.

"I don't want to be unkind, Mrs. Bergen, but there's something here that needs explaining. Who was the man you talked to outside the door?"

"I—I can't tell ye," she muttered.

"You must. It's better. I'm your friend and Beth's——"

The woman raised her haggard face to his.

"Beth's friend! Are ye? Then ask me no more."

"But I've got to know. I'm here to protect Mr. McGuire, but I'd like to protect you too. Who is this stranger?"

The woman lowered her head and then shook it violently. "No, no. I'll not tell."

He frowned down at her head.

"Did you know that to-night McGuire saw the stranger—the man that *you* saw—and that he's even more frightened than you?"

The woman raised her head, gazed at him helplessly, then lowered it again, but she did not speak. The kitchen was silent, but an obbligato to this drama, like the bray of the ass in the overture to "Midsummer Night's Dream," came from the drawing-room, where Freddy Mordaunt was now singing a sentimental ballad.

"I'm sorry, Mrs. Bergen, but if Mr. McGuire is in danger to-night, I've got to know it."

"To-night!" she gasped, as though clutching at a straw. "Not to-night. Nothin'll happen to-night. I'm sure of that, Mr. Nichols."

"How do you know?"

She threw out her arms in a wide gesture of desperation. "For the love o' God, go 'way an' leave me in peace. Don't ye see I ain't fit to talk to anybody?" She gasped with a choking throat. "*He* ain't comin' back again—not to-night. I'll swear it on th' Bible, if ye want me to."

Their glances met, hers weary and pleading, and he believed her.

"All right, Mrs. Bergen," he said soothingly. "I'll take your word for it, but you'll admit the whole thing is very strange—very startling."

"Yes—strange. God knows it is. But I—I can't tell ye anything."

"But what shall I say to Mr. McGuire—upstairs. I've got to go up—now."

"Say to him——?" she gasped helplessly, all her terrors renewed. "Ye can't tell him I was talkin' to anybody." And then more wildly, "Ye mustn't. I wasn't. I was talkin' to myself—that's the God's truth, I was—when ye come in. It was so strange—an' all. Don't tell him, Mr. Nichols," she pleaded at last, with a terrible earnestness, and clutching at his hand. "For my sake, for Beth's——"

"What has Beth to do with it?"

"More'n ye think. Oh, God——" she broke off. "What am I sayin'——? Beth don't know. She mustn't. He don't know either——"

"Who? McGuire?"

"No—no. Don't ask any more questions, Mr. Nichols," she sobbed. "I can't speak. Don't ye see I can't?"

So Peter gave up the inquisition. He had never liked to see a woman cry.

"Oh, all right," he said more cheerfully, "you'd better be getting to bed. Perhaps daylight will clear things up."

"And ye won't tell McGuire?" she pleaded.

"I can't promise anything. But I won't if I'm not compelled to."

She gazed at him uncertainly, her weary eyes wavering, but she seemed to take some courage from his attitude.

"God bless ye, sir."

"Good-night, Mrs. Bergen."

And then, avoiding the drawing-room, Peter made his way up the stairs with a great deal of mental uncertainty to the other room of terror.

CHAPTER VII
MUSIC

Stryker, who kept guard at the door of McGuire's room, opened it cautiously in response to Peter's knock. He found McGuire sitting rigidly in a rocking-chair at the side of the room, facing the windows, a whisky bottle and glass on the table beside him. His face had lost its pallor, but in his eyes was the same look of glassy bewilderment.

"Why the H——— couldn't you come sooner?" He whined the question, not angrily, but querulously, like a child.

"I was having a look around," replied Peter coolly.

"Oh! And did you find anybody?"

"No."

"H-m! I thought you wouldn't."

Peter hesitated. He meant to conceal the housekeeper's share in the night's encounters, but he knew that both Andy and the chauffeur would talk, and so,

"There *was* somebody outside, Mr. McGuire," he said. "You were not mistaken, a man prowling in the dark near the kitchen. Andy thought it was the chauffeur, who was in the garage washing the cars."

"Ah!"

McGuire started up, battling for his manhood. It seemed to Peter that his gasp was almost one of relief at discovering that his eyes had not deceived him, that the face he had seen was that of a real person, instead of the figment of a disordered mind.

"Ah! Why didn't they shoot him?"

"I've just said, sir, Andy thought it was the chauffeur."

McGuire was pacing the floor furiously.

"He has no business to think. I pay him to act. And you—what did you do?"

"Three of us searched the whole place—every tree, every bush—every shadow———. The man has gone."

"Gone," sneered the other. "A H——— of a mess you're making of this job!"

Peter straightened angrily, but managed to control himself.

"Very well, Mr. McGuire," he said. "Then you'd better get somebody else at once."

He had never given notice before but the hackneyed phrase fell crisply from his lips. For many reasons, Peter didn't want to go, but he bowed and walked quickly across the room. "Good-night," he said.

Before he had reached the door the frightened man came stumbling after him and caught him by the arm.

"No, no, Nichols. Come back. D'ye hear? You mustn't be so d—— touchy. Come back. You can't go. I didn't mean anything. Come now!"

Peter paused, his hand on the knob, and looked down into the man's flabby, empurpled countenance.

"I thought you meant it," he said.

"No. I—I didn't. I—I like you, Nichols—liked you from the very first—yesterday. Of course you can't be responsible for all the boneheads here."

Peter had "called the bluff." Perhaps the lesson might have a salutary effect. And so, as his good humor came back to him, he smiled pleasantly.

"You see, Mr. McGuire, you could hardly expect Andy to shoot the chauffeur. They're on excellent terms."

McGuire had settled down into a chair near the table, and motioned Peter to another one near him.

"Sit down, Nichols. Another glass, Stryker. So." He poured the whisky with an assumption of ease and they drank.

"You see, Nichols," he went on as he set his empty glass down, "I know what I'm about. There *is* somebody trying to get at me. It's no dream—no hallucination. You know that too, now. I saw him—I would have shot him through the window—if it hadn't been for Peggy—and the others—but I—I didn't dare—for reasons. She mustn't know——" And then eagerly, "She doesn't suspect anything yet, does she, Nichols?"

Peter gestured over his shoulder in the direction of the sounds which still came from below.

"No. They're having a good time."

"That's all right. To-morrow they'll be leaving for New York, I hope. And then we'll meet this issue squarely. You say the man has gone. Why do you think so?"

"Isn't it reasonable to think so? His visit was merely a reconnoissance. I think he had probably been lying out in the underbrush all day, getting the lay of the land, watching what we were doing—seeing where the men were placed. But he must know now that he'll have to try something else—that he hasn't a chance of getting to you past these guards, if you don't want him to."

"But he nearly succeeded to-night," mumbled McGuire dubiously.

Peter was silent a moment.

"I'm not supposed to question and I won't. But it seems to me, Mr. McGuire, that if this visitor's plan were to murder you, to get rid of you, he would have shot you down to-night, through the window. From his failure to do so, there is one definite conclusion to draw—and that is that he wants to see you—to talk with you——"

McGuire fairly threw himself from his chair as he roared,

"I can't see him. I won't. I won't see anybody. I've got the law on my side. A man's house is his castle. A fellow prowls around here in the dark. He's been seen—if he's shot it's his own lookout. And he *will* be shot before he reaches me. You hear me? Your men must shoot—shoot to kill. If they fail I'll—— "

He shrugged as if at the futility of his own words, which came stumbling forth, born half of fear, half of braggadocio.

Peter regarded him soberly. It was difficult to conceive of this man, who talked like a madman and a spoiled child, as the silent, stubborn, friendless millionaire, as the power in finance that Sheldon, Senior, had described him to be. The love of making money had succumbed to a more primitive passion which for the time being had mastered him. From what had been revealed, it seemed probable that it was not death or bodily injury that he feared, for Peter had seen him stand up at the window, a fair target for any good marksman, but an interview with this nocturnal visitor who seemed bent upon bringing it about. Indeed, the childish bravado of his last speech had voiced a wish, but beneath the wish Peter had guessed a protest against the inevitable.

Peter acknowledged McGuire's right to seclusion in his own house, but he found himself wondering whether death for the intruder as proposed by his employer were a justifiable means of preserving it, especially if the strange visitor did not himself use violence to gain his ends. And so, when McGuire presently poured himself another glass of whisky, and drank it, Peter took the liberty of asking the question.

"I am ignorant of your laws in this country, Mr. McGuire, but doesn't it seem that short of forcible entry of this house we would hardly be justified in shooting the man?"

"I take the responsibility for that."

"I understand. But what I was going to propose was a hunt through the woods to-morrow. A description of this man would be helpful. For instance, whether he was smoothly shaven or whether he had a beard—or—or a mustache?"

McGuire scowled.

"The man has a slight growth of beard—of mustache. But what difference does that make? No one has a right here—without my permission."

Peter sipped at his glass. As he had suspected, there were two of them.

"That's true. But even with this, we can move with more intelligence. This forest is your property. If we find any person who can't give an account of himself, we could take him into custody and turn him over to the proper authorities."

"No. No," cried McGuire. "And have him set loose after a trivial examination? Little good that would do. This man who is trying to reach me——"

McGuire stopped suddenly, glaring at his superintendent with bloodshot eyes, and Peter very politely waited for him to go on. But he brought his empty glass down on the table with a crash which shattered it.

"He mustn't reach me," he roared. "I won't see him. That's understood. He's a man I'd have no more compunction about shooting than——"

McGuire, with a curious suddenness, stopped again. Then rose and resumed his habit of pacing the floor. For a moment it had almost seemed as if he were on the point of a revelation. But the mood passed. Instead of speaking further he threw out his arms in a wide gesture.

"I've said enough," he growled, "more than enough. You know your duty." And he gestured toward the door. "Do it!" he finished brusquely.

Peter had already risen, and Stryker unemotionally opened the door for him.

"I'll stay on duty all night, Mr. McGuire," he said quietly. "I'd advise you to turn in and get some sleep. You need it."

"Yes. Yes, I will. Thanks, Nichols," said McGuire, following him to the door and offering a flabby hand. "Don't mind what I've said to-night. I think we understand each other. Stryker will see that the house is locked when the young people come up. Keep your men to the mark and take no chances."

"Good-night."

The remainder of the night, as Mrs. Bergen had predicted, proved uneventful, and at daylight Peter went to his cabin and tumbled into bed, too tired to think further of McGuire's visitors—or even of the man with the black mustache.

The next day he lay abed luxuriously for a while after he had awakened, but no amount of quiet thinking availed to clarify the mystery. There were two men, one bearded, interested in watching McGuire, another with a black mustache, interested in Peter. And so, after wondering again for some puzzling moments as to how Mrs. Bergen, the housekeeper, had come to be involved in McGuire's fortunes, he gave the problem up.

Foreseeing difficulties over breakfast at the house, he had arranged to make his own coffee on a small oil stove which happened to be available, and so Peter set the pot on to boil and while he dressed turned over in his mind the possibilities of the future. It seemed quite certain that the antagonism, whatever its nature, between his employer and the prowling stranger must come to an issue of some sort almost at once. The intruder, if he were the sort of man who could inspire terror, would not remain content merely to prowl fruitlessly about with every danger of being shot for his pains, and McGuire could hardly remain long in his present situation without a physical or mental collapse.

Why hadn't McGuire taken flight? Why indeed had he come to Black Rock House when it seemed that he would have been much safer amongst the crowds of the city, where he could fall back upon the protection of the police and their courts for immunity from this kind of persecution?

Pieced together, the phrases his employer had let slip suggested the thought that he had come to Black Rock to escape publicity in anything that might happen. And McGuire's insistence upon the orders that the guards should shoot to kill also suggested, rather unpleasantly, the thought that McGuire knew who the visitor was and earnestly desired his death.

But Mrs. Bergen could have no such wish, for, unlike McGuire, she had shown a reticence in her fears, as though her silence had been intended to protect rather than to accuse. Beth Cameron, too, was in some way unconsciously involved in the adventure. But how? He drank his coffee and ate his roll, a prey to a very lively curiosity. Beth interested him. And if Aunt Tillie Bergen, her only near relative, showed signs of inquietude on the girl's account, the mysterious visitor surely had it in his power to make her unhappy. As he washed up the dishes and made his bed, Peter decided that he would find Beth to-night when she came back from work and ask her some questions about her Aunt Tillie.

Beth Cameron saved him that trouble. He was sitting at the piano, awaiting a telephone call to Black Rock House, where he was to have a conference with his employer on the forestry situation. He was so deeply absorbed in his music that he was unaware of the figure that had stolen through the underbrush and was now hidden just outside the door. It was Beth. She stood with the fingers of one hand lightly touching the edge of the door-jamb, the other hand at her breast, while she listened, poised lightly as though for flight. But a playful breeze twitched at the hem of her skirt, flicking it out into the patch of sunlight by the doorsill, and Peter caught the glint of white from the tail of his eye.

The music ceased suddenly and before Beth could flee into the bushes Peter had caught her by the hand.

Now that she was discovered she made no effort to escape him.

"I—I was listening," she gasped.

"Why, Beth," he exclaimed, voicing the name in his thoughts. "How long have you been here?"

"I—I don't know. Not long."

"I'm so glad."

She was coloring very prettily.

"You—you told me you—you'd play for me sometime," she said demurely.

"Of course. Won't you come in? It's rather a mess here, but——"

He led her in, glancing at her gingham dress, a little puzzled.

"I thought you'd be farmeretting," he said.

But she shook her head.

"I quit—yesterday."

He didn't ask the reason. He was really enjoying the sight of her. Few women are comely in the morning hours, which have a merciless way of exaggerating minute imperfections. Beth hadn't any minute imperfections except her freckles, which were merely Nature's colorings upon a woodland flower. She seemed to fill the cabin with morning fragrance, like a bud just brought in from the garden.

"I'm very glad you've come," he said gallantly, leading her over to the double window where there was a chintz-covered seat. "I've wanted very much to talk to you."

She followed him protestingly.

"But I didn't come to be talked to. I came to listen to you play."

"You always arrive in the midst of music," he laughed. "I played you in, without knowing it. That was an Elfentanz——"

"What's that?"

"A dance of the Elves—the fairies." And then, with a laugh, "And the little devils."

"The little devils? You mean *me*!"

"Elf—fairy and devil too—but mostly elf."

"I'm not sure I like that—but I *do* like the music. Please play it again."

She was so lovely in her eagerness that he couldn't refuse, his fingers straying from the dance by slow transitions into something more quiet, the "Romance" of Sibelius, and then after that into a gay little *scherzo*, at the end of which he turned suddenly to find her flushed and breathless, regarding him in a kind of awe.

"How lovely!" she whispered. "There were no devils in that."

"No, only fairies."

"Angels too—but somethin' else—that quiet piece—like the—the memory of a—a—sorrow."

"'Romance,' it's called," he explained gently.

"Oh!"

"The things we dream. The things that ought to be, but aren't."

She took a deep breath. "Yes, that's it. That's what it meant. I felt it." And then, as though with a sudden shyness at her self-revelation, she glanced about. "What a pretty place! I've never been here before."

"How did you find your way?"

"Oh, I knew where the cabin was. I came through the woods and across the log-jam below the pool. Then I heard the music. I didn't think you'd mind."

"Mind! Oh, I say. I don't know when I've been so pleased."

"Are you really? You *say* a lot."

"Didn't I play it?"

That confused her a little.

"Oh!" she said demurely.

"And now, will you talk to me?"

"Yes, of course. But——"

"But what——?"

"I—I'm not sure that I ought to be here."

"Why not?"

"It's kind of—unusual."

He laughed. "You wouldn't be you, if you weren't unusual."

She glanced at him uneasily.

"You see, I don't know you very well."

"You're very exclusive in Black Rock!" he laughed.

"I guess we *have* to be exclusive whether we want to or not," she replied.

"Don't you think I'll do?"

"Maybe. I oughtn't to have come, but I just couldn't keep away."

"I'm glad you did. I wanted to see you."

"It wasn't that," she put in hastily. "I had to hear you play again. That's what I mean."

"I'll play for you whenever you like."

"Will you? Then play again, now. It makes me feel all queer inside."

Peter laughed. "Do you feel that way when you sing?"

"No. It all comes out of me then."

"Would you mind singing for me, Beth?" he asked after a moment.

"I—I don't think I dare."

He got up and went to the piano.

"What do you sing?"

But she hadn't moved and she didn't reply. So he urged her.

"In the woods when you're coming home——?"

"Oh, I don't know——It just comes out—things I've heard—things I make up——"

"What have you heard? I don't know that I can accompany you, but I'll try."

She was flushing painfully. He could see that she wanted to sing for him—to be a part of this wonderful dream-world in which he belonged, and yet she did not dare.

"What have you heard?" he repeated softly, encouraging her by running his fingers slowly over the simple chords of a major key.

Suddenly she started up and joined him by the piano.

"That's it—'The long, long trail a-windin'——" and in a moment was singing softly. He had heard the air and fell in with her almost at once.

"There's a long, long trail a-windingInto the land of my dreams,Where the nightingale is singingAnd a bright moon beams——"

Like the good musician that he was, Peter submerged himself, playing gently, his gaze on his fingers, while he listened. He had made no mistake. The distances across which he had heard her had not flattered. Her voice was untrained, of course, but it seemed to Peter that it had lost nothing by the neglect, for as she gained confidence, she forgot Peter, as he intended that she should, and sang with the complete abstraction of a thrush in the deep wood. Like the thrush's note, too, Beth's was limpid, clear, and sweet, full of forest sounds—the falling brook, the sigh of night winds....

When the song ended he told her so.

"You do say nice things, don't you?" she said joyously.

"Wouldn't you—if it cost you nothing and was the truth? You must have your voice trained."

"Must! I might jump over the moon if I had a broomstick."

"It's got to be managed somehow."

"Then you're not disappointed in the way it sounds, close up?"

She stood beside him, leaning against the piano, her face flushed, her breath rapid, searching his face eagerly. Peter knew that it was only the dormant artist in her seeking the light, but he thrilled warmly at her nearness, for she was very lovely. Peter's acquaintance with women had been varied, but, curiously enough, each meeting with this girl instead of detracting had only added to her charm.

"No. I'm not disappointed in it," he said quite calmly, every impulse in him urging a stronger expression. But he owed a duty to himself. *Noblesse oblige!* It was one of the mottoes of his House—(not always followed—alas!). With a more experienced woman he would have said what was in his mind. He would probably have taken her in his arms and kissed her at once, for that was really what he would have liked to do. But Beth....

Perhaps something in the coolness of his tone disconcerted her, for she turned away from the piano.

"You're very kind," she said quietly.

He had a feeling that she was about to slip away from him, so he got up.

"Won't you sing again, Beth?"

But she shook her head. For some reason the current that had run between them was broken. As she moved toward the door, he caught her by the hand.

"Don't go yet. I want to talk to you."

"I don't think I ought." And then, with a whimsical smile, "And you ought to be out makin' the trees grow."

He laughed. "There's a lot of time for that."

She let him lead her to the divan again and sat, her fingers dovetailed around a slender knee.

"I—I'm sorry I made fun of you the other day," she confessed immediately.

"I didn't mind in the least."

"But you *did* seem to know it all," she said. And then smiled in the direction of the piano. "Now—I'm comin' to think you do. Even Shad says you're a wonder. I—I don't think he likes you, though——" she admitted.

"I'm sorry to hear that."

"Don't you care. Shad don't like anybody but himself and Goda'mighty— with God trailin' a little."

Peter smiled. Her singing voice may have been impersonal but one could hardly think that of her conversation.

"And you, Beth—where do *you* come in?"

She glanced at him quickly.

"Oh, I——," she said with a laugh, "I just trail along after God."

Her irony meant no irreverence but a vast derogation of Shad Wells. Somehow her point of view was very illuminating.

"I'm afraid you make him very unhappy," he ventured.

"That's *his* lookout," she finished.

Peter was taking a great delight in watching her profile, the blue eyes shadowed under the mass of her hair, eyes rather deeply set and thoughtful in repose, the straight nose, the rather full underlip ending in a precipitous dent above her chin. He liked that chin. There was courage there and strength, softened at once by the curve of the throat, flowing to where it joined the fine deep breast. Yesterday she had seemed like a boy. To-day she was a woman grown, feminine in every graceful conformation, on tiptoe at the very verge of life.

But there was no "flapper" here. What she lacked in culture was made up in refinement. He had felt that yesterday—the day before. She belonged elsewhere. And yet to Peter it would have seemed a pity to have changed her in any particular. Her lips were now drawn in a firm line and her brows bore a curious frown.

"You don't mind my calling you Beth, do you?"

She flashed a glance at him.

"That's what everybody calls me."

"My name is Peter."

"Yes, I know." And then, "That's funny."

"Funny!"

"You look as if your name ought to be Algernon."

"Why?" he asked, laughing.

"Oh, I don't know. It's the name of a man in a book I read—an Englishman. You're English, you said."

"Half English," said Peter.

"What's the other half?"

"Russian." He knew that he ought to be lying to her, but somehow he couldn't.

"Russian! I thought Russians all had long hair and carried bombs."

"Some of 'em do. I'm not that kind. The half of me that's English is the biggest half, and the safest."

"I'm glad of that. I'd hate to think of you as bein' a Bolshevik."

"H-m. So would I."

"But Russia's where you get your music from, isn't it? The band leader at Glassboro is a Russian. He can play every instrument. Did you learn music in Russia?"

Beth was now treading dangerous ground and so it was time to turn the tables.

"Yes, a little," he said, "but music has no nationality. Or why would I find a voice like yours out here?"

"Twenty miles from nowhere," she added scornfully.

"How did you come here, Beth? Would you mind telling me? You weren't born here, were you? How did you happen to come to Black Rock?"

"Just bad luck, I guess. Nobody'd ever come to Black Rock just because they want to. We just came. That's all."

"Just you and Aunt Tillie? Is your father dead?" he asked.

She closed her eyes a moment and then clasped her knees again.

"I don't like to talk about family matters."

"Oh, I——"

And then, gently, she added,

"I never talk about them to any one."

"Oh, I'm sorry," said Peter, aware of the undercurrent of sadness in her voice. "I didn't know that there was anything painful to you——"

"I didn't know it myself, until you played it to me, just now, the piece with the sad, low voices, under the melody. It was like somebody dead speakin' to me. I can't talk about the things I feel like that."

"Don't then——Forgive me for asking."

He laid his fingers softly over hers. She withdrew her hand quickly, but the look that she turned him found his face sober, his dark eyes warm with sympathy. And then with a swift inconsequential impulse born of Peter's recantation,

"I don't s'pose there's any reason why I shouldn't tell you," she said more easily. "Everybody around here knows about me—about us. Aunt Tillie and I haven't lived here always. She brought me here when I was a child."

She paused again and Peter remained silent, watching her intently. As she glanced up at him, something in the expression of his face gave her courage to go on.

"Father's dead. His name was Ben Cameron. He came of nice people," she faltered. "But he—he was no good. We lived up near New Lisbon. He used to get drunk on 'Jersey Lightnin'' and tear loose. He was all right between whiles—farmin'—but whisky made him crazy, and then—then he would come home and beat us up."

"Horrible!"

"It was. I was too little to know much, but Aunt Tillie's husband came at last and there was a terrible fight. Uncle Will was hurt—hurt so bad—cut with a knife—that he never was the same again. And my—my father went away cursing us all. Then my mother died—Uncle Will too—and Aunt Tillie and I came down here to live. That's all. Not much to be proud of," she finished ruefully.

Peter was silent. It was a harrowing, sordid story of primitive passion. He was very sorry for her.

Beth made an abrupt graceful movement of an arm across her brows, as though to wipe out the memory.

"I don't know why I've told you," she said. "I never speak of this to any one."

"I'm so sorry."

He meant it. And Beth knew that he did.

CHAPTER VIII
THE PLACARD

The look that she had given him showed her sense of his sympathy. So he ventured,

"Did you hear from your father before he died?"

"Aunt Tillie did,—once. Then we got word he'd been killed in a railway accident out West. I was glad. A man like that has no right to live."

"You and Aunt Tillie have had a pretty hard time——" he mused.

"Yes. She's an angel—and I love her. Why is it that good people have nothin' but trouble? She had an uncle who went bad too—he was younger than she was—my great-uncle—Jack Bray—he forged a check—or somethin' up in Newark—and went to the penitentiary."

"And is he dead too?"

"No—not at last accounts. He's out—somewhere. When I was little he used to come to Aunt Tillie for money—a tall, lantern-jawed man. I saw him once three years ago. He was here. Aunt Tillie tried to keep me out of the kitchen. But I thought he was up to some funny business and stayed. He took a fancy to me. He said he was camera man in the movies. He wanted me to go with him—thought I could be as good as Mary Pickford. I'm glad I didn't go— from what I know now. He was a bad man. Aunt Tillie was scared of him. Poor soul! She gave him all she had—most of what was left from the old farm, I guess."

"Do you think——" began Peter, then paused. And as she glanced at him inquiringly, "Did you notice that your Aunt Tillie seemed—er—frightened last night?" he asked at last.

"I thought so for a while, but she said she was only sick. She never lies to me."

"She seemed very much disturbed."

"Her nerve's not what it used to be—especially since Mr. McGuire's taken to seein' things——"

"You don't believe then that she could have seen John Bray—that he had come back again last night?"

"Why, no," said Beth, turning in surprise. "I never thought of it—and yet," she paused, "yes,—it might have been——"

She became more thoughtful but didn't go on. Peter was on the trail of a clew to the mystery, but she had already told him so much that further questions seemed like personal intrusion. And so,

"I'd like to tell you, Beth," he said, "that I'm your friend and Mrs. Bergen's. If anything should turn up to make you unhappy or to make your aunt unhappy and I can help you, won't you let me know?"

"Why—do you think anything is goin' to happen?" she asked.

His reply was noncommittal.

"I just wanted you to know you could count on me——" he said soberly. "I think you've had trouble enough."

"But I'm not afraid of Jack Bray," she said with a shrug, "even if Aunt Tillie is. He can't do anything to me. He can't *make* me go to New York if I don't want to."

She had clenched her brown fists in her excitement and Peter laughed.

"I think I'd be a little sorry for anybody who tried to make you do anything you didn't want to do," he said.

She frowned. "Why, if I thought that bandy-legged, lantern-jawed, old buzzard was comin' around here frightenin' Aunt Tillie, I'd—I'd——"

"What would you do?"

"Never you mind what I'd do. But I'm not afraid of Jack Bray," she finished confidently.

The terrors that had been built up around the house of McGuire, the mystery surrounding the awe-inspiring prowler, the night vigils, the secrecy—all seemed to fade into a piece of hobbledehoy buffoonery at Beth's contemptuous description of her recreant relative. And he smiled at her amusedly.

"But what would you say," he asked seriously, "if I told you that last night Mr. McGuire saw the same person your Aunt Tillie did, and that he was terrified—almost to the verge of collapse?"

Beth had risen, her eyes wide with incredulity.

"Merciful Father! McGuire! Did he have another spell last night? You don't mean——?"

"I went up to his room. He was done for. He had seen outside the drawing-room window the face of the very man he's been guarding himself against."

"I can't believe——," she gasped. "And you think Aunt Tillie——?"

"Your Aunt Tillie talked to a man outside the door of the kitchen. You didn't hear her. I did. The same man who had been frightening Mr. McGuire."

"Aunt Tillie!" she said in astonishment.

"There's not a doubt of it. McGuire saw him. Andy saw him too,—thought he was the chauffeur."

Beth's excitement was growing with the moments.

"Why, Aunt Tillie didn't know anything about what was frightening Mr. McGuire—no more'n I did," she gasped.

"She knows now. She wasn't sick last night, Beth. She was just bewildered—frightened half out of her wits. I spoke to her after you went home. She wouldn't say a word. She was trying to conceal something. But there was a man outside and she knows who he is."

"But what could Jack Bray have to do with Mr. McGuire?" she asked in bewilderment.

Peter shrugged. "You know as much as I do. I wouldn't have told you this if you'd been afraid. But Mrs. Bergen is."

"Well, did you *ever?*"

"No, I never did," replied Peter, smiling.

"It does beat *anything.*"

"It does. It's most interesting, but as far as I can see, hardly alarming for you, whatever it may be to Mr. McGuire or Mrs. Bergen. If the man is only your great-uncle, there ought to be a way to deal with him——"

"I've just got to talk to Aunt Tillie," Beth broke in, moving toward the door. Peter followed her, taking up his hat.

"I'll go with you," he said.

For a few moments Beth said nothing. She had passed through the stages of surprise, anger and bewilderment, and was now still indignant but quite self-contained. When he thought of Beth's description of the Ghost of Black Rock House, Peter was almost tempted to forget the terrors of the redoubtable McGuire. A man of his type hardly lapses into hysteria at the mere thought of a "bandy-legged buzzard." And yet McGuire's terrors had been so real and were still so real that it was hardly conceivable that Bray could have been the cause of them. Indeed it was hardly conceivable that the person Beth described could be a source of terror to any one. What was the answer?

"Aunt Tillie doesn't know anything about McGuire," Beth said suddenly. "She just couldn't know. She tells me everything."

"But of course it's possible that McGuire and this John Bray could have met in New York——"

"What would Mr. McGuire be doin' with him?" she said scornfully.

Peter laughed.

"It's what he's doing with McGuire that matters."

"I don't believe it's Bray," said Beth confidently. "I don't believe it."

They had reached a spot where the underbrush was thin, and Beth, who had been looking past the tree trunks toward the beginnings of the lawns, stopped suddenly, her eyes focusing upon some object closer at hand.

"What's that?" she asked, pointing.

Peter followed the direction of her gaze. On a tree in the woods not far from the path was a square of cardboard, but Beth's eyes were keener than Peter's, and she called his attention to some writing upon it.

They approached curiously. With ironic impudence the message was scrawled in red crayon upon the reverse of one of Jonathan McGuire's neat trespass signs, and nailed to the tree by an old hasp-knife. Side by side, and intensely interested, they read:

TO MIKE McGUIRE

I'VE COME BACK.

YOU KNOW WHAT I'VE GOT AND I KNOW WHAT YOU'VE GOT. ACT PRONTO. I'LL COME FOR MY ANSWER AT ELEVEN FRIDAY NIGHT—AT THIS TREE. NO TRICKS. IF THERE'S NO ANSWER—YOU KNOW WHAT I'LL DO.

HAWK.

"Hawk!" muttered Beth, "who on earth——?"

"Another——," said Peter cryptically.

"You see!" cried Beth triumphantly, "I knew it couldn't be Jack Bray!"

"This chap seems to be rather in earnest, doesn't he? *Pronto!* That means haste."

"But it's only a joke. It must be," cried Beth.

Peter loosened the knife, took the placard down and turned it over, examining it critically.

"I wonder." And then, thoughtfully, "No, I don't believe it is. It's addressed to McGuire. I'm going to take it to him."

"Mike McGuire," corrected Beth. And then, "But it really does look queer."

"It does," assented Peter; "it appears to me as if this message must have come from the person McGuire saw last night."

Beth looked bewildered.

"But what has Aunt Tillie got to do with—with Hawk? She never knew anybody of that name."

"Probably not. It isn't a real name, of course."

"Then why should it frighten Mr. McGuire?" she asked logically.

Peter shook his head. All the props had fallen from under his theories.

"Whether it's real to McGuire or not is what I want to know. And I'm going to find out," he finished.

When they reached a path which cut through the trees toward the creek, Beth stopped, and held out her hand.

"I'm not goin' up to the house with you and I don't think I'll see Aunt Tillie just now," she said. "Good-by, Mr.——"

"Peter——," he put in.

"Good-by, Mr. Peter."

"Just Peter——" he insisted.

"Good-by, Mr. Just Peter. Thanks for the playin'. Will you let me come again?"

"Yes. And I'm going to get you some music——"

"Singin' music?" she gasped.

He nodded.

"And you'll let me know if I can help—Aunt Tillie or you?"

She bobbed her head and was gone.

Peter stood for a while watching the path down which she had disappeared, wondering at her abrupt departure, which for the moment drove from his mind all thought of McGuire's troubles. It was difficult to associate Beth with the idea of prudery or affectation. Her visit proved that. She had come to the Cabin because she had wanted to hear him play, because she had wanted to sing for him, because too his promises had excited her curiosity about him, and inspired a hope of his assistance. But the visit had flattered Peter. He wasn't inured to this sort of frankness. It was perhaps the greatest single gift of tribute and confidence that had ever been paid him—at least by a woman. A visit of this sort from a person like Anastasie Galitzin or indeed from almost any woman in the world of forms and precedents in which he had lived would have been equivalent to unconditional surrender.

The girl had not stopped to question the propriety of her actions. That the Cabin was Peter's bedroom, that she had only seen him twice, that he might not have understood the headlong impulse that brought her, had never occurred to Beth. The self-consciousness of the first few moments had been wafted away on the melody of the music he had played, and after that he knew they were to be friends. There seemed to be no doubt in Peter's mind that she could have thought they would be anything else.

And Peter was sure that he had hardly been able, even if he had wished, to conceal his warm admiration for her physical beauty. She had been very near him. All he would have had to do was to reach out and take her. That he hadn't done so seemed rather curious now. And yet he experienced a sort of mild satisfaction that he had resisted so trying a temptation. If she hadn't been so sure of him.... Idealism? Perhaps. The same sort of idealism that had made Peter believe the people at Zukovo were fine enough to make it worth while risking his life for them—that had made him think that the people of Russia could emerge above Russia herself. He had no illusions as to Zukovo now, but Beth was a child—and one is always gentle with children.

He puzzled for another moment over her decision not to be seen coming with him from the Cabin. Had this sophistication come as an afterthought, born of something that had passed between them? Or was it merely a feminine instinct seeking expression? Peter didn't care who knew or saw, because he really liked Beth amazingly. She had a gorgeous voice. He would have to develop it. He really would.

All the while Peter was turning over in his fingers the placard bearing the strange message to "Mike" McGuire from the mysterious "Hawk." He read and reread it, each time finding a new meaning in its wording. Blackmail? Probably. The "*pronto*" was significant. This message could hardly have come from Beth's "bandy-legged buzzard." He knew little of movie camera men, but imagined them rather given to the depiction of villainies than the accomplishment of them. And a coward who would prey upon an old woman and a child could hardly be of the metal to attempt such big game as McGuire. The mystery deepened. The buzzard was now a hawk. "Hawk," whatever his real name, was the man McGuire had seen last night through the window. Was he also the man who had frightened Mrs. Bergen? And if so, how and where had she known him without Beth's being aware of it? And why should Beth be involved in the danger?

Peter was slowly coming to the belief that there had been two men outside the house last night, "Hawk" and John Bray. And yet it seemed scarcely possible that the men on guard should not have seen the second man and that both men could have gotten away without leaving a trace. And where was the man with the black mustache? Was he John Bray? Impossible. It was all very perplexing. But here in his hand he held the tangible evidence of McGuire's fears. "You know what I've got and I know what you've got." The sentence seemed to have a cabalistic significance—a pact—a threat which each man held over the other. Perhaps it wasn't money only that "Hawk" wanted. Whatever it was, he meant to have it, and soon. The answer the man expected was apparently something well understood between himself and McGuire, better understood perhaps since the day McGuire had seen him in New York and had fled in terror to Sheldon, Senior's, office. And if McGuire didn't send the desired answer to the tree by Friday night, there would be the very devil to pay—if not "Hawk."

Peter was to be the bearer of ill tidings and with them, he knew, all prospect of a business discussion would vanish. The situation interested him, as all things mysterious must, and he could not forget that he was, for the present, part policeman, part detective; but forestry was his real job here and every day that passed meant so many fewer days in which to build the fire towers. And these he considered to be a prime necessity to the security of the estate.

He rolled the placard up and went toward the house. On the lawn he passed the young people, intent upon their own pursuits. He was glad that none of them noticed him and meeting Stryker, who was hovering around the lower hall, he sent his name up to his employer.

"I don't think Mr. McGuire expects you just yet, sir," said the man.

"Nevertheless, tell him I must see him," said Peter. "It's important."

Though it was nearly two o'clock, McGuire was not yet dressed and his looks when Peter was admitted to him bespoke a long night of anxiety and vigil. Wearing an incongruous flowered dressing gown tied at the waist with a silken cord, he turned to the visitor.

"Well," he said rather peevishly.

"I'm sorry to disturb you, Mr. McGuire, but something has happened that I thought——"

"What's happened?" the other man snapped out, eying the roll of cardboard in Peter's hand. "What——?" he gasped.

Peter smiled and shrugged coolly.

"It may be only a joke, sir—and I hardly know whether I'm even justified in calling it to your attention, but I found this placard nailed to a tree near the path to the Cabin."

"Placard!" said McGuire, his sharp glance noting the printing of the trespass sign. "Of course—that's the usual warning——"

"It's the other side," said Peter, "that is unusual." And unrolling it carefully, he laid it flat on the table beside his employer's breakfast tray and then stood back to note the effect of the disclosure.

McGuire stared at the headline, starting violently, and then, as though fascinated, read the scrawl through to the end. Peter could not see his face, but the back of his neck, the ragged fringe of moist hair around his bald spot were eloquent enough. And the hands which held the extraordinary document were far from steady. The gay flowers of the dressing gown mocked the pitiable figure it concealed, which seemed suddenly to sag into its chair. Peter waited. For a long while the dressing gown was dumb and then as though its occupant were slowly awakening to the thought that something was required of him it stirred and turned slowly in the chair.

"You—you've read this?" asked McGuire weakly.

"Yes, sir. It was there to read. It was merely stuck on a tree with this hasp-knife," and Peter produced the implement and handed it to McGuire.

McGuire took the knife—twisting it slowly over in his fingers. "A hasp-knife," he repeated dully.

"I thought it best to bring them to you," said Peter, "especially on account of——"

"Yes, yes. Of course." He was staring at the red crayon scrawl and as he said nothing more Peter turned toward the door, where Stryker stood on guard.

"If there's nothing else just now, I'll——"

"Wait!" uttered the old man, and Peter paused. And then, "Did any one else see this—this paper?"

"Yes—Mrs. Bergen's niece—she saw it first."

"My housekeeper's niece. Any one else?"

"I don't know. I hardly think so. It seemed quite freshly written."

"Ah——" muttered McGuire. He was now regarding Peter intently. "Where—where is the tree on which you found it?"

"A maple—just in the wood—at the foot of the lawn."

"Ah!" He stumbled to the window, the placard still clutched in his hands, and peered at the woods as though seeking to pick out the single tree marked for his exacerbation. Then jerked himself around and faced the bearer of these tidings, glaring at him as though he were the author of them.

"G—— d—— you all!" he swore in a stifled tone.

"I beg pardon," said Peter with sharp politeness.

McGuire glanced at Peter and fell heavily into the nearest armchair. "It can't—be done," he muttered, half to himself, and then another oath. He was showing his early breeding now.

"I might 'a' known——," he said aloud, staring at the paper.

"Then it isn't a joke?" asked Peter, risking the question.

"Joke!" roared McGuire. And then more quietly, "A joke? I don't want it talked about," he muttered with a senile smile. And then, "You say a woman read it?"

"Yes."

"She must be kept quiet. I can't have all the neighborhood into my affairs."

"I think that can be managed. I'll speak to her. In the meanwhile if there's anything I can do——"

McGuire looked up at Peter and their glances met. McGuire's glance wavered and then came back to Peter's face. What he found there seemed to satisfy him for he turned to Stryker, who had been listening intently.

"You may go, Stryker," he commanded. "Shut the door, but stay within call."

The valet's face showed surprise and some disappointment, but he merely bowed his head and obeyed.

"I suppose you're—you're curious about this message, Nichols—coming in such a way," said McGuire, after a pause.

"To tell the truth, I am, sir," replied Peter. "We've done all we could to protect you. This 'Hawk' must be the devil himself."

"He is," repeated McGuire. "Hell's breed. The thing can't go on. I've got to put a stop to it—and to him."

"He speaks of coming again Friday night——"

"Yes—yes—Friday." And then, his fingers trembling along the placard, "I've got to do what he wants—this time—just this time——"

McGuire was gasping out the phrases as though each of them was wrenched from his throat. And then, with an effort at self-control,

"Sit down, Nichols," he muttered. "Since you've seen this, I—I'll have to tell you more. I—I think—I'll need you—to help me."

Peter obeyed, flattered by his employer's manner and curious as to the imminent revelations.

"I may say that—this—this 'Hawk' is a—an enemy of mine, Nichols—a bitter enemy—unscrupulous—a man better dead than alive. I—I wish to God you'd shot him last night."

"Sorry, sir," said Peter cheerfully.

"I—I've got to do what he wants—this time. I can't have this sort of thing goin' on—with everybody in Black Rock reading these damn things. You're sure my daughter Peggy knows nothing?"

"I'd be pretty sure of that——"

"But she might—any time—if he puts up more placards. I've got to stop that, Nichols. This thing mustn't go any further."

"I think you may trust me."

"Yes. I think I can. I've *got* to trust you now, whether I want to or no. The man who wrote this scrawl is the man I came down here to get away from." Peter waited while McGuire paused. "You may think it's very strange. It is strange. I knew this man—called 'Hawk,' many years ago. I—I thought he was dead, but he's come back."

McGuire paused again, the placard in his hands, reading the line which so clearly announced that fact.

"He speaks of something I've got—something he's got, Nichols. It's a paper—a—er—a partnership paper we drew up years ago—out West and signed. That paper is of great value to me. As long as he holds it I——," McGuire halted to wipe the sweat from his pallid brow. "He holds it as a— well—not exactly as a threat—but as a kind of menace to my happiness and Peggy's."

"I understand, sir," put in Peter quietly. "Blackmail, in short."

"Exactly—er—blackmail. He wanted five thousand dollars—in New York. I refused him—there's no end to blackmail once you yield—and I came down here—but he followed me. But I've got to get that paper away from him."

"If you were sure he had it with him——"

"That's just it. He's too smart for that. He's got it hidden somewhere. I've got to get this money for him—from New York—I haven't got it in the house—before Friday night———"

"But blackmail———!"

"I've got to, Nichols—this time. I've got to."

"I wouldn't, sir," said Peter stoutly.

"But you don't know everything. I've only told you part," said McGuire, almost whining. "This is no ordinary case—no ordinary blackmail. I've got to be quick. I'm going to get the money—I'm going to get you to go to New York and get it."

"Me!"

"Yes. Yes. This is Wednesday. I can't take any chances of not having it here Friday. Peggy is going back this afternoon. I'll get her to drive you up. I'll 'phone Sheldon to expect you—he'll give you the money and you can come back to-morrow."

"But to-night———"

"He knows the danger of trying to reach me. That's why he wrote this. I won't be bothered to-night. I'll shut the house tight and put some of the men inside. If he comes, we'll shoot."

"But Friday———Do you mean, sir, that you'll go out to him with five thousand dollars and risk———"

"No, I won't. *You* will," said McGuire, watching Peter's face craftily.

"Oh, I see," replied Peter, aware that he was being drawn more deeply into the plot than he had wished. "You want me to meet him."

McGuire noted Peter's dubious tone and at once got up and laid his hands upon his shoulders.

"You'll do this for me, won't you, Nichols? I don't want to see this man. I can't explain. There wouldn't be any danger. He hasn't anything against you. Why should he have? I haven't any one else that I can trust—but Stryker. And Stryker—well—I'd have to tell Stryker. *You* know already. Don't say you refuse. It's—it's a proof of my confidence. You're just the man I want here. I'll make it worth your while to stay with me—well worth your while."

Peter was conscious of a feeling partly of pity, partly of contempt, for the cringing creature pawing at his shoulders. Peter had never liked to be pawed. It had always rubbed him the wrong way. But McGuire's need was great and pity won.

"Oh, I'll do it if you like," he said, turning aside and releasing himself from the clinging fingers, "provided I assume no responsibility——"

"That's it. No responsibility," said McGuire, in a tone of relief. "You'll just take that money out—then come away——"

"And get nothing in return?" asked Peter in surprise. "No paper—no receipt——?"

"No—just this once, Nichols. It will keep him quiet for a month or so. In the meanwhile——" The old man paused, a crafty look in his eyes, "In the meanwhile we'll have time to devise a way to meet this situation."

"Meaning—precisely what?" asked Peter keenly.

McGuire scowled at him and then turned away toward the window.

"That needn't be your affair."

"It won't be," said Peter quickly. "I'd like you to remember that I came here as a forester and superintendent. I agreed also to guard your house and yourself from intrusion, but if it comes to the point of——"

"There, there, Nichols," croaked McGuire, "don't fly off the handle. We'll just cross this bridge first. I—I won't ask you to do anything a—a gentleman shouldn't."

"Oh, well, sir," said Peter finally, "that's fair enough."

McGuire came over and faced Peter, his watery eyes seeking Peter's.

"You'll swear, Nichols, to say nothing of this to any one?"

"Yes. I'll keep silent."

"Nothing to Sheldon?"

"No."

"And you'll see this—this niece of the housekeeper's?"

"Yes."

The man gave a gasp of relief and sank into his chair.

"Now go, Nichols—and shift your clothes. Peggy's going about four. Come back here and I'll give you a letter and a check."

Peter nodded and reached the door. As he opened it, Stryker straightened and bowed uncomfortably. But Peter knew that he had been listening at the keyhole.

CHAPTER IX
SHAD IS UNPLEASANT

Peter returned from New York on Thursday night, having accomplished his curious mission. He had first intercepted Beth on her way to the kitchen and sworn her to secrecy, advising her to say nothing to Mrs. Bergen about the events of the previous night. And she had agreed to respect his wishes. On the way to New York he had sat in the rumble of the low red runabout, Miss Peggy McGuire at the wheel, driving the fashionable Freddy. Miss McGuire after having yielded, the night before, to the musical predilections of Miss Delaplane, had apparently reconsidered Peter's social status and had waved him to the seat in the rear with a mere gesture and without apologies. And Peter, biting back a grin and touching his hat, had obeyed. The familiarities tolerable in such a wilderness as Black Rock could not of course be considered in the halls of the fashionable hotel where Miss Peggy lived in New York, and where by dint of great care and exclusiveness she had caught a hold of the fringe of society. But Peter sat up very straight, trying not to hear what was said in front. If he could only have worn his Colonel's uniform and decorations, or his Grand Ducal coronet, and have folded his arms, the irony would have been perfection.

He had gone to Sheldon, Senior, in the morning and in return for McGuire's check had been given cash in the shape of ten virginal five hundred dollar bills. This money had been put into an envelope and was now folded carefully in Peter's inside pocket. Sheldon, Senior, to be sure, had asked questions, but with a good grace Peter had evaded him. Dick Sheldon was out of town, so Peter put in the remaining period before his train-time in a music store where he spent all the money that remained of his salary, on books, a few for the piano but most of them for Beth. Peter had wasted, as he had thought, two perfectly good years in trying to learn to sing. But those two years were not going to be wasted now—for Beth was to be his mouthpiece. He knew the beginnings of a training—how to give her the advantage of the instruction he had received from one of the best teachers in Milan. He was lucky enough to find books on the Italian method of voice production and on the way back to McGuire's, armed with these, he stopped off at the Bergen house in Black Rock village and returned Beth's call.

There he found Shad Wells, in his shirt-sleeves, smoking a pipe in the portico, and looking like a thundercloud. In response to Peter's query, he moved his right shoulder half an inch in the direction of the door, and then spat in the geranium bed. So Peter knocked at the door, softly at first, then loudly, when

Beth emerged, her sleeves rolled to her shoulders and her arms covered with soapsuds.

"Why, Shad," she said witheringly, after she had greeted Peter, "you might have let me know! Come in, Mr. Nichols. Excuse my appearance. Wash-day," she explained, as he followed her into the dark interior.

"I can't stop," said the visitor, "I just came to bring these books——"

"For *me*!" she exclaimed, hurriedly wiping her arms on her apron.

"I got them in New York——"

She pulled up the shade at the side, letting in the sunlight, an act permissible in the parlors of Black Rock only on state occasions, for the sunlight (as every one knew) was not kind to plush-covered furniture.

"For *me*!" Beth repeated softly. "I didn't think you meant it."

"*Tone production—Exercises*," explained Peter, "and here's one on *The Lives of the Great Composers*. I thought you might be interested in reading it."

"Oh, yes. I am—I will be. Thank you ever so much——"

"Of course you can't do much by yourself just yet—not without a piano—to get the pitch—the key—but I've brought a tuning fork and——"

"But I've got the harmonium——," Beth broke in excitedly. "It's a little out of tune, but——"

"The harmonium!" asked the bewildered Peter. "What's that?"

Beth proudly indicated a piece of furniture made of curly walnut which stood in the corner of the room. There were several books on the top of it—*Gospel Tunes—Moody and Sankey*, a Methodist Episcopal hymn book, and a glass case containing wax flowers.

"We play it Sundays——," said Beth, "but it ought to help——"

"You play——!" he said in surprise.

"Aunt Tillie and I—oh, just hymns——." She sat, while Peter watched, began pumping vigorously with her feet and presently the instrument emitted a doleful sound. "It has notes anyhow," said Beth with a laugh.

"Splendid!" said Peter. "And when I've told you what to do you can practice here. You'll come soon?"

She nodded. "When?"

"To-morrow—sometime?" And then, "What's the matter with Wells?" he asked.

She frowned. "He just asked me to marry him. It's the twenty-seventh time."

"Oh——"

"I can't be botherin' with Shad—not on wash-day—or any other day," she added as though in an afterthought.

Peter laughed. He was quite sure that nobody would ever make her do anything she didn't want to do.

"He knows I was at the Cabin yesterday," she said in a low voice. "He was watchin'."

Peter was silent a moment, glancing at the books he had just brought her.

"Of course if he has any claim on you, perhaps——," he began, when she broke in.

"Claim! He hasn't," she gasped. "I'll do as I please. And he'd better quit pesterin' me or I'll——"

"What?"

She laughed.

"I'll put him through the clothes-wringer."

Peter grinned. "He almost looks as though you'd done that already."

And as she followed him to the door, "I thought I ought to tell you about Shad. When he gets ugly—he's ugly an' no mistake."

"Do you still think he'll—er—swallow me at one gobble?" he asked.

She stared at him a moment and then laughed with a full throat. "I hope he don't—at least not 'til I've had my singin' lessons."

"I think I can promise you that," said Peter.

She followed him out to the porch, where they looked about for Shad. He had disappeared. And in the "Lizzie," which had been panting by the side of the road, Peter was conducted by the soiled young man at the wheel to Black Rock House.

Nothing unusual had happened in his absence, nor had any other message or warning been posted, for Stryker, released for this duty, had searched all the morning and found nothing. "Hawk" was waiting, biding his hour.

Curiously enough, an astonishing calm seemed to have fallen over the person of Jonathan K. McGuire. When Peter arrived he found his employer seated on the portico in a wicker chair, smoking his after-supper cigar. True, the day guards were posted near by and Stryker hovered as was his wont, but the change in his employer's demeanor was so apparent that Peter wondered how such a stolid-looking creature could ever have lost his self-control. It was difficult to understand this metamorphosis unless it could be that, having come to a decision and aware of the prospect of immunity, if only a temporary one, McGuire had settled down to make the best of a bad job and await with stoicism whatever the future was to bring. This was Peter's first impression, nothing else suggesting itself, but when he followed the old man up to his room and gave him the money he had brought he noted the deeply etched lines at nostril and jaw and felt rather than saw the meaning of them— that Jonathan McGuire was in the grip of some deep and sinister resolution. There was a quality of desperation in his calmness, a studied indifference to the dangers which the night before last had seemed so appalling.

He put the money in the safe, carefully locked the combination and then turned into the room again.

"Thanks, Nichols," he said. "You'd better have some supper and get to bed to-night. I don't think you'll be needed." And then, as Peter's look showed his surprise, "I know my man better than you do. To-morrow night we shall see."

He closed his lips into a thin line, shot out his jaw and lowered his brows unpleasantly. Courage of a sort had come back to him, the courage of the animal at bay, which fights against the inevitable.

To Peter the time seemed propitious to state the need for the observation towers and he explained in detail his projects. But McGuire listened and when Peter had finished speaking merely shook his head.

"What you say is quite true. The towers must be built. I've thought so for a long time. In a few days we will speak of that again—*after to-morrow night*," he finished significantly.

"As you please," said Peter, "but every day lost now may——"

"We'll gain these days later," he broke in abruptly. "I want you to stay around here now."

On Friday morning he insisted on having Peter show him the tree where the placard had been discovered, and Peter, having taken lunch with him, led him down to the big sugar maple, off the path to the cabin. Peter saw that he scanned the woods narrowly and walked with a hand in his waist-band, which Peter knew held an Army Colt revolver, but the whine was gone from his voice, the trembling from his hands. He walked around the maple with Peter, regarding it with a sort of morbid abstraction and then himself led the way to the path and to the house. Why he wanted to look at the tree was more than Peter could understand, for it was Peter, and not he, who was to keep this costly assignation.

"You understand, Nichols," he said when they reached the portico, "you've agreed to go—to-night—at eleven."

"I wish you'd let me meet him—without the money."

"No—no. I've made up my mind———," gasped McGuire with a touch of his old alarm, "there can't be any change in the plan—no change at all."

"Oh, very well," said Peter, "it's not my money I'm giving away."

"It won't matter, Nichols. I—I've got a lot more———"

"But the principle———" protested Peter.

"To H—— with the principle," growled the old man.

Peter turned and went back to the Cabin, somewhat disgusted with his whole undertaking. Already he had been here for five days and, except for two walks through the woods for purposes of investigation, nothing that he had come to do had been accomplished. He had not yet even visited the sawmills which were down on the corduroy road five miles away. So far as he could see, for the present he was merely McGuire's handy man, a kind of upper servant and messenger, whose duties could have been performed as capably by Stryker or Shad Wells, or even Jesse Brown. The forest called him. It needed him. From what he had heard he knew that down by the sawmills they were daily cutting the wrong trees. He had already sent some instructions to the foreman there, but he could not be sure that his orders had been obeyed. He knew that he ought to spend the day there, making friends with the men and explaining the reasons for the change in orders, but as long as McGuire wanted him within telephone range, there was nothing to do but to obey.

He reached the Cabin, threw off his coat, and had hardly settled down at the table to finish his drawing, a plan of the observation towers, when Beth appeared. He rose and greeted her. Her face was flushed, for she had been running.

"Has Shad been here?" she asked breathlessly.

"No."

"Oh!" she gasped. "I was afraid he'd get here before me. I took the short cut through the woods."

"What's the matter?"

"He said he—he was going to break you to bits———"

"To bits! Me? Why?"

"Because he—he says I oughtn't to come here———"

"Oh, I see," he muttered, and then, with a grin, "and what do *you* think about it, Beth?"

"I'll do what I please," she said. "So long as I think it's all right. What business has he got to stop me!"

Peter laughed. "Don't let's bother then. Did you bring your books?"

She hadn't brought them. She had come in such a hurry.

"But aren't you afraid—when he comes?" she asked.

"I don't know," said Peter. "Do you think I ought to be?"

"Well, Shad's—he's what they call a Hellion around here."

"What's a—er—Hellion?"

"A—a scrapper."

"Oh, a fighting man?"

"Yes."

Peter sat down at the piano and struck loudly some strident discords in the bass. "Like this!" he laughed. "Isn't it ugly, Beth—that's what fighting is—I had it day and night for years. If Shad had been in the war he wouldn't ever want to fight again."

"Were you in the war?" asked Beth in amazement.

"Of course. Where would I have been?" And before she could reply he had swept into the rumbling bass of the "Revolutionary Étude." She sank into a chair and sat silent, listening, at first watching the door, and then as the soul of the artist within her awoke she forgot everything but the music.

There was a long silence at the end when Peter paused, and then he heard her voice, tense, suppressed.

"I could see it—you made me see it!" she gasped, almost in a whisper. "War—revolution—the people—angry—mumbling—crowding, pushing ... a crowd with guns and sticks howling at a gate ... and then a man trying to speak to them—appealing———"

Peter turned quickly at the words and faced her. Her eyes were like stars, her soul rapt in the vision his music had painted. Peter had lived that scene again and again, but how could Beth know unless he had made her see it? There was something strange—uncanny—in Beth's vision of the great drama of Peter's life. And yet she had seen. Even now her spirit was afar.

"And what happened to the man who was appealing to them?" he asked soberly.

She closed her eyes, then opened them toward him, shaking her head. "I—I don't know—it's all gone now."

"But you saw what I played. That is what happened."

"What do you mean?" She questioned, startled in her turn.

Peter shrugged himself into the present moment. "Nothing. It's just—revolution. War. War is like that, Beth," he went on quietly after a moment. "Like the motif in the bass—there is no end—the threat of it never stops—day or night. Only hell could be like it."

Beth slowly came out of her dream.

"You fought?" she asked.

"Oh, yes."

Another silence. "I—I think I understand now why you're not afraid."

"But I *am* afraid, Beth," he said with a smile. "I was always afraid in the war. Because Death is always waiting just around the corner. Nobody who has been in the war wants ever to fight again."

He turned to the piano. "They all want happiness, Beth. Peace. This!" he finished, and his roving fingers played softly the Tschaikowsky "Reverie."

When he had finished he turned to her, smiling.

"What vision do you see in that, Beth?"

She started as though from a dream. "Oh, happiness—and sadness, too."

"Yes," said Peter soberly. "No one knows what it is to be happy unless one has been sad."

"That's true, isn't it?" she muttered, looking at him in wonder. "I never knew what unhappiness was for—but I guess that's it."

He caught the minor note in her voice and smiled.

"Come now," he said, "we'll have our first lesson."

"Without the books?"

"Yes. We'll try breathing."

"Breathing?"

"Yes—from the diaphragm."

And as she looked bewildered, "From the stomach—not from the chest—breathe deeply and say 'Ah.'"

She obeyed him and did it naturally, as though she had never breathed in any other way.

"Fine," he cried and touched a note on the piano. "Now sing it. Throw it forward. Softly first, then louder——"

It was while she was carrying out this instruction that a shadow appeared on the doorsill, followed in a moment by the figure of Shad Wells. Beth's "Ah" ceased suddenly. The visitor stood outside, his hands on his hips, in silent rage.

Peter merely glanced at him over his shoulder.

"How are you, Wells?" he said politely. "Won't you come in? We've having a singing lesson."

Shad did not move or speak as Peter went on, "Take the chair by the door, old man. The cigarettes are on the table. Now, Beth——"

But Beth remained as she was, uneasily regarding the intruder, for she knew that Shad was there for no good purpose. Peter caught her look and turned toward the door, deliberately ignoring the man's threatening demeanor.

"We won't be long," he began coolly, "not over half an hour——"

"No, I know ye won't," growled Shad. And then to the girl, "Beth, come out o' there!"

If Shad's appearance had caused Beth any uncertainty, she found her spirit now, for her eyes flashed and her mouth closed in a hard line.

"Who are you to say where I come or go?" she said evenly.

But Shad stood his ground.

"If you don't know enough to know what's what I'm here to show you."

"Oh, I say——," said Peter coolly.

"You can say what you like, Mister. And I've got somethin' to say to you when this lady goes."

"Oh,——" and then quietly to Beth, "Perhaps you'd better go. Bring the books to-morrow—at the same time."

But Beth hadn't moved, and only looked at Peter appealingly. So Peter spoke.

"This man is impolite, not to say disagreeable to you. Has he any right to speak to you like this?"

"No," said Beth uneasily, "but I don't want any trouble."

Peter walked to the door and faced Shad outside.

"There won't be any trouble unless Wells makes it." And then, as if a new thought had come to him, he said more cheerfully, "Perhaps he doesn't quite understand——"

"Oh, I understand, all right. Are you goin', Beth?"

She glanced at Peter, who nodded toward the path, and she came between them.

"Go on back, Shad," she said.

"No."

"Do you mean it? If you do I'm through with you. You understand?"

Peter took the girl by the arm and led her gently away.

"Just wait a minute, Wells," he flung over his shoulder at the man, "I'll be back in a second."

The careless tone rather bewildered the woodsman, who had expected to find either fear or anger. The forester-piano-player showed neither—only careless ease and a coolness which could only be because he didn't know what was coming to him.

"D—n him! I'll fix him!" muttered Shad, quivering with rage. But Peter having fortified himself with a cigarette was now returning. Wells advanced into an open space where there was plenty of room to swing his elbows and waited.

"Now, Wells," said Peter alertly, "you wanted to see me?"

"Yes, I did, ye stuck-up piano-playin', psalm-singin' —— —— —— —— ——." And suiting the action to the word leaped for Peter, both fists flying.

The rugged and uncultured often mistake politeness for effeminacy, sensibility for weakness. Shad was a rough and tumble artist of a high proficiency, and he had a reputation for strength and combativeness. He was going to make short work of this job.

But Peter had learned his boxing with his cricket. Also he had practiced the *Savate* and was familiar with *jiu jitsu*—but he didn't need either of them.

Wells rushed twice but Peter was not where he rushed. The only damage he had done was to tear out the sleeve of Peter's shirt.

"Stand up an' fight like a man," growled Shad.

"There's no hurry," said Peter, calmly studying Shad's methods.

"Oh, *ain't* there!"

This bull-like rush Peter stopped with a neat uppercut, straightening Shad's head which came up with a disfigured nose and before he could throw down his guard, Peter landed hard on his midriff. Shad winced but shot out a blow which grazed Peter's cheek. Then Peter countered on Shad's injured nose. Shad's eyes were now regarding Peter in astonishment. But in a moment only one of them was, for Peter closed the other.

"We'd better stop now," gasped Peter, "and talk this over."

"No, you —— —— ——," roared Shad, for he suspected that somewhere in the bushes Beth was watching.

Peter lost what remained of his shirt in the next rush and sprained a thumb. It didn't do to fight Shad "rough and tumble." But he got away at last and stood his man off, avoiding the blind rushes and landing almost at will.

"Had enough?" he asked again, as politely as ever.

"No," gulped the other.

So Peter sprang in and struck with all the force of his uninjured hand on the woodsman's jaw, and then Shad went down and lay quiet. It had been ridiculously easy from the first and Peter felt some pity for Shad and not a little contempt for himself. But he took the precaution of bending over the man and extracting the revolver that he found in Shad's hip pocket.

As he straightened and turned he saw Beth standing in the path regarding him.

"Beth!" he exclaimed with a glance at Shad. "You saw?"

"Yes." She covered her face with her hands. "It was horrible."

"I tried to avoid it," he protested.

"Yes, I know. It was his own fault. Is he badly hurt?"

"No, I think not. But you'd better go."

"Why?"

"It will only make matters worse if he sees you."

She understood, turned and vanished obediently.

Then Peter went to the house, got a basin and, fetching some water from the creek, played the Samaritan. In a while Shad gasped painfully and sat up, looking at the victor.

"Sorry," said Peter, "but you *would* have it."

Shad blinked his uninjured eye and rose, feeling at his hip.

"I took your revolver," said Peter calmly.

"Give it here."

"A chap with a bad temper has no business carrying one," said Peter sternly.

"Oh——." The man managed to get to his feet.

"I'm sorry, Shad," said Peter again, and held out his hand. "Let's be friends."

Shad looked at the hand sullenly for a moment. "I'll fix *you*, Mister. I'll fix you yet," he muttered, then turned and walked away.

If Peter had made one friend he had also made an enemy.

The incident with Shad Wells was unfortunate, but Peter didn't see how it could have been avoided. He was thankful nevertheless for his English schooling, which had saved him from a defeat at the hands of a "roughneck" which could have been, under the circumstances, nothing less than ignominious. For if Shad Wells had succeeded in vanquishing him, all Peter's authority, all his influence with the rest of the men in McGuire's employ would have gone forever, for Shad Wells was not the kind of man upon whom such a victory would have lightly sat. If he had thrashed Peter, Shad and not Peter would have been the boss of Black Rock and Peter's position would have been intolerable.

As Peter laved his broken knuckles and bruised cheek, he wondered if, after all, the affair hadn't been for the best. True, he had made an enemy of Shad, but then according to the girl, Shad had already been his enemy. Peter abhorred fighting, as he had told Beth, but, whatever the consequences, he was sure that the air had cleared amazingly. He was aware too that the fact that he had been the champion of Beth's independence definitely stood forth. Whatever the wisdom or the propriety, according to the standards of Black Rock society, of Beth's visits to the Cabin, for the purpose of a musical education or for any other purposes, Peter was aware that he had set the seal of his approval upon them, marked, that any who read might run, upon the visage of Mr. Wells. Peter was still sorry for Shad, but still more sorry for Beth, whose name might be lightly used for her share in the adventure.

He made up his mind to say nothing of what had happened, and he felt reasonably certain that Shad Wells would reach a similar decision. He was not at all certain that Beth wouldn't tell everybody what had happened for he was aware by this time that Beth was the custodian of her own destinies and that she would not need the oracles of Black Rock village as censors of her behavior.

But when he went up to the house for supper he made his way over the log-jam below the pool and so to the village, stopping for a moment at the Bergen house, where Beth was sitting on the porch reading *The Lives of the Great Composers*. She was so absorbed that she did not see him until he stood at the little swing gate, hat in hand.

She greeted him quietly, glancing up at his bruised cheek.

"I'm so sorry," she said, "that it was on my account."

"I'm not—now that I've done the 'gobbling,'" he said with a grin. And then, "Where's Shad?"

"I haven't seen him. I guess he's gone in his hole and pulled it in after him."

Peter smiled. "I just stopped by to say that perhaps you'd better say nothing. It would only humiliate him."

"I wasn't goin' to—but it served him right———"

"And if you think people will talk about your coming to the Cabin, I thought perhaps I ought to give you your lessons here."

"Here!" she said, and he didn't miss the note of disappointment in her tone.

"If your cousin Shad disapproves, perhaps there are others."

She was silent for a moment and then she looked up at him shyly.

"If it's just the same to you—I—I'd rather come to the Cabin," she said quietly. "It's like—like a different world—with your playin' an' all———" And then scornfully, "What do I care what they think!"

"Of course—I'm delighted. I thought I ought to consult you, that's all. And you'll come to-morrow?"

"Yes—of course."

He said nothing about the meeting that was to take place that night with the mysterious "Hawk" at the maple tree. He meant to find out, if possible, how Beth could be concerned (if she was concerned) in the fortunes of the mysterious gentleman of the placard, but until he learned something definite he thought it wiser not to take Beth further into his confidence.

CHAPTER X
"HAWK"

Three months ago it would have been difficult for His Highness, Grand Duke Peter Nicholaevitch, to imagine himself in his present situation as sponsor for Beth Cameron. He had been no saint. Saintly attributes were not usually to be found in young men of his class, and Peter's training had been in the larger school of the world as represented in the Continental capitals. He had tasted life under the tutelage of a father who believed that women, bad as well as good, were a necessary part of a gentleman's education, and Peter had learned many things.... Had it not been for his music and his English love of fair play, he would have stood an excellent chance of going to the devil along the precipitous road that had led the Grand Duke Nicholas Petrovitch there.

But Peter had discovered that he had a mind, the needs of which were more urgent than those of his love of pleasure. Many women he had known, Parisian, Viennese, Russian—and one, Vera Davydov, a musician, had enchained him until he had discovered that it was her violin and not her soul that had sung to him ... Anastasie Galitzin ... a dancer in Moscow ... and then—the War.

In that terrible alembic the spiritual ingredients which made Peter's soul had been stirred until only the essential remained. But that essence was the real Peter—a wholesome young man steeped in idealism slightly tinged with humor. It was idealism that had made him attempt the impossible, humor that had permitted him to survive his failure, for no tragedy except death itself can defy a sense of humor if it's whimsical enough. There was something about the irony of his position in Black Rock which interested him even more than the drama that lay hidden with McGuire's Nemesis in the pine woods. And he couldn't deny the fact that this rustic, this primitive Beth Cameron was as fine a little lady as one might meet anywhere in the wide world. She had amused him at first with originality, charmed him with simplicity, amazed him later with talent and now had disarmed him with trust in his integrity. If at any moment the idea had entered Peter's head that here was a wild-flower waiting to be gathered and worn in his hat, she had quickly disabused his mind of that chimera. Curious. He found it as difficult to conceive of making free with Beth as with the person of the Metropolitan of Moscow, or with that of the President of the Pennsylvania Railroad. She had her dignity. It was undeniable. He imagined the surprise in her large blue eyes and the torrent of ridicule of which her tongue could be capable. He had felt the sting of its humor at their first meeting. He had no wish to test it again.

And now, after a few days of acquaintanceship, he found himself Beth's champion, the victor over the "Hellion" triplet, and the guardian of her good repute. He found, strangely enough, the responsibility strengthening his good resolves toward Beth and adding another tie to those of sympathy and admiration. The situation, while not altogether of his making, was not without its attractions. He had given Beth her chance to withdraw from the arrangement and she had persisted in the plan to come to the Cabin. Very well. It was his cabin. She should come and he would teach her to sing. But he knew that Peter Nichols was throwing temptation in the way of Peter Nicholaevitch.

McGuire was quiet that night and while they smoked Peter talked at length on the needs of the estate as he saw them. Peter went down to the Cabin and brought up his maps and his plans for the fire towers. McGuire nodded or assented in monosyllables, but Peter was sure that he heard little and saw less, for at intervals he glanced at the clock, or at his watch, and Peter knew that his obsession had returned. Outside, somewhere in the woods, "Hawk" was approaching to keep his tryst and McGuire could think of nothing else. This preoccupation was marked by a frowning thatch of brow and a sullen glare at vacancy which gave no evidence of the fears that had inspired him, but indicated a mind made up in desperation to carry out his plans, through Peter, whatever happened later. Only the present concerned him. But underneath his outward appearance of calm, Peter was aware of an intense alertness, for from time to time his eyes glowed suddenly and the muscles worked in his cheeks as he clamped his jaws shut and held them so.

As the clock struck ten McGuire got to his feet and walked to the safe, which he opened carefully and took out the money that Peter had brought. Then he went to a closet and took out an electric torch which he tested and then put upon the table.

"You're armed, Nichols?" he asked.

Peter nodded. "But of course there's no reason why your mysterious visitor should take a pot at me," he said. And then, curiously, "Do you think so, Mr. McGuire?"

"Oh, no," said the other quickly. "You have no interest in this affair. You're my messenger, that's all. But I want you to follow my instructions carefully. I've trusted you this far and I've got to go the whole way. This man will say something. You will try to remember word for word what he says to you, and you're to repeat that message to me."

"That shouldn't be difficult."

McGuire was holding the money in his hand and went on in an abstraction as though weighing words.

"I want you to go at once to the maple tree. I want you to go now so that you will be there when this man arrives. You will stand waiting for him and when he comes you will throw the light into his face, so that you can see him when you talk to him, and so that he can count this money and see that the amount is correct. I do not want you to go too close to him nor to permit him to go too close to you—you are merely to hand him this package and throw the light while he counts the money. Then you are to say to him these words, 'Don't forget the blood on the knife, Hawk Kennedy.'"

"'Don't forget the blood on the knife, Hawk Kennedy,'" murmured Peter in amazement. And then, "But suppose he wants to tell me a lot of things you don't want me to know——"

"I'll have to risk that," put in McGuire grimly. "I want you to watch him carefully, Nichols. Are you pretty quick on the draw?"

"What do you mean?"

"I mean, can you draw your gun and shoot quickly—surely? If you can't, you'd better have your gun in your pocket, keep him covered and at the first sign, shoot through your coat."

Peter took out his revolver and examined it quizzically. "I thought you said, Mr. McGuire," he put in coolly, "that I was not to be required to do anything a gentleman couldn't do."

"Exactly," said the old man jerkily.

"I shouldn't say that shooting a defenseless man answers that requirement."

McGuire threw up his hands wildly.

"There you go—up in the air again. I didn't say you were to shoot him, did I?" he whined. "I'm just warning you to be on the lookout in case he attacks you. That—that's all."

"Why should he attack me?"

"He shouldn't, but he might be angry because I didn't come myself."

"I see. Perhaps you'd better go, sir. Then you can do your killing yourself."

McGuire fell back against the table, to which he clung, his face gray with apprehension, for he saw that Peter had guessed what he hoped.

"You want this man killed," Peter went on. "It's been obvious to me from the first night I came here. Well, I'm not going to be the one to do it."

McGuire's glance fell to the rug as he stammered hoarsely, "I—I never asked you to do it. Y-you must be dreaming. I—I'm merely making plans to assure your safety. I don't want you hurt, Nichols. That's all. You're not going to back out now?" he pleaded.

"Murder is a little out of my line——"

"You're not going to fail me——?" McGuire's face was ghastly. "You *can't*," he whispered hoarsely. "You can't let me down now. *I* can't see this man. I can't tell Stryker all you know. You're the only one. You promised, Nichols. You promised to go."

"Yes. And I'll keep my word—but I'll do it in my own way. I'm not afraid of any enemy of yours. Why should I be? But I'm not going to shoot him. If that's understood give me the money and I'll be off."

"Yes—yes. That's all right, Nichols. You're a good fellow—and honest. I'll make it worth your while to stay with me here." He took up the money and handed it to Peter, who counted it carefully and then put it in an inside pocket. "I don't see why you think I wanted you to kill Hawk Kennedy," McGuire went on, whining. "A man's got a right to protect himself, hasn't he? And you've got a right to protect *yourself*, if he tries to start anything."

"Have you any reason to believe that he might?"

"No. I can't say I have."

"All right. I'll take a chance. But I want it understood that I'm not responsible if anything goes wrong."

"That's understood."

Peter made his way downstairs, and out of the front door to the portico. Stryker, curiously enough, was nowhere to be seen. Peter went out across the dim lawn into the starlight. Jesse Brown challenged him by the big tree and Peter stopped for a moment to talk with him, explaining that he would be returning to the house later.

"The old man seems to be comin' to life, Mister," said Jesse.

"What do you mean?"

"Not so skeered-like. He was out here when you went to the Cabin for them plans——"

"Out here?" said Peter in amazement.

Andy nodded. "He seemed more natural-like,—asked what the countersign was and said mebbe we'd all be goin' back to the mills after a night or so."

"Oh, did he? That's good. You're pretty tired of this night work?"

"Not so long as it pays good. But what did he mean by changin' the guards?"

"He didn't say anything to me about it," said Peter, concealing his surprise.

"Oh, didn't he? Well, he took Andy off the privet hedge and sent him down to the clump of pines near the road."

"I see," said Peter. "Why?"

"You've got me, Mister. If there's trouble to-night, there ain't no one at the back of the house at all. We're one man short."

"Who?"

"Shad Wells. He ain't showed up."

"Ah, I see," muttered Peter. And then, as he lighted a cigarette, "Oh, well, we'll get along somehow. But look sharp, just the same."

Peter went down the lawn thoughtfully. From the first he hadn't been any too pleased with this mission. Though Peter was aware that in the realm of big business it masqueraded under other names, blackmail, at the best, was a dirty thing. At the worst—and McGuire's affair with the insistent Hawk seemed to fall into this classification,—it was both sinister and contemptible. To be concerned in these dark doings even as an emissary was hardly in accordance with Peter's notion of his job, and he had acceded to McGuire's request without thinking of possible consequences, more out of pity for his employer in his plight than for any other reason. But he remembered that it usually required a guilty conscience to make blackmail possible and that the man who paid always paid because of something discreditable which he wished to conceal.

McGuire's explanations had been thin and Peter knew that the real reason for the old man's trepidations was something other than the ones he had given. He had come to Black Rock from New York to avoid any possible publicity that might result from the visits of his persecutor and was now paying this sum of money for a respite, an immunity which at the best could only be temporary. It was all wrong and Peter was sorry to have a hand in it, but he couldn't deny that the interest with which he had first approached Black Rock House had now culminated in a curiosity which was almost an obsession. Here, close at hand, was the solution of the mystery, and whether or not he learned anything as to the facts which had brought McGuire's discomfiture, he would at least see and talk with the awe-inspiring Hawk who had been the cause of them. Besides, there was Mrs. Bergen's share in the adventure which indicated that Beth's happiness, too, was in some way involved. For Peter, having had time to weigh Beth's remarks with the housekeeper's, had come to the conclusion that there had been but one man near the house that night. The man who had talked with Mrs. Bergen at the kitchen door was not John Bray the camera-man, or the man with the dark mustache, but Hawk Kennedy himself.

Peter entered the path to the Cabin, and explored it carefully, searching the woods on either side and then, cutting into the scrub oak at the point where he and Beth had first seen the placard, made his way to the maple tree. There was no one there. A glance at his watch under the glare of the pocket torch showed that he was early for the tryst, so he walked around the maple, flashing his light into the undergrowth and at last sat down, leaning against the trunk of the tree, lighted another cigarette and waited.

Under the depending branches of the heavy foliage it was very dark, and he could get only the smallest glimpses of the starlit sky. At one point toward Black Rock House beyond the boles of the trees he could see short stretches of the distant lawn and, in the distance, a light which he thought must be that of McGuire's bedroom, for to-night, Peter had noticed, the shutters had been left open. It was very quiet too. Peter listened for the sounds of approaching footsteps among the dry leaves, but heard only the creak of branches overhead, the slight stir of the breeze in the leaves and the whistle of a locomotive many miles away, on the railroad between Philadelphia and Atlantic City.

The sound carried his mind beyond the pine-belt out into the great world from which he had come, and he thought of many things that might have been instead of this that was—the seething yeast that was Russia, the tearing down of the idols of centuries and the worship of new gods that were no gods at all—not even those of brass or gold—only visions—will-o'-the-wisps.... The madness had shown itself here too. Would the fabric of which the American Ideal was made be strong enough to hold together against the World's new madness? He believed in American institutions. Imperfect though they were, fallible as the human wills which controlled them, they were as near Liberty, Equality, Fraternity as one might yet hope to attain in a form of government this side of the millennium.

Peter started up suddenly, for he was sure that he had heard something moving in the underbrush. But after listening intently and hearing nothing more he thought that his ears had deceived him. He flashed his lantern here and there as a guide to Hawk Kennedy but there was no sound. Complete silence had fallen again over the woods. If McGuire's mysterious enemy was approaching he was doing it with the skill of an Indian scout. And it occurred to Peter at this moment that Hawk Kennedy too might have his reasons for wishing to be sure that he was to be fairly dealt with. The placard had indicated the possibility of chicanery on the part of McGuire. "No tricks," Hawk had written. He would make sure that Peter was alone before he showed himself. So Peter flashed his lamp around again, glanced at his watch, which showed that the hour of the appointment had passed, then lighted a third cigarette and sank down on the roots of the tree to wait.

There was no other sound. The breeze which had been fitful at best had died and complete silence had fallen. Peter wasn't in the least alarmed. Why should he be? He had come to do this stranger a favor and no one else except McGuire could know of the large sum of money in his possession. The trees were his friends. Peter's thoughts turned back again, as they always did when his mind was at the mercy of his imagination. What was the use of it all? Honor, righteousness, pride, straight living, the ambition to do, to achieve something real by his own efforts—to what end? He knew that he could have been living snugly in London now, married to the Princess Galitzin, drifting with the current in luxury and ease down the years, enjoying those things——

Heigho! Peter sat up and shrugged the vision off. He must not be thinking back. It wouldn't do. The new life was here. *Novaya Jezn*. Like the seedling from the twisted oak, he was going to grow straight and true—to be himself, the son of his mother, who had died with a prayer on her lips that Peter might not be what his father had been. Thus far, he had obeyed her. He had grown straight, true to the memory of that prayer.

Yes, life was good. He tossed away his cigarette, ground it into the ground with his heel, then lay back against the tree, drinking in great drafts of the clean night air. The forest was so quiet that he could hear the distant tinkle of Cedar Creek down beyond the Cabin. The time was now well after eleven. What if Hawk Kennedy failed to appear? And how long must——?

A tiny sound close at hand, clear, distinct. Peter took a chance and called out,

"Is that you, Hawk Kennedy?"

Silence and then a repetition of the sound a little louder now and from directly overhead. Peter rose, peering upward in amazement.

"Yes, I'm here," said a low voice among the leaves above him.

And presently a foot appeared, followed by legs and a body, emerging from the gloom above. Peter threw the light of his torch up into the tree.

"Hey! Cut that," commanded a voice sharply.

And Peter obeyed. In a moment a shape swung down and stood beside him. After the glare of the torch Peter couldn't make out the face under the brim of the cap, but he could see that it wore a mustache and short growth of beard. In size, the stranger was quite as tall as Peter.

Hawk Kennedy stood for a moment listening intently and Peter was so astonished at the extraordinary mode of his entrance on the scene that he did not speak.

"You're from McGuire?" asked the man shortly.

"Yes."

"Why didn't he come himself?"

The voice was gruff, purposely so, Peter thought, but there was something about it vaguely reminiscent.

"Answer me. Why didn't he come?"

Peter laughed.

"He didn't tell me why. Any more than you'd tell me why you've been up this tree."

"I'm takin' no chances this trip. I've been watchin'—listenin'," said the other grimly. "Well, what's the answer? And who—who the devil are you?"

The bearded visage was thrust closer to Peter's as though in uncertainty, but accustomed as both men now were to the darkness, neither could make out the face of the other.

"I'm McGuire's superintendent. He sent me here to meet you—to bring you something——"

"Ah—he comes across. Good. Where is it?"

"In my pocket," said Peter coolly, "but he told me to tell you first not to forget the blood on the knife, Hawk Kennedy."

The man recoiled a step.

"The blood on the knife," he muttered. And then, "McGuire asked you to say that?"

"Yes."

"Anything else?"

"No. That's all."

Another silence and then he demand in a rough tone,

"Well, give me the money!"

Impolite beggar! What was there about this shadow that suggested to Peter the thought that this whole incident had happened before? That this man belonged to another life that Peter had lived? Peter shrugged off the illusion, fumbled in his pocket and produced the envelope containing the bills.

"You'd better count it," said Peter, as the envelope changed hands.

"It's not 'phoney'——?" asked Hawk's voice suspiciously.

"Phoney?"

"Fake money——?"

"No. I got it in New York myself yesterday."

"Oh——." There was a silence in which the shade stood uncertainly fingering the package, peering into the bushes around him and listening intently. And then, abruptly,

"I want to see the color of it. Switch on your light."

Peter obeyed. "You'd better," he said.

In the glow of lamp Hawk Kennedy bent forward, his face hidden by his cap brim, fingering the bills, and Peter saw for the first time that his left hand held an automatic which covered Peter now, as it had covered him from the first moment of the interview.

"Five hundreds—eh," growled Kennedy. "They're real enough, all right. One—two—three—four——"

A roar from the darkness and a bullet crashed into the tree behind them.... Another shot! Peter's startled finger relaxed on the button of the torch and they were in darkness. A flash from the trees to the right, the bullet missing Peter by inches.

"A trick! By ——!" said Hawk's voice in a fury, "but I'll get _you_ for this."

Peter was too quick for him. In the darkness he jumped aside, striking Kennedy with his torch, and then closed with the man, whose shot went wild. They struggled for a moment, each fighting for the possession of the weapon, McGuire's money ground under their feet, but Peter was the younger and the stronger and when he twisted Hawk's wrist the man suddenly relaxed and fell, Peter on his chest.

The reason for this collapse was apparent when Peter's hand touched the moisture on Kennedy's shoulder.

"Damn you!" Hawk was muttering, as he struggled vainly.

Events had followed so rapidly that Peter hadn't had time to think of anything but his own danger. He had acted with the instinct of self-preservation, which was almost quicker than his thought, but as he knew now what had happened he realized that he, too, had been tricked by McGuire and that the murderous volley directed at Hawk Kennedy had come perilously near doing for himself. With the calm which followed the issue of his struggle with Kennedy, came a dull rage at McGuire for placing him in such danger, which only showed his employer's desperate resolve and his indifference to Peter's fate. For Hawk Kennedy had been within his rights in supposing Peter to be concerned in the trick and only the miracle of the expiring torch which had blinded the intruder had saved Peter from the fate intended for Hawk. Peter understood now the meaning of McGuire's explicit instructions and the meaning of the changing of the guards. The old man had hoped to kill his enemy with one shot and save himself the recurrence of his terror. What had become of him now? There was no sound among the bushes or any sign of him. He had slipped away like the poltroon that he was, leaving Peter to his fate.

"Damn you!" Hawk muttered again. "What did *you* want to come meddling for!"

The man couldn't be dangerously hurt if he possessed the power of invective and so, having possessed himself of Hawk's automatic, Peter got off his chest and fumbled around for the electric torch.

"It won't do you any good to lie there cursing me. Get up, if you're able to."

"Got me in the shoulder," muttered the man.

"And he might have gotten *me*," said Peter, "which would have been worse."

"You mean—you didn't—*know*," groaned Hawk, getting up into a sitting posture.

"No. I didn't," replied Peter.

He had found the torch now and was flashing it around on the ground while he picked up the scattered money.

"I'll fix him for this," groaned the stranger.

Peter glanced at him.

"His men will be down here in a moment. You'd better be getting up."

"I'm not afraid. They can't do anything to *me*. They'd better leave me alone. McGuire don't want me to talk. But I'll squeal if they bother me." Peter was aware that the man was watching him as he picked up the bills and heard him ask haltingly, "What are you—going to do—with that money?"

"My orders were to give it to you. Don't you want it?"

Peter turned and for the first time flashed the lamp full in the injured man's face. Even then Peter didn't recognize him, but he saw Hawk Kennedy's eyes open wide as he stared at Peter.

"Who——?" gasped the man. And then, "*You* here! '*Cré nom!* It's Pete, the waiter!"

Peter started back in astonishment.

"Jim Coast!" he said.

Hawk Kennedy chuckled and scrambled to his feet, halfway between a laugh and a groan.

"Well, I'm damned!"

Peter was still staring at him, the recovered bills loose in his hand. Jim Coast thrust out an arm for them.

"The money," he demanded. "The money, Pete."

Without a word Peter handed it to him. It was none of his. Coast counted the bills, the blood dripping from his fingers and soiling them, but he wiped them off with a dirty handkerchief and put them away into his pocket. Blood money, Peter thought, and rightly named.

"And now, *mon gars*, if it's all the same to you, I'd like you to take me to some place where we can tie up this hole in my shoulder."

This was like Coast's impudence. He had regained his composure again and, in spite of the pain he was suffering, had become his proper self, the same Jim Coast who had bunked with Peter on the *Bermudian*, full of smirking assertiveness and sinister suggestion. Peter was too full of astonishment to make any comment, for it was difficult to reconcile the thought of Jim Coast with Hawk Kennedy, and yet there he was, the terror of Black Rock House revealed.

"Well, Pete," he growled, "goin' to be starin' at me all night?"

"You'd better be off," said Peter briefly.

"Why?"

"They'll be here in a minute. You've got your money."

"Let 'em come. They'll have to take me to McGuire——"

"Or the lock-up at Egg Harbor——"

"All right. I'll go. But when I open my mouth to speak, McGuire will wish that Hell would open for him." And then, "See here, Pete, do you know anything of what's between me and McGuire?"

"No—except that he fears you."

"Very well. If you're workin' for him you'll steer these guys away from me. I mean it. Now think quick."

Peter did. Angry as he was at McGuire, he knew that Jim Coast meant what he said and that he would make trouble. Also Peter's curiosity knew no subsidence.

"You go to my cabin. It's hidden in the woods down this path at the right——"

"That's where you live, is it?"

"Yes. You'll find water there and a towel on the washstand. I'll be there to help you when I sheer these men off."

Coast walked a few steps and then turned quickly.

"No funny business, Pete."

"No. You can clear out if you like. I don't care. I only thought if you were badly hurt——"

"Oh, all right. Thanks."

Peter watched the dim silhouette merge into the shadows and disappear. Then flashed his light here and there that the men who must be approaching now might be guided to him. In a moment they were crashing through the undergrowth, Jesse and Andy in the lead.

"What's the shootin'?" queried Jesse Brown breathlessly.

"A man in the woods. I'm looking for him," said Peter. "He got away."

"Well, don't it beat Hell——"

"But it may be a plan to get you men away from the house," said Peter as the thought came to him. "Did you see McGuire?"

"McGuire! No. What——?"

"All right. You'd better hurry back. See if he's all right. I'll get along——"

"Not if you go flashin' *that* thing. I could a got ye with my rifle as easy as——"

"Well, never mind. Get back to the house. I'll poke around here for a while. Hurry!"

In some bewilderment they obeyed him and Peter turned his footstep toward the Cabin.

CHAPTER XI
ANCIENT HISTORY

Peter wasn't at all certain that he had done the right thing. One event had followed another with such startling rapidity that there hadn't been time to deliberate. Jim Coast was wounded, how badly Peter didn't know, but the obvious duty was to give him first aid and sanctuary until Peter could get a little clearer light on Coast's possibilities for evil. None of this was Peter's business. He had done what McGuire had asked him to do and had nearly gotten killed for his pains. Two fights already and he had come to Black Rock to find peace!

In his anger at McGuire's trick he was now indifferent as to what would happen to the old man. There was no doubt that Jim Coast held all the cards and, unless he died, would continue to hold them. It was evident that McGuire, having failed in accomplishing the murder, had placed himself in a worse position than before, for Coast was not one to relax or to forgive, and if he had gotten his five thousand dollars so easily as this, he would be disposed to make McGuire pay more heavily now. Peter knew nothing of the merits of the controversy, but it seemed obvious that the two principals in the affair were both tarred with the same stick. *Arcades Ambo*. He was beginning to believe that Coast was the more agreeable villain of the two. At least he had made no bones about the fact of his villainy.

Peter found Coast stripped to the waist, sitting in a chair by the table, bathing his wounded shoulder. But the hemorrhage had stopped and Peter saw that the bullet had merely grazed the deltoid, leaving a clean wound, which could be successfully treated by first aid devices. So he found his guest a drink of whisky, which put a new heart into him, then tore up a clean linen shirt, strips from which he soaked in iodine and bandaged over the arm and shoulder.

Meanwhile Coast was talking.

"Well, *mon vieux*, it's a little world, ain't it? To think I'd find *you*, my old bunkie, Pete, the waiter, out here in the wilds, passin' the buck for Mike McGuire! Looks like the hand o' Fate, doesn't it? Superintendent, eh? Some job! Twenty thousand acres—if he's got an inch. An' me thinkin' all the while you'd be slingin' dishes in a New York chop house!"

"I studied forestry in Germany once," said Peter with a smile, as he wound the bandage.

"Right y'are! Mebbe you told me. I don't know. Mebbe there's a lot o' things you *didn't* tell me. Mebbe there's a lot of things I didn't tell *you*. But I ought to 'a' known a globe trotter like you never would 'a' stayed a waiter. A waiter! *Nom de Dieu!* Remember that (sanguine) steward on the *Bermudian*? Oily, fat little beef-eater with the gold teeth? Tried to make us 'divy' on the tips? But we beat him to it, Pete, when we took French leave. H-m! I'm done with waitin' now, Pete. So are you, I reckon. Gentleman of leisure, *I* am!"

"There you are," said Peter as he finished the bandage, "but you'll have to get this wound dressed somewhere to-morrow."

"Right you are. A hospital in Philly will do the trick. And McGuire pays the bill."

Jim Coast got up and moved his arm cautiously.

"Mighty nice of you, Pete. That's fine. I'll make him pay through the nose for this." And then turning his head and eyeing Peter narrowly, "You say McGuire told you nothin'!"

"Nothing. It's none of my affair."

The ex-waiter laughed. "He knows his business. Quiet as death, ain't he? He's got a right to be. And scared. He's got a right to be scared too. I'll scare him worse before I'm through with him."

He broke off with a laugh and then, "Funny to find you guardin' *him* against *me*. House all locked—men with guns all over the place. He wanted one of those guys to kill me, didn't he? But I'm too slick for him. No locked doors can keep out what's scarin' Mike McGuire——"

He broke off suddenly and held up his empty glass. "Another drink of the whisky, *mon gars*, and I'm yer friend for life."

Peter was still curious, so he obeyed and after cleaning up the mess they had made he sank into a chair, studying the worn features of his old companion. He had taken the precaution to pull in the heavy shutter of the window which had been opened and to lock the door. Peter did not relish the idea of a murder committed in this cabin.

"Not apt to come now, are they, Pete? Well, let 'em," he answered himself with a shrug. "But they won't if McGuire has his way. Murder is the only thing that will suit McGuire's book. He can't do that—not with witnesses around. Ain't he the slick one, though? I was watchin' for just what happened. That's why I stayed in the tree so long—listenin'. He must of slipped in like a snake. How he did it I don't know. I'm a worse snake than he is but I always rattle before I strike."

He laughed again dryly.

"I've got *him* rattled all O. K. Mebbe he'd of shot straighter if he hadn't been. He used to could—dead shot. But I reckon his talents are runnin' different *now*. Millions he has they say, *mon vieux*, millions. And I'll get my share of 'em."

Jim Coast smoked for a moment in contented silence.

"See here, Pete. I like you. Always did. Straight as a string—you are. You've done me a good turn to-night. You might of put me out—killed me when you had me down——"

"I'm no murderer, Jim."

"Right. Nor I ain't either. I don't want to hurt a hair of McGuire's head. Every one of 'em is precious as refined gold. I want him to live—to keep on livin' and makin' more money because the more money he's got the more I'll get—see."

"Blackmail," said Peter shortly.

Coast glanced at him, shrugged and laughed.

"Call it that if you like. It's a dirty word, but I'll stand for it, seein' it's you. Blackmail! What's a waiter's tip but blackmail for good service? What's a lawyer's fee from a corporation but money paid by men to keep them out of the jail? What's a breach of promise case? Blackmail—legal blackmail. I'm doin' nothin' less an' nothin' more than a million other men—but I'm not workin' with a lawyer. I'll turn the trick alone. What would you say if I told you that half of every dollar McGuire has got is mine—a full half—to say nothin' of payment for the years I was wanderin' an' grubbin' over the face of the earth, while he was livin' easy. Oh! You're surprised. You'd better be. For that's the God's truth, *mon ami*."

"You mean—he—he——" Peter's credulity was strained and he failed to finish his query.

"Oh, you don't believe? Well, you needn't. But there's no blackmail when you only take what belongs to you. The money—the money that made his millions was as much mine as his. I'm going to have my share with compound interest for fifteen years—and perhaps a bit more."

"You surprise me. But it seems that if there's any justice in your claim, you could establish it legally."

Jim Coast laughed again.

"There's a quicker—a safer way than that. I'm takin' it." He filled his glass again and went on, leaning far over the table toward Peter. "*Voyons*, Pete. When we came ashore, I made you an offer to play my game. You turned me down. It's not too late to change your mind. The old man trusts you or he wouldn't of sent you out with that money. I may need some help with this business and you're fixed just right to lend me a hand. Throw in with me, do what I want, and I'll see that you're fixed for life."

Peter shook his head slowly from side to side.

"No, Jim. He pays me well. I'm no traitor."

"H-m. Traitor!" he sneered. "*He* wasn't overparticular about *you*. He might of killed you or *I* might of, if you hadn't been too damn quick for me. What do you think Mike McGuire cares about *you*?" he laughed bitterly.

"Nothing. But that makes no difference. I——"

A loud jangle of a bell from the corner and Jim Coast sprang to his feet.

"The telephone," explained Peter, indicating the instrument. "That's McGuire now." He rose and moved toward it, but Coast caught him by the arm.

"Worried, eh?" he said with a grin. "Wants to know what's happened! All right. Tell him—tell the——." And then, as Peter released himself, "Wait a minute. Tell him you've got me here," laughed Coast, "a prisoner. Tell him I'm talking. Ask for instructions. He'll tell you what to do with me, damn quick," he sneered.

Peter waited a moment, thinking, while the bell tinkled again, and then took down the receiver. He was in no mood to listen to McGuire.

"Hello—Yes, this is Nichols.... All right, yes. Shot at from the dark—while paying the money. You hit Hawk Kennedy in the shoulder.... Yes, *you*. I'm no fool, McGuire.... He's here—at the Cabin. I've just fixed his shoulder——. All right——. What shall I do with him——? Yes—Yes, he's talking.... Let him go——! Hello! Let him go, you say? Yes——"

"Let me get to him——," growled Coast, pushing close to the transmitter. "Hello—Mike McGuire—hello——"

"He's gone," said Peter.

"'Let him go,'" sneered Coast. "You'd bet he'd let me go." Then he looked at Peter and laughed. "He's scared all right—beat it like a cottontail. Seems a shame to take the money, Pete—a real shame."

He laughed uproariously, then sauntered easily over to the table, took another of Peter's cigarettes and sank into the easy chair again. Peter eyed him in silence. He was an unwelcome guest but he hadn't yet gratified Peter's curiosity.

"Well, what are you going to do?" asked Peter.

"Me?" Coast inhaled Peter's cigarette luxuriously, and smiled. "I'm goin' West, *pronto*—to get my facts straight—all at the expense of the party of the first part. I might stop off at the Grand Cañon first for the view. I need a rest, Pete. I ain't as young as I was—or I mightn't of let you put me out so easy to-night. I'm glad of that, though. Wouldn't like to of done you hurt——"

"And then——?" asked Peter steadily.

"Then? Oh, I'll beat it down to Bisbee and ask a few questions. I just want to hook up a few things I *don't* know with the things I *do* know. I'll travel light but comfortable. Five thousand dollars makes a heap of difference in your point of view—and other people's. I'll be an eastern millionaire lookin' for investments. And what I won't know about Jonathan K. McGuire, alias Mike McGuire—won't be worth knowin'." He broke off and his glance caught the interested expression on the face of his host.

"H-m. Curious, ain't you, Pete?"

"Yes," said Peter frankly. "I am. Of course it's none of my business, but——"

"But you'd like to know, just the same. I get you." He flicked off the ash of his cigarette and picked up his whisky glass. "Well——," he went on, "I don't see why I shouldn't tell you—some of it—that is. It won't do any harm for you to know the kind of skunk you're workin' for. There's some of it that nobody on God's earth will ever know but me and Mike McGuire—unless he slips up on one of his payments, and then everybody's goin' to know. *Everybody*—but his daughter first of all."

Coast was silent a long moment while he drained the whisky and slowly set the glass down upon the table. The shadows upon his face were unpleasant, darkened perceptibly as they marked the years his thoughts followed, and the lines at his lips and nostrils became more deeply etched in bitterness and ugly resolve.

"It was down in the San Luis valley I first met up with Mike McGuire. He was born in Ireland, of poor but honest parents, as the books tell us. He changed his name to 'Jonathan K.' when he made his first 'stake.' That meant he was comin' up in the world—see? Me and Mike worked together up in Colorado, punchin' cattle, harvestin', ranchin' generally. We were 'buddies,' *mon gars*, like you an' me, eatin', sleepin' together as thick as thieves. He had a family somewhere, same as me—the wife had a little money but her old man made him quit—some trouble. After awhile we got tired of workin' for wages, grub staked, and beat it for the mountains. That was back in nineteen one or two, I reckon. We found a vein up above Wagon Wheel Gap. It looked good and we staked out claims and worked it, hardly stoppin' to eat or sleep." Coast stopped with a gasp and a shrug. "Well, the long an' short of that, *mon vieux*, was a year of hard work with only a thousand or so apiece to show for it. It was only a pocket. Hell!" He broke off in disgust and spat into the fireplace. "Don't talk to me about your gold mines. There ain't any such animal. Well, Mike saved his. I spent mine. Faro. You know—an' women. Then I got hurt. I was as good as dead—but I pulled through. I ain't easy to kill. When I came around, I 'chored' for a while, doin' odd jobs where I could get 'em and got a little money together and went to Pueblo. When I struck town I got pretty drunk and busted a faro bank. I never *did* have any luck when I was sober."

"Yes, you've told me about that," said Peter.

"So I did—on the *Bermudian*. Well, it was at Pueblo I met up with Mike McGuire, and we beat it down into Arizona where the copper was. Bisbee was only a row of wooden shacks, but we got some backin', bought an outfit and went out prospectin' along the Mexican border. And what with 'greasers' and thievin' redskins it was some job in those days. But we made friends all right enough and found out some of the things we wanted to know.

"Now, Pete, if I was to tell you all that went on in that long trail into the Gila Desert and what happened when we got what we went for, you'd know as much as I do. You'd know enough to hold up Mike McGuire yourself if you'd a mind to. This is where the real story stops. What happened in between is my secret and Mike McGuire's. We found the mine we were lookin' for.... That's sure——How we got it you'll never know. But we got it. And here's where the real story begins again. We were miles out in the Gila Desert and if ever there's a Hell on earth, it's there. Sand, rocks, rocks and sand and the sun. It was Hell with the cover off and no mistake! No water within a hundred miles.

"Now, this is where the fine Eyetalian hand of Mike McGuire shows itself. We were rich. Any fool with half an eye could see that. The place was lousy— fairly lousy! It was ours——," Coast's brow darkened and his eyes glittered strangely as a darting demon of the past got behind them. "Yes—*ours. Sacré bleu!* Any man who went through what we did deserved it, by G——! We were rich. There was plenty enough for two, but McGuire didn't think so. And here's what he does to me. In the middle of the night while I'm asleep he sneaks away as neat as you please, with the horses and the pack-mules and the water, leavin' me alone with all the money in the world, and a devourin' thirst, more than a hundred miles from nowhere."

"Murder," muttered Peter.

Coast nodded. "You bet you. Murder. Nothin' less. Oh, he knew what *he* was about all right. And I saw it quick. Death! That's what it meant. Slow but sure. Hadn't I seen the bones bleaching all along the trail? He left me there to die. He thought I would die. *Dios!* That thirst!" Coast reached for the pitcher and splashed rather than poured a glass of water which he gulped down avidly. "There was nothin' for it but to try afoot for Tucson, which was due east. Every hour I waited would of made me an hour nearer to bein' a mummy. So I set out through the hot sand, the sun burnin' through me, slowly parchin' my blood. My tongue swelled. I must of gone in circles. Days passed—nights when I lay gaspin' on my back, like a fish out of water, tryin' to suck moisture out of dry air.... Then the red sun again—up over the edge of that furnace, mockin' at me. I was as good as dead and I knew it. Only the mummy of me, parched black, stumbled on, fallin', strugglin' up again, fallin' at last, bitin' at the sand like a mad dog...."

"Horrible," muttered Peter.

"It was. I reckon I died—the soul of me, or what was left of it. I came to life under the starlight, with a couple of 'greasers' droppin' water on my tongue. They brought me around, but I was out of my head for a week. I couldn't talk the lingo anyhow. I just went with 'em like a child. There wasn't anything else to do. Lucky they didn't kill me. I guess I wasn't worth killin'. We went South. They were makin' for Hermosillo. Revolutionists. They took all my money—about three hundred dollars. But it was worth it. They'd saved my life. But I couldn't go back now, even if I wanted to. I had no money, nor any way of gettin' any."

Jim Coast leaned forward, glowering at the rag carpet.

"But I—I didn't want to go back just then. The fear of God was in me. I'd looked into Hell."

He laughed bitterly.

"Then I joined the 'greasers' against Diaz. I've told you about that. And the 'Rurales' cleaned us up all right. A girl saved my life. Instead of shootin' me against a mud wall, they put me to work on a railroad. I was there three years. I escaped at last and reached the coast, where I shipped for South America. It was the only way out, but all the while I was thinkin' of Mike McGuire and the copper mine. You know the rest, Pete—the Argentine deal that might of made me rich an' how it fell through. Don't it beat Hell how the world bites the under dog!"

"But why didn't you go back to America and fight your claim with McGuire?" asked Peter, aware of the sinister, missing passage in the story.

Coast shot a sharp glance at his questioner.

"There were two reasons—one of which you won't know. The other was that I couldn't. I was on the beach an' not too popular. The only ships out of Buenos Aires were for London. That was the easiest way back to America anyhow. So I shipped as a cattle hand. And there you are. I lived easy in London. That's me. Easy come easy go. There it was I wrote a man I knew out in Bisbee—the feller that helped stake us—and he answered me that McGuire was dead, and that the mine was a flivver—too far away to work. You see he must of showed the letter to McGuire, and McGuire told him what to write. That threw me off the track. I forgot him and went to France...."

Coast paused while he filled his glass again.

"It wasn't until I reached New York that I found out McGuire was alive. It was just a chance while I was plannin' another deal. I took it. I hunted around the brokers' offices where they sell copper stocks. It didn't take me long to find that my mine was the 'Tarantula.' McGuire had developed it with capital from Denver, built a narrow gauge in. Then after a while had sold out his share for more than half a million clear."

Peter was studying Coast keenly, thinking hard. But the story held with what he already knew of the man's history.

"That's when Mike McGuire tacked the 'Jonathan K.' onto his name," Coast went on. "And that money's mine, the good half of it. Figure it out for yourself. Say five hundred thou, eight per cent, fifteen years—I reckon I could worry along on that even if he wouldn't do better—which he will.

"Well, Pete—to shorten up—I found McGuire was here—in New York— and I laid for him. I watched for a while and then one day I got my nerve up and tackled him on the street. You ought to of seen his face when I told him who I was and what I'd come for. We were in the crowd at Broadway and Wall, people all about us. He started the 'high and mighty' stuff for a minute until I crumpled him up with a few facts. I thought he was goin' to have a stroke for a minute, when I made my brace for the five thou—then he turned tail and ran into the crowd pale as death. I lost him then. But it didn't matter. I'd find him again. I knew where his office was—and his hotel. It was dead easy. But he beat it down here. It took me awhile to pick up the trail. But here I am, Pete—here I am—safe in harbor at last."

Coast took the bills out of his pocket and slowly counted them again.

"And when you come back from the West, what will you do?" asked Peter.

"Oh, now you're talkin', Pete. I'm goin' to settle down and live respectable. I like this country around here. I came from Jersey, you know, in the first place. I might build a nice place—keep a few horses and automobiles and enjoy my old age—run over to gay Paree once a year—down to Monte Carlo in the season. Oh, I'd know how to *live* now. You bet you. I've seen 'em do it—those swells. They won't have anything on me. I'll live like a prince——"

"On blackmail——," said Peter.

"See here, Pete——!"

"I meant it." Peter had risen and faced Coast coolly. "Blackmail! You can't tell me that if you had any legal claim on McGuire you couldn't prove it."

"I mightn't be able to——," he shrugged.

"What is McGuire frightened about? Not about what he owes you. He could pay that ten times over. It's something else—something that happened out there at the mine that you dare not tell——"

"That I *won't* tell," laughed Coast disagreeably.

"That you *dare* not tell—that McGuire dares not tell. Something that has to do with his strange message about the blood on the knife, and your placard about what you've got holding over him——"

"Right you are," sneered the other.

"It's dirty money, I tell you—bloody money. I know it. And I know who you are, Jim Coast."

Coast started up and thrust the roll deep into his trousers pocket.

"You don't know anything," he growled.

Peter got up too. His mind had followed Coast's extraordinary story, and so far as it had gone, believed it to be true. Peter wanted to know what had happened out there at the mine in the desert, but more than that he wanted to know how the destinies of this man affected Beth. And so the thought that had been growing in his mind now found quick utterance.

"I know this—that you've come back to frighten McGuire, but you've also come back to bring misery and shame to others who've lived long in peace and happiness without you——"

"What——?" said Coast incredulously.

"I know who you are. You're Ben Cameron," said Peter distinctly.

The effect of this statement upon Jim Coast was extraordinary. He started back abruptly, overturning a chair, and fell rather than leaned against the bedpost—his eyes staring from a ghastly face.

"What—what did—you say?" he gasped chokingly.

"You're Ben Cameron," said Peter again.

Coast put the fingers of one hand to his throat and straightened slowly, still staring at Peter. Then uneasily, haltingly, he made a sound in his throat that grew into a dry laugh——

"Me—B-Ben Cameron! That's damn good. Me—Ben Cameron! Say, Pete, whatever put *that* into your head?"

"The way you frightened the old woman at the kitchen door."

"Oh!" Coast straightened in relief. "I get you. You've been talkin' to *her*."

"Yes. What did you say to her?"

"I—I just gave her a message for McGuire. I reckon she gave it to him."

"A message?"

"Oh, you needn't say you don't know, Pete. It didn't fetch him. So I put up the placard."

Peter was now more bewildered than Coast. "Do you deny that you're Ben Cameron?" he asked.

Coast pulled himself together and took up his coat.

"Deny it? Sure! I'm not—not him—not Ben Cameron—not Ben Cameron. Don't I know who I am?" he shouted. Then he broke off with a violent gesture and took up his cap. "Enough of your damn questions, I say. I've told you what I've told you. You can believe it or not, as you choose. I'm Jim Coast to you or Hawk Kennedy, if you like, but don't you go throwin' any more of your dirty jokes my way. Understand?"

Peter couldn't understand but he had had enough of the man. So he pointed toward the door.

"Go," he ordered. "I've had enough of you—get out!"

Coast walked a few paces toward the door, then paused and turned and held out his hand.

"Oh, Hell, Pete. Don't let's you and me quarrel. You gave me a start back there. I'm sorry. Of course, you knew. You been good to me to-night. I'm obliged. I need you in my business. More'n ever."

"No," said Peter.

"Oh, very well. Suit yourself," said Coast with a shrug. "There's plenty of time. I'll be back in a month or six weeks. Think it over. I've made you a nice offer—real money—to help me a bit. Take it or leave it, as you please. I'll get along without you, but I'd rather have you with me than against me."

"I'm neither," said Peter. "I want nothing to do with it."

Coast shrugged. "I'm sorry. Well, so long. I've got a horse back in the dunes. I'll take the milk train from Hammonton to Philadelphia. You won't tell, Pete?"

"No."

"Good-night."

Peter didn't even reply. And when the man had gone he opened the door and windows to let in the night air. The room had been defiled by the man's very presence. Ben Cameron? Beth's father? The thing seemed impossible, but every fact in Peter's knowledge pointed toward it. And yet what the meaning of Jim Coast's strange actions at the mention of his name? And what were the facts that Jim Coast *didn't* tell? What had happened at the mine that was too terrible even to speak about? What was the bond between these two men, which held the successful one in terror, and the other in silence? Something unspeakably vile. A hideous pact——

The telephone bell jangled again. Peter rose and went to it. But he was in no humor to talk to McGuire.

"Hello," he growled. "Yes—he's gone. I let him go. You told me to.... Yes, he talked—a long while.... No. He won't be back for a month.... We'll talk that over later.... No. Not to-night. I'm going to bed.... No. Not until to-morrow. I've had about enough of this.... All right. Good-night."

And Peter hung up the receiver, undressed and went to bed.

It had been rather a full day for Peter.

CHAPTER XII
CONFESSION

In spite of his perplexities, Peter slept soundly and was only awakened by the jangling of the telephone bell. But Peter wanted to do a little thinking before he saw McGuire, and he wanted to ask the housekeeper a few questions, so he told McGuire that he would see him before ten o'clock. The curious part of the telephone conversation was that McGuire made no mention of the shooting. "H-m," said Peter to himself as he hung up, "going to ignore that trifling incident altogether, is he? Well, we'll see about that. It doesn't pay to be too clever, old cock." His pity for McGuire was no more. At the present moment Peter felt nothing for him except an abiding contempt which could hardly be modified by any subsequent revelations.

Peter ran down to the creek in his bath robe and took a quick plunge, then returned, shaved and dressed while his coffee boiled, thinking with a fresh mind over the events and problems of the night before. Curiously enough, he found that he considered them more and more in their relation to Beth. Perhaps it was his fear for her happiness that laid stress on the probability that Jim Coast was Ben Cameron, Beth's father. How otherwise could Mrs. Bergen's terror be accounted for? And yet why had Coast been so perturbed at the mere mention of Ben Cameron's name? That was really strange. For a moment the man had stared at Peter as though he were seeing a ghost. If he *were* Ben Cameron, why shouldn't he have acknowledged the fact? Here was the weak point in the armor of mystery. Peter had to admit that even while Coast was telling his story and the conviction was growing in Peter's mind that this was Beth's father, the very thought of Beth herself seemed to make the relationship grotesque. This Jim Coast, this picturesque blackguard who had told tales on the *Bermudian* that had brought a flush of shame even to Peter's cheeks—this degenerate, this scheming blackmailer—thief, perhaps murderer, too, the father of Beth! Incredible! The merest contact with such a man must defile, defame her. And yet if this were the fact, Coast would have a father's right to claim her, to drag her down, a prey to his vile tongue and drunken humors as she had once been when a child. Her Aunt Tillie feared this. And Aunt Tillie did not know as Peter now did of the existence of the vile secret that sealed Coast's lips and held McGuire's soul in bondage.

Instead of going directly up the lawn to the house Peter went along the edge of the woods to the garage and then up the path, as Coast must have done a few nights before. The housekeeper was in the pantry and there Peter sought her out. He noted the startled look in her eyes at the moment he entered the room and then the line of resolution into which her mouth was immediately drawn. So Peter chose a roundabout way of coming to his subject.

"I wanted to talk to you about Beth, Mrs. Bergen," he began cheerfully. She offered him a chair but Peter leaned against the windowsill looking out into the gray morning. He told her what he had discovered about her niece's voice, that he himself had been educated in music and that he thought every opportunity should be given Beth to have her voice trained.

He saw that Mrs. Bergen was disarmed for the moment as to the real purpose of his visit and he went on to tell her just what had happened at the Cabin with Shad Wells the day before, and asking her, as Beth's only guardian, for permission to carry out his plan to teach her all that he knew, after which he hoped it would be possible for her to go to New York for more advanced training.

Mrs. Bergen listened in wonder, gasping at the tale of Shad Wells's undoing, which Peter asked her to keep in confidence. From Mrs. Bergen's comments he saw that she took little stock in Shad, who had been bothering Beth for two years or more, and that her own love for the girl amounted to a blind adoration which could see no fault in anything that she might do. It was clear that she was delighted with the opportunities Peter offered, for she had always known that Beth sang "prettier than anybody in the world." As to going to the Cabin for the lessons, that was nobody's business but Beth's. She was twenty-two—and able to look out for herself.

"I'm an old woman, Mr. Nichols," she concluded timidly, "an' I've seen a lot of trouble, one kind or another, but I ain't often mistaken in my judgments. I know Beth. She ain't nobody's fool. And if she likes you, you ought to be glad of it. If she's willin' to come to your cabin, I'm willin' that she should go there—no matter who don't like it or why. She can look after herself—aye, better than I can look after her." She sighed. And then with some access of spirit, "You're different from most of the folks around here, but I don't see nothin' wrong with you. If you say you want to help Beth, I'm willin' to believe you. But if I thought you meant her any harm——"

She broke off and stared at him with her mild eyes under brows meant to be severe.

"I hope you don't want to think that, Mrs. Bergen," said Peter gently.

"No. I don't want to. Beth don't take up with every Tom, Dick and Harry. And if she likes you, I reckon she knows what's she's about."

"I want to help her to make something of herself," said Peter calmly. "And I know I can. Beth is a very unusual girl."

"Don't you suppose I know that? She always was. She ain't the same as the rest of us down here. She always wanted to learn. Even now when she's through school, she's always readin'—always."

"That's it. She ought to complete her education. That's what I mean. I want to help her to be a great singer. I can do it if you'll let me."

"Where's the money comin' from?" sighed Mrs. Bergen.

"No need to bother about that, yet. I can give her a beginning, if you approve. After that——" Peter paused a moment and then, "We'll see," he finished.

He was somewhat amazed at the length to which his subconscious thought was carrying him, for his spoken words could infer nothing less than his undertaking at his own expense the completion of the girl's education. The housekeeper's exclamation quickly brought him to a recognition of his meaning.

"You mean—that *you*——!" she halted and looked at him over her glasses in wonder.

"Yes," he said blandly, aware of an irrevocable step. "I do, Mrs. Bergen."

"My land!" she exclaimed. And then again as though in echo, "My land!"

"That's one of the reasons why I've come here to you to-day," he went on quickly. "I want to help Beth and I want to help *you*. I know that everything isn't going right for you at Black Rock House. I've been drawn more deeply into—into McGuire's affairs than I expected to be and I've learned a great many things that aren't any business of mine. And one of the things I've learned is that your peace of mind and Beth's happiness are threatened by the things that are happening around you."

The housekeeper had risen and stood leaning against the dresser, immediately on her guard.

"Mrs. Bergen," he went on firmly, "there's no use of trying to evade this issue—because it's here! I know more than you think I do. I'm trying to get at the root of this mystery because of Beth. You told me the other night that Beth's happiness was involved when that stranger came to the kitchen porch——"

"No, no," gasped the woman. "Don't ask me. I'll tell you nothin'."

"You saw this man—outside the kitchen door in the dark," he insisted. "You talked with him——"

"No—no. Don't ask me, Mr. Nichols."

"Won't you tell me what he said? I saw him last night—talked with him for an hour——"

"*You*—talked—with him!" she gasped in alarm. And then, haltingly, "What did he say to you? What did he do? Is he coming back?"

She was becoming more disturbed and nervous, so Peter brought a chair and made her sit in it.

"No. He's not coming back—not for a month or more," he replied reassuringly. "But if I'm to help you, I've got to know something more about him, and for Beth's sake you've got to help me." And then quietly, "Mrs. Bergen, was this man who came to the kitchen door, Ben Cameron, Beth's father?"

"My God!" said the housekeeper faintly, putting her face in her hands.

"Won't you tell me just what happened?" Peter asked.

"I—I'm scared, Mr. Nichols," she groaned. "The whole thing has been too much for me—knowin' how scared Mr. McGuire is too. I can't understand, I can't even—think—no more."

"Let me do your thinking for you. Tell me what happened the other night, Mrs. Bergen."

The woman raised a pallid face, her colorless eyes blinking up at him beseechingly.

"Tell me," he whispered. "It can do no possible harm."

She glanced pitifully at him once more and then haltingly told her story.

"I—I was sittin' in the kitchen there, the night of the supper party—by the door—restin' and tryin' to get cool—when—when a knock come on the door-jamb outside. It sounded queer—the door bein' open—an' my nerves bein' shook sorter with the goin's on here. But I went to the door an' leaned out. There was a man standin' in the shadow——"

Mrs. Bergen paused in a renewed difficulty of breathing.

"And then——?" Peter urged.

"He—he leaned forward toward me an' spoke rough-like. 'You're the cook, ain't you?' he says. I was that scared I—I couldn't say nothin'. An' he went on. 'You tell McGuire to meet me at the end of the lawn to-morrow night.'"

"And what did you say?"

"Nothin'. I couldn't."

"What else did he tell you?"

Mrs. Bergen bent her head but went on with an effort.

"He says, 'Tell McGuire Ben—Ben Cameron's come back.'"

"I see. And you were more frightened than ever?"

"Yes. More frightened—terrible. I didn't know what to do. I mumbled somethin'. Then you an' Beth come in——"

"And *was* it Ben Cameron that you saw?"

The poor creature raised her gaze to Peter's again.

"B-Ben Cameron? Who else could it 'a' been? An' I thought he was dead, Mr. Nichols—years ago."

"You didn't recognize him, then?"

"I—I don't know. It was all so sudden—like seein' a corpse—speakin' that name."

"He wore a short beard?"

"Yes. But Ben Cameron was smooth shaved."

"Did Ben Cameron have any distinguishing mark—anything you could remember him by?"

"Yes. Ben Cameron's little finger of his left hand was missin'——. But of course, Mr. Nichols, I couldn't see nothin' in the dark."

"No, of course," said Peter with a gasp of relief. "But his voice——?"

"It was gruff—hoarse—whisperin'-like."

"Was the Ben Cameron you knew, your brother-in-law—was he tall?"

She hesitated, her brows puckering.

"That's what bothered me some. Beth's father wasn't over tall——"

"I see," Peter broke in eagerly, "and this man was tall—about my size—with a hook nose—black eyes and——"

"Oh, I—I couldn't see his face," she muttered helplessly. "The night was too dark."

"But you wouldn't swear it was Ben Cameron?"

She looked up at him in a new bewilderment. "But who else could it 'a' been—sayin' that name—givin' that message?"

Peter rubbed his chin thoughtfully.

"Queer, isn't it? I don't wonder that you were alarmed—especially for Beth, knowing the kind of man he was."

"It's terrible, Mr. Nichols. A man like Ben Cameron never gets made over. He's bad clear through. If you only knew——" Mrs. Bergen's pale eyes seemed to be looking back into the past. "He means no good to Beth—that's what frightens me. He could take her away from me. She's his daughter——"

"Well—don't worry," said Peter at last. "We'll find a way to protect you." And then, "Of course you didn't take that message to McGuire?" he asked.

"Why, no—Mr. Nichols. I couldn't. I'd 'a' died first. But what does it all mean? *Him* bein' scared of Ben Cameron, too. I can't make it out—though I've thought and thought until I couldn't think no more."

She was on the point of tears now, so Peter soothed her gently.

"Leave this to me, Mrs. Bergen." And then, "You haven't said anything of this to any one?"

"Not a soul—I—I was hopin' it might 'a' been just a dream."

Peter was silent for a moment, gazing out of the window and thinking deeply.

"No. It wasn't a dream," he said quietly at last. "You saw a man by the kitchen door, and he gave you the message about Ben Cameron, *but the man you saw wasn't Ben Cameron*, Mrs. Bergen, because, unless I'm very much mistaken, Ben Cameron is dead——"

"How do you——?"

"He didn't die when you thought he did, Mrs. Bergen—but later. I can't tell you how. It's only a guess. But I'm beginning to see a light in this affair—and I'm going to follow it until I find the truth. Good-by. Don't worry."

And Peter, with a last pat on the woman's shoulder and an encouraging smile, went out of the door and into the house.

Eagerly Peter's imagination was trying to fill the gap in Jim Coast's story, and his mind, now intent upon the solution of the mystery, groped before him up the stair. And what it saw was the burning Gila Desert ... the mine among the rocks—"lousy" with outcroppings of ore ... "Mike" McGuire and "Hawk" Kennedy, devious in their ways, partners in a vile conspiracy....

But Peter's demeanor was careless when Stryker admitted him to McGuire's room and his greeting in reply to McGuire's was casual enough to put his employer off his guard. After a moment's hesitation McGuire sent the valet out and went himself and closed and locked the door. Peter refused his cigar, lighting one of his own cigarettes, and sank into the chair his host indicated.

After the first words Peter knew that his surmise had been correct and that his employer meant to deny all share in the shooting of the night before.

"Well," began the old man, with a glance at the door, "what did he say?"

Peter shook his head judicially. He had already decided on the direction which this conversation must take.

"No. It won't do, Mr. McGuire," he said calmly.

"What do you mean?"

"Merely that before we talk of what Hawk Kennedy said to me, we'll discuss your reasons for unnecessarily putting my life in danger——"

"This shooting you've spoken of——"

"This attempted *murder*!"

"You're dreaming."

Peter laughed at him. "You'll be telling me in a moment that you didn't hear the shots." And then, leaning forward so that he stared deep into his employer's eyes, "See here, Mr. McGuire, I'm not to be trifled with. I know too much of your affairs—more than you think I do——"

"He talked——?" McGuire's poise was slipping from him.

"One moment, if you please. I want this thing perfectly understood. Your arrangements were cleverly made—changing the guards—your instructions to me—the flashlight and all the rest. You didn't want to kill me if you could help it. I'm obliged for this consideration. You forgot that your hand isn't as steady now as it was when you were a dead shot out in Arizona—Ah! I see that you already understand what I mean."

McGuire had started forward in his chair, his face livid.

"You know——?"

"Yes. More than I wanted to know—more than I would ever have known if you'd played fair with me. You cared nothing for my life. You shot, twice, missed killing your man and then when the light went out, sneaked away like the coward that you are——"

"D——n you," croaked McGuire feebly, falling back in his chair.

"Leaving me to the mercies of your ancient enemy in the dark—who thought *me* your accomplice. You can hardly blame him under the circumstances. But I got the best of him—luckily for me, and disarmed him. If you had remained a few moments longer you might have taken part in our very interesting conversation. Do you still deny all this?"

McGuire, stifled with his fear and fury, was incapable of a reply.

"Very good. So long as we understand each other thus far, perhaps you will permit me to go on. As you know, I came to you in good faith. I wanted to help you in any way that a gentleman could do. Last night you tricked me, and put my life in danger. If you had killed Kennedy everything would have been all right for *you*. And I would have been accused of the killing. If *I* had been killed no harm would have been done at all. That was your idea. It was a clever little scheme. Pity it didn't work out."

McGuire's faltering courage was coming back.

"Go on!" he muttered desperately.

"Thanks," said Peter, "I will. One shot of yours scraped Kennedy's shoulder. He was bleeding badly, so I took him to the Cabin and fixed him up. He was rather grateful. He ought to have been. I gave him a drink too—several drinks. You said he wouldn't talk, but he did."

"You *made* him talk, d——n you," McGuire broke in hoarsely.

"No. He volunteered to talk. I may say, he insisted upon it. You see, I happened to have the gentleman's acquaintance——"

"You——!"

"We met on the steamer coming over when we were escaping from Russia. His name was Jim Coast then. He was a waiter in the dining saloon. So was I. Funny, isn't it?"

To McGuire it seemed far from that, for at this revelation his jaw dropped and he stared at Peter as though the entire affair were beyond his comprehension.

"You knew him! A waiter, *you*!"

"Yes. Misfortune makes strange bedfellows. It was either that or starvation. I preferred to wait."

"For—for the love of God—go on," growled McGuire. His hands were clutching the chair arm and there was madness in his shifting eyes, so Peter watched him keenly.

"I will. He told me how you and he had worked together out in Colorado, up in the San Luis valley, of the gold prospect near Wagon Wheel Gap, of its failure—how you met again in Pueblo and then went down into the copper country—Bisbee, Arizona."

Peter had no pity now. He saw McGuire straighten again in his chair, his gaze shifting past Peter from left to right like a trapped animal. His fingers groped along the chair arms, along the table edge, trembling, eager but uncertain. But the sound of Peter's narrative seemed to fascinate—to hypnotize him.

"Go on———!" he whispered hoarsely. "Go on!"

"You got an outfit and went out into the Gila Desert," continued Peter, painting his picture leisurely, deliberately. "It was horrible—the heat, the sand, the rocks—but you weren't going to fail this time. There was going to be something at the end of this terrible pilgrimage to repay you for all that you suffered, you and Hawk Kennedy. There was no water, but what you carried on your pack-mules—no water within a hundred miles, nothing but sand and rocks and the heat. No chance at all for a man, alone without a horse, in that desert. You saw the bones of men and animals bleaching along the trail. That was the death that awaited any man———"

"You lie!"

Peter sprang for the tortured man as McGuire's fingers closed on something in the open drawer of the table, but Peter twisted the weapon quickly out of his hand and threw it in the corner of the room.

"You fool," he whispered quickly as he pinioned McGuire in his chair, "do you want to add another murder to what's on your conscience?"

But McGuire had already ceased to resist him. Peter hadn't been too gentle with him. The man had collapsed. A glance at his face showed his condition. So Peter poured out a glass of whisky and water which he poured between his employer's gaping lips. Then he waited, watching the old man. He seemed really old now to Peter, a hundred at least, for his sagging facial muscles seemed to reveal the lines of every event in his life—an old man, though scarcely sixty, yet broken and helpless. He came around slowly, his heavy gaze slowly seeking Peter's.

"What—what are you going to do?" he managed at last.

"Nothing. I'm no blackmailer." And then, playing his high card, "I've heard what Hawk said about Ben Cameron," said Peter. "Now tell me the truth."

At the sound of the name McGuire started and then his eyes closed for a moment.

"You know—everything," he muttered.

"Yes, *his* side," Peter lied. "What's yours?"

McGuire managed to haul himself upright in his chair, staring up at Peter with bloodshot eyes.

"He's lied to you, if he said I done it———," he gasped, relapsing into the vernacular of an earlier day. "It was Hawk. He stabbed him in the back. I

never touched him. I never had a thing to do with the killin'. I swear it——
"

Peter's lips set in a thin line.

"So Hawk Kennedy killed Ben Cameron!" he said.

"He did. I swear to God——"

"And then *you* cleared out with all the water, leaving Hawk to die. *That* was murder—cold-blooded murder——"

"My God, don't, Nichols!" the old man moaned. "If you only knew——"

"Well, then—tell me the truth."

Their glances met. Peter's was compelling. He had, when he chose, an air of command. And there was something else in Peter's look, inflexible as it was, that gave McGuire courage, an unalterable honesty which had been so far tried and not found wanting.

"You know—already," he stammered.

"Tell me your story," said Peter bluntly.

There was a long moment of hesitation, and then,

"Get me a drink, Nichols. I'll trust you. I've never told it to a living man. I'll tell—I'll tell it all. It may not be as bad as you think."

He drank the liquor at a gulp and set the glass down on the table beside him.

"This—this thing has been hanging over me for fifteen years, Nichols— fifteen years. It's weighted me down, made an old man of me before my time. Maybe it will help me to tell somebody. It's made me hard—silent, busy with my own affairs, bitter against every man who could hold his head up. I knew it was going to come some day. I knew it. You can't pull anything like that and get away with it forever. I'd made the money for my kids—I never had any fun spending it in my life. I'm a lonely man, Nichols. I always was. No happiness except when I came back to my daughters—to Peggy and my poor Marjorie...."

McGuire was silent for a moment and Peter, not taking his gaze from his face, patiently waited. McGuire glanced at him just once and then went on, slipping back from time to time into the speech of a bygone day.

"I never knew what his first name was. He was always just 'Hawk' to us boys on the range. Hawk Kennedy was a bad lot. I knew it up there in the San Luis valley but I wasn't no angel from Heaven myself. And he had a way with him. We got on all right together. But when the gold mine up at the Gap petered out he quit me—got beaten up in a fight about a woman. I didn't see him for some years, when he showed up in Pueblo, where I was workin' in a smelter. He was all for goin' South into the copper country. He had some money—busted a faro bank he said, and talked big about the fortune he was goin' to make. Ah, he could talk, when he had something on his mind.... I had some money saved up too and so I quit my job and went with him down to Bisbee, Arizona. I wish to God I never had. I'd gotten pretty well straightened out up in Pueblo, sendin' money East to the wife and all———. But I wanted to be rich. I was forty-five and I had to hurry. But I could do it yet. Maybe this was my chance. That's the way I thought. That's why I happened to listen to Hawk Kennedy and his tales of the copper country.

"Well, we got an outfit in Bisbee and set out along the Mexican border. We had a tip that let us out into the desert. It was just a tip, that's all. But it was worth following up. It was about this man Ben Cameron. He'd come into town all alone, get supplies and then go out again next day. He let slip something over the drink one night. That was the tip we were followin' up. We struck his trail all right—askin' questions of greasers and Indians. We knew he'd found somethin' good or he wouldn't have been so quiet about it.

"I swear to God, I had no idea of harmin' him. I wanted to find what Ben Cameron had found, stake out near him and get what I could. Maybe Hawk Kennedy had a different idea even then. I don't know. He never said what he was thinkin' about.

"We found Ben Cameron. Perched up in a hill of rocks, he was, livin' in the hole he'd dug where he'd staked his claim. But we knew he hadn't taken out any papers. He never thought anybody'd find him out there in that Hell-hole. It was Hell all right. Even now whenever I think of what Hell must be I think of what that gulch looked like. Just rocks and alkali dust and heat.

"It all comes back to me. Every little thing that was said and done—every word. Ben Cameron saw us first—and when we came up, he was sittin' on a rock, his rifle acrost his knees, a hairy man, thin, burnt-out, black as a greaser. Hawk Kennedy passed the time of day, but Ben Cameron only cursed at him and waved us off. 'Get the Hell out of here,' he says—ugly. But we only laughed at him—for didn't we both see the kind of an egg Ben Cameron was settin' on?

"'Don't be pokin' jokes at the Gila Desert, my little man,' say Hawk, polite as you please. 'It's Hell that's here and here it will remain.' And then we said we were short of water—which we were not—and had he any to spare? But he waved us on with his rifle, never sayin' a word. So we moved down the gulch a quarter of a mile and went into camp. There was ore here, too, but nothin' like what Ben Cameron had.

"Hawk was quiet that night—creepin' about among the rocks, but he didn't say what was on his mind. In the mornin' he started off to talk to Ben Cameron an' I went with him. The man was still sittin' on his rock, with the rifle over his knees—been there all night, I reckon. But he let us come to hailin' distance.

"'Nice claim you got there, pardner,' says Hawk.

"'Is it?' says he.

"'Ain't you afraid of rubbin' some o' that verdigris off onto your pants,' says Hawk.

"'They're my pants,' says Cameron. 'You ain't here for any good. Get out!' And he brings his rifle to his hip. We saw he was scared all right, maybe not so much at what we'd do to him as at sharin' what he'd found.

"'The Gila Desert ain't *all* yours, is it, pardner? Or maybe you got a mortgage on the earth!' says Hawk, very polite. 'You ain't got no objection to our stakin' alongside of you, have you? Come along, now. Let's be neighbors. We see what you've got. That's all right. We'll take your leavin's. We've got a right to them.'

"And so after a while of palaverin' with him, he lets us come up and look over his claim. It didn't take any eye at all to see what he'd got. He wasn't much of a man—Ben Cameron—weak-eyed, rum-dum—poor too. You could see that by his outfit—worse off than we were. Hawk told him we had a lot of friends with money—big money in the East. Maybe we could work it to run a railroad out to tap the whole ridge. That kind of got him and we found he had no friends in this part of the country—so we sat down to grub together, Ben Cameron, like me, unsuspectin' of what was to happen.

"My God, Nichols, I can see it all like it had happened yesterday. Hawk Kennedy stood up as though to look around and then before I knew what he was about had struck Ben Cameron in the back with his knife.

"It was all over in a minute. Ben Cameron reached for his gun but before his hand got to it he toppled over sideways and lay quiet.

"I started up to my feet but Hawk had me covered and I knew from what had happened that he'd shoot, too.

"'Don't make a fuss,' he says. 'Give me your gun.' I knew he had me to rights and I did what he said. 'Now,' he says, 'it's yours and mine.'"

McGuire made a motion toward the glass. Peter filled it for him and he drank.

"And then—what happened?" asked Peter quietly.

"Hawk Kennedy had me dead to rights. There was only one thing to do—to make believe I was 'with him.' We buried Ben Cameron, then went down and brought our outfit up, Hawk watchin' me all the while. He'd taken my gun and Ben Cameron's and unloaded them and carried all the ammunition about him. But I didn't know what I was in for. That night he made me sit down while he drew up a paper, torn from an old note book of Ben Cameron's— a partnership agreement, a contract."

McGuire broke off suddenly and got up, moving nervously to the safe, from one of the drawers of which he took a blue linen envelope and brought forth a paper which he handed to Peter.

"That's the hellish thing, Nichols," he said hoarsely. "That's why I'm afraid of Hawk Kennedy. A lie that he forced me to sign! And there's another paper like this in his possession. Read it, Nichols."

Peter took the paper in his fingers and looked at it curiously. It was soiled and worn, broken at the edges, written over in lead pencil, but still perfectly legible.

AGREEMENT BETWEEN HAWK KENNEDY AND MIKE McGUIRE

Us two found Ben Cameron on his copper claim in Madre Gulch. We killed him. Both of us had a hand in it. This mine is Hawk Kennedy's and Mike McGuire's and we are pardners in the same until death us do part, so help us God.

(Signed) MIKE McGUIRE.
HAWK KENNEDY.

"He wanted it on me——" McGuire gasped. "You see? To keep me quiet."

"I understand," said Peter. "This is 'what you've got and what I've got' referred to in the placard."

"Yes," said McGuire. "A partnership agreement and a confession—of something I didn't do."

Peter's eyes were searching him through and through.

"You swear it?"

McGuire held up his right hand and met Peter's gaze without flinching.

"Before God, I do."

Peter was silent for a moment, thinking.

"And then, you left Hawk Kennedy there to die," he said slowly, watching the man.

McGuire sank into his chair with a sigh, the perspiration now beaded on his pale forehead.

"I didn't know what to do, I tell you," he almost whispered. "He had me. I was unarmed. I'd 'a' killed him if I'd had a gun. But I waited a few days after we buried Cameron—makin' believe I was satisfied with everything and he believed me, and at last he fell asleep tired with keepin' watch on me. He was all in. I bored holes in Ben Cameron's barrels, lettin' the water out down the rocks, then took the three horses and the mules with all the water that was left and got away before he woke up.

"It was a terrible thing to do, Nichols—call it murder if you like. But it served him right. It was comin' to him—and I got away with it. At first when I reached water I had a thought of goin' back—to save him before he died— to get that paper I couldn't get that was inside his shirt."

McGuire leaned forward, his face in his hands for a moment, trying to finish.

"But I didn't go back, Nichols. I didn't go back. That's the crime I'm payin' for now—not the other—not the murder of Ben Cameron—I didn't do that—the murder of Hawk Kennedy—who has come back."

"What happened then?"

"I turned Ben Cameron's horse and burros loose where there was water and grass and went on to Bisbee. I told them my buddy had died of a fever. I thought he had by now. They didn't ask any questions. I was safe. The rest was easy. I filed a claim, found some real money and told what I'd found. I waited a month, then went back to Madre Gulch with Bill Munroe, the fellow that helped stake us. There was no one there. We searched the rocks and plains for miles around for signs of Hawk Kennedy's body, for we knew he couldn't have got far in that heat without water. But we found nothin'. Hawk Kennedy had disappeared."

"Then," said Peter, "you built a railroad in and sold out for half a million dollars——?"

McGuire looked up, mystified.

"Or thereabouts," he muttered. "But Hawk Kennedy was alive. I found that out later when he wrote from London. We steered him off the track. But I knew he'd come back some day with that paper I'd signed. That's what's been hangin' over me. An' now it's fallen. I've told you the truth. I had to. You believe me, don't you?" he asked appealingly.

Peter had watched him keenly. There seemed little doubt that what he told was the truth. There was no flaw in the tale.

"Yes," he said after a pause. "I believe you've told me the truth. But you can hardly blame Hawk Kennedy, murderer though he is, for hating you and wanting what he thinks is his."

"No. That's true."

"And you can't blame me for being angry at the trick you played me——"

"I was desperate. I've been desperate since I saw him in New York. Sometimes I've been a bit queer, I reckon—thinkin' about Peggy hearin' this. I wanted to kill him. It was a good chance last night. Nobody would have blamed me, after his being around the place. It was an easy shot—but my hand wasn't steady——"

"Pity you didn't know that before you put me in danger."

"I'm sorry, Nichols—sorry. I'll do anything you like. What do you want me to do?"

Instead of replying at once Peter took out a cigarette and lighted it carefully. And then,

"You've never taken the trouble to make any inquiries as to the whereabouts of the family of Ben Cameron?" he asked.

The old man shook his head.

"Why not?"

"I was afraid to ask."

"I see. Don't you think it's about time you did? It's *his* money that made your fortune."

"He was no good. Nobody knew him. So far as I ever heard, nobody ever asked about him."

"Nevertheless he must have had some friends somewhere."

"Maybe. I don't know. I'm willing to help them if I can, providing this thing can be kept quiet." And then, pleadingly, "You're not going to talk—to use it against me, Nichols?"

Peter's pity for McGuire had come back. The man's terror, his desperation of the past weeks had burned him out, worn him to a shell.

"No, I'm not going to talk. Hawk Kennedy didn't dare tell what you've told me. That's why I believe you."

"And you'll stay on here and help me?"

"Yes——We'll see how we can balk Hawk Kennedy."

"I'll pay him fifty thousand—a hundred thousand—for that agreement——
"

"Not a dollar. I've got a better use for your money than that."

McGuire thought Peter referred to the necessary improvements of the estate. But Peter had another idea in mind.

CHAPTER XIII
THE CHASE

Peter had discovered the means of providing for Beth's musical education. Upon inquiry he had found that McGuire hardly knew Beth except as a dependent relative of Mrs. Bergen, who came in sometimes to help her aunt with the cleaning—usually before McGuire came down from New York. Their little home was not on his visiting list.

He delayed telling McGuire. There was plenty of time and there was no doubt of his employer's doing the right thing by the daughter of the murdered man. Meanwhile, having completed his plans for the estate, he had suggested that McGuire go off for a trip somewhere to rest and recover his poise. Peter had promised his allegiance to McGuire when Hawk Kennedy returned, but he knew that he would have to fight fire with fire. For Hawk had proved himself both skillful and dangerous, and would struggle desperately to get what he thought was his own. It was his last chance to make a big stake—to be independent for the rest of his life. He was tasting luxury now and wouldn't give up without a fight to the death. Something must be thought of—some plan to outwit him, to circumvent the schemes which would come out of his visit of investigation to the copper country.

Peter had said nothing to Beth or to Mrs. Cameron of what he had discovered. He was under no oath of secrecy to the old man, but he realized that while Hawk Kennedy held the "confession" McGuire was in a predicament which would only be made more difficult if the facts got abroad. And so Peter had gone about his work silently, aware that the burden of McGuire's troubles had been suddenly shifted to his own shoulders. He spent most of his days at the lumber camp and now had every detail of the business at his fingers' ends. Timbers had been hauled to the appointed sites and under his direction the fire towers were now half way to completion.

He had found Shad Wells down at the mills, morose, sullen and disposed to question his authority, but McGuire had visited the bunk-house one night before he went away, and it was soon discovered that Peter and no other was the boss of the job. Peter for reasons of his own retained Shad, much to that gentleman's surprise, as foreman of the lumbering gang, but Peter wasn't at all satisfied with conditions as he had found them at the lumber camp and mills and, as he discovered later, the continuance of Shad in the foreman's job was a mistake. If Peter had hoped by this act of conciliation to heal Shad's wounds and bring about a spirit of useful coöperation with the man, he soon found that the very reverse of this had been accomplished. The lumbermen were an unregenerate lot, some of them "pineys," a few Italians, but most of them the refuse of the factories and shipyards, spoiled by the fatal "cost plus" contracts of war time. All of these facts Peter learned slowly, aware of an undercurrent moving against him and yet entirely dependent upon this labor—which was the best, indeed the only labor, to be had. He made some improvements in the bunk-house for their comfort, increased the supply of food and posted notices that all complaints of whatever nature would be promptly investigated. But day after day new stories came to him of shirking, of dissatisfaction and continued trouble-making.

This labor trouble was no new thing at Black Rock, and had existed practically since the beginning of the work on the lumber contract six months before Peter had been employed. But it was not long before Peter discovered through Jesse Brown, whose confidence he had gained, that there were agitators in the camp, undoubtedly receiving their inspiration and pay from sources inimical to all capital in the abstract and to all order and decency at Black Rock in the concrete, who were fomenting the unrest and dissatisfaction among the men. In order to investigate the difficulties personally Peter went down to the camp and lived there for a time, bunking with the men and listening to their stories, winning some of them to his side and tracing as far as he could the troubles to their sources, two men named Flynn and Jacobi. He discharged these two men and sent them out of the camp over Wells's protest. But even then he had a sense of failure. The trouble was deeper than was manifest upon the surface. No mere raise in wages would clear it away. It was born of the world's sickness, with which the men from the cities had been inoculated.

One night while he sat in the bunk-house smoking a pipe and talking with Jesse Brown, Shad Wells suddenly appeared in the doorway, framed against the darkness. Shad's gaze and Peter's met—then Peter's glance turned to Shad's companion. As this man saw Peter he turned his head and went down the length of the bunk-house. Peter got up at once, followed him and faced him. The man now wore a dark beard, but there was no mistake. It was the fellow of the black mustache—the stranger whom Peter had seen in the Pennsylvania Station in New York, the same man he had caught prowling some weeks ago around his cabin in the darkness.

Peter stared at him for a moment but the man would not meet his gaze.

"Who are you?" asked Peter at last. And then, as he made no reply, "What were you doing prowling around my cabin up by the creek?"

The stranger shook his head from side to side.

"No understan'," he muttered.

At this point, Shad Wells, who had followed with Jesse Brown, came in between them.

"That's right, Nichols," he growled. "No understan'—He's a 'guinea.'" To Wells all men were "guineas" who didn't speak his own language.

"Italian? Are you? French? Spanish? Slovak?"

Each time the man shook his head. And then, with an inspiration, Peter shot at him a quick phrase in Russian. But the man gave no sign of comprehension.

"Who put this man on?" asked Peter, turning to Wells.

"I did," said the native sullenly.

"Why?" said Peter, growing warmer. "Didn't I tell you that in future I would hire all the men myself?"

"We're short-handed, since you fired two of the best axmen we got——"

"You disobeyed orders——"

"*Orders*—Hell!"

"All right. We'll see who's running this camp, you or me. To-morrow morning Jesse Brown starts as foreman here. Understand?"

Shad's eyes shot fire, then smoldered and went out as he turned with a sneering laugh and walked away.

"As for you," said Peter to the stranger, who stood uncertainly, "you go to the office in the morning and get your envelope." Then repeated the sentence in Russian. "If you don't understand—find somebody who does."

That the stranger had understood Peter's demeanor if not his language was evident, for in the morning he had vanished.

After that clearing of the air things went somewhat better at the camp. Jesse Brown, though not aggressive, was steady and honest and had a certain weight with the Jerseymen. As to the others, there was doubt as to whether anything would have satisfied them. For the present, at least, it was a question of getting on as well as possible with the means at hand. There was a limit to Peter's weekly pay roll and other men were not to be had. Besides, Peter had promised McGuire to keep the sawmills busy. He knew that when he had come to Black Rock the work on the lumber contract had already fallen behind the schedule, and that only by the greatest perseverance could he make up the time already lost.

As he rode back to his cabin on the afternoon after his encounter with Shad Wells and the stranger with the black mustache, he found himself quite satisfied with regard to his summary dismissal of them both. On Beth's account he had hesitated to depose Shad. He knew that before he had come to Black Rock they had been friends as well as distant relatives, and Beth in her frequent meetings with Peter had expressed the hope that Shad would "come around." Peter had given him every chance, even while he had known that the Jerseyman was working against both McGuire's and Peter's interests. Flynn and Jacobi, the men Peter had sent away, were radicals and agitators. Flynn had a police record that did not bear close inspection, and Jacobi was an anarchist out and out. Before Peter had come to Black Rock they had abused Shad's credulity and after the fight at the Cabin, he had been their willing tool in interrupting the completion of the contract. For of course Shad had hoped that if Peter couldn't get the lumber out when promised, McGuire would put the blame on the new superintendent and let him go. That was Shad's idea. If he had ever been decent enough to warrant Beth's friendship, his jealousy had warped his judgment. Peter was no longer sorry for Shad Wells. He had brought all his troubles on himself.

As to the stranger with the black mustache, that was a more serious matter. Every circumstance—the recognition in New York, the skill with which the man had traced him to Black Rock, the craft with which he had watched Peter and his success in finally getting into the camp and gaining Shad's confidence, made a certainty in Peter's mind that the stranger had some object in remaining near Peter and keeping him under observation. And what other object than a political one? The trail he had followed had begun with the look of recognition in the Pennsylvania Station in New York. And where could that look of recognition have sprung from unless he had identified Peter Nichols as the Grand Duke Peter Nicholaevitch? It seemed incredible, but there could be no other explanation. The man had seen him somewhere—perhaps in Russia—perhaps in Paris or London, or perhaps had only identified him by his portraits which had been published frequently in the Continental magazines and newspapers. But that he had really identified him there could not be the slightest doubt and Peter's hope that he would have been able to lose his identity in the continent of America and become merged into a different civilization where he could work out the personal problem of existence in his own time, by his own efforts and in his own way, seemed destined to failure.

If the stranger knew that Peter was in New Jersey there was no doubt that there were others who knew it also, those who employed him—those in whose interests he was working. Who? The same madmen who had done Nicholas to death and had killed one by one the misguided Empress, Olga, Tania, the poor little Czarevitch and the rest.... Did they consider him, Peter Nichols, lumber-jack extraordinary, as a possible future claimant to the throne of Russia? Peter smiled grimly. They were "straining at a gnat while swallowing the camel." And if they feared him, why didn't they strike? The stranger had already had ample opportunity to murder him if he had been so disposed, could still do it during Peter's daily rides back and forth from the Cabin to the camp and to the Upper Reserve.

All of these thoughts percolated slowly, as a result of the sudden inspiration at the bunk-house which had liberated a new train of ideas, beginning with the identification of the Russian characteristics of the new lumberman, which were more clearly defined under the beard and workman's shirt than under the rather modish gray slouch hat and American clothing in which Peter had seen him earlier. And Peter had merely let the man go. He had no proof of the fellow's purposes, and if he had even discovered exactly what those purposes were, there was no recourse for Peter but to ask for the protection of Washington, and this he had no desire to do.

If the man suspected from the quickly spoken Russian sentence that Peter now guessed his mission, he had given no sign of it. But that meant nothing. The fellow was clever. He was doubtless awaiting instructions. And unless Peter took his case to the Department of Justice he could neither expect any protection nor hope for any security other than his own alertness.

At the Cabin Beth was waiting for him. These hours of music and Beth were now as much a part of Peter's day as his breakfast or his dinner. And he had only failed her when the pressure of his responsibilities was too great to permit of his return to the Cabin. The hour most convenient for him was that at the close of the day, and though weary or discouraged, Peter always came to the end of this agreeable hour rested and refreshed, and with a sense of something definitely achieved. For whatever the days brought forth of trouble and disappointment, down at the logging camp or the mills, here was Beth waiting for him, full of enthusiasm and self-confidence, a tangible evidence of success.

The diligence with which she applied his instructions, the ease with which she advanced from one step to another, showed her endowed with an intelligence even beyond his early expectations. She was singing simple ballads now, English and French, and already evinced a sense of interpretation which showed the dormant artist. He tried at first, of course, to eliminate all striving for effect, content to gain the purity of tone for which he was striving, but she soared beyond him sometimes, her soul defying limitations, liberated into an empyrean of song. If anything, she advanced too rapidly, and Peter's greatest task was to restrain her optimism and self-confidence by imposing the drudgery of fundamental principles. And when he found that she was practicing too long, he set her limits of half-hour periods beyond which she must not go. But she was young and strong and only once had he noted the slightest symptom of wear and tear on her vocal chords, when he had closed the piano and prohibited the home work for forty-eight hours.

As to their personal relations, Peter had already noticed a difference in his own conduct toward Beth, and in hers toward him,—a shade of restraint in Beth's conversation when not on the topic of music, which contrasted rather strangely with the candor of their first meetings. Peter couldn't help smiling at his memories, for now Beth seemed to be upon her good behavior, repaying him for her earlier contempt with a kind of awe at his attainments. He caught her sometimes in unguarded moments looking at him curiously, as though in wonder at a mystery which could not be explained. And to tell the truth, Peter wondered a little, too, at his complete absorption in the task he had set himself. He tried to believe that it was only the music that impelled him, only the joy of an accomplished musician in the discovery of a budding artist, but he knew that it was something more than these. For reducing the theorem to different terms, he was obliged to confess that if the girl had been any one but Beth, no matter how promising her voice, he must have been bored to extinction. No. He had to admit that it was Beth that interested him, Beth the primitive, Beth the mettlesome, Beth the demure. For if now demure she was never dull. The peculiarity of their situation—of their own choosing—lent a spice to the relationship which made each of them aware that the other was young and desirable—and that the world was very far away.

However far Beth's thoughts may have carried her in the contemplation of the personal pulchritude of her music master (somewhat enhanced by the extirpation of the Hellion triplet in her own behalf) it was Peter Nicholaevitch who made the task of Peter Nichols difficult. It was the Grand Duke Peter who wanted to take this peasant woman in his arms and teach her what other peasant girls had been taught by Grand Dukes since the beginning of the autocratic system of which he had been a part—but it was Peter Nichols who restrained him. Peter Nicholaevitch feared nothing, knew no restraint, lived only for the hour—for the moment. Peter Nichols was a coward—or a gentleman—he was not quite certain which.

When Peter entered the Cabin on the evening after the appointment of Jesse Brown as foreman at the lumber camp, Beth could not help noticing the clouds of worry that hung over Peter's brows.

"You're tired," she said. "Is anything wrong at the camp?"

But he only shook his head and sat down at the piano. And when she questioned him again he evaded her and went on with the lesson. Music always rested him, and the sound of her voice soothed. It was the "Elégie" of Massenet that he had given her, foolishly perhaps, a difficult thing at so early a stage, because of its purity and simplicity, and he had made her learn the words of the French—like a parrot—written them out phonetically, because the French words were beautiful and the English, as written, abominable. And now she sang it to him softly, as he had taught her, again and again, while he corrected her phrasing, suggesting subtle meanings in his accompaniment which she was not slow to comprehend.

"I didn't know that music could mean so much," she sighed as she sank into a chair with a sense of failure, when the lesson was ended. "I always thought that music just meant happiness. But it means sorrow too."

"Not to those who hear you sing, Beth," said Peter with a smile, as he lighted and smoked a corncob pipe, a new vice he had discovered at the camp. Already the clouds were gone from his forehead.

"No! Do you really think that, Mr. Nichols?" she asked joyously.

She had never been persuaded to call him by his Christian name, though Peter would have liked it. The "Mr." was the tribute of pupil to master, born also of a subtler instinct of which Peter was aware.

"Yes," he replied generously, "you'll sing that very well in time——"

"When I've suffered?" she asked quickly.

He glanced up from the music in his hand, surprised at her intuition.

"I don't like to tell you so——"

"But I think I understand. Nobody can sing what she doesn't feel—what she hasn't felt. Oh, I know," she broke off suddenly. "I can sing songs of the woods—the water—the pretty things like you've been givin' me. But the deep things—sorrow, pain, regret—like this—I'm not 'up' to them."

Peter sat beside her, puffing contentedly.

"Don't worry," he muttered. "Your voice will ripen."

"And will I ripen too?"

He laughed. "I don't want you ever to be any different from what you are."

She was thoughtful a moment, for Peter had always taken pains to be sparing in personalities which had nothing to do with her voice.

"But I don't want always to be what I am," she protested, "just growin' close to the ground like a pumpkin or a squash."

He laughed. "You might do worse."

"But not much. Oh, I know. You're teachin' me to think—and to feel—so that I can make other people do the same—the way you've done to me. But it don't make me any too happy to think of bein' a—a squash again."

"Perhaps you won't have to be," said Peter quietly.

"And the factory—I've got to make some money next winter. I can't use any of Aunt Tillie's savin's. But when I know what I *might* be doin', it's not any too easy to think of goin' back *there*!"

"Perhaps you won't have to go," said Peter again.

Her eyes glanced at him quickly, looked away, then returned to his face curiously.

"I don't just understand what you mean."

"I mean," said Peter, "that we'll try to find the means to keep you out of the glass factory—to keep on with the music."

"But how——? I can't be dependent on——" She paused with a glance at him. And then quickly, with her characteristic frankness that always probed straight to her point, "You mean that *you* will pay my way?"

"Merely that I'm going to find the money—somehow."

But she shook her head violently. "Oh, no, I couldn't let you do that, Mr. Nichols. I couldn't think of it."

"But you've got to go on, Beth. I've made up my mind to that. You'll go pretty fast. It won't be long before you'll know all that I can teach you. And then I'm going to put you under the best teacher of this method in New York. In a year or so you'll be earning your own way——"

"But I can't let you do this for me. You're doin' too much as it is—too much that I can't pay back."

"We won't talk of money. You've given me a lot of enjoyment. That's my pay."

"But this other—this studyin' in New York. No, I couldn't let you do that. I couldn't—I can't take a cent from you or from any man—woman either, for that matter. I'll find some way—workin' nights. But I'm not goin' back," she added almost fiercely between her teeth, "not to the way I was before. I won't. I can't."

"Good. That's the way great careers are made. I don't intend that you shall. I'm going to make a great singer of you, Beth."

She colored with joy.

"Are you, Mr. Nichols? Are you? Oh, I want to make good—indeed I do—to learn French and Italian——" And then, with a sharp sigh, "O Lord, if wishes were horses——!" She was silent again, regarding him wistfully. "Don't think I'm not grateful. I'm afraid you might. I *am* grateful. But—

sometimes I wonder what you're doin' it all for, Mr. Nichols. And whether——"

As she paused again Peter finished for her.

"Whether it wouldn't have been better if I hadn't let you just remain——er," he grinned, "a peach, let's say? Well, I'll tell you, Beth," he went on, laying his pipe aside, "I came here, without a friend, to a strange job in a strange country. I found you. Or rather *you* found *me*—lost like a babe in the woods. You made fun of me. Nobody had ever done that before in my life, but I rather liked it. I liked your voice too. You were worth helping, you see. And then along came Shad. I couldn't have him ordering you about, you know—not the way he did it—if he hadn't any claim on you. So you see, I had a sense of responsibility for you after that——About you, too——," he added, as though thinking aloud.

His words trailed off into silence while Beth waited for him to explain about his sense of responsibility. She wasn't altogether accustomed to have anybody responsible for her. But as he didn't go on, she spoke.

"You mean that you—that I—that Shad forced me on you?"

"Bless your heart, child—no."

"Then what *did* you mean?" she insisted.

Peter thought he had a definite idea in his mind about what he felt as to their relationship. It was altruistic he knew, gentle he was sure, educational he was positive. But half sleepily he spoke, unaware that what he said might sound differently to one of Beth's independent mind.

"I mean," he said, "that I wanted to look after you—that I wanted our friendship to be what it has proved to be—without the flaw of sentiment. I wouldn't spoil a single hour by any thought of yours or mine that led us away from the music."

And then, while her brain worked rapidly over this calm negation of his, "But you can't be unaware, Beth, that you're very lovely."

Now "sentiment" is a word over which woman has a monopoly. It is her property. She understands its many uses as no mere man can ever hope to do. The man who tosses it carelessly into the midst of a delicate situation is courting trouble. Beth perked up her head like a startled fawn. What did he mean? All that was feminine in her was up in arms, nor did she lay them down in surrender at his last phrase, spoken with such an unflattering air of commonplace.

Suddenly she startled Peter with a rippling laugh which made him sit up blinking at her. "Are you apologizin' for not makin' love to me?" she questioned impertinently. "Say—that's funny." And she went off into another disconcerting peal of laughter.

But it wasn't funny for Peter, who was now made aware that she had turned his mind inside out upon the table between them, so to speak, that she might throw dust in the wheels. And so he only gasped and stared at her—startlingly convinced that in matters of sentiment the cleverest man is no match for even the dullest woman and Beth could hardly be considered in this category. At the challenge of his half expressed thought the demureness and sobriety of the lesson hour had fallen from her like a doffed cloak.

Peter protested blandly.

"You don't understand what——"

But she broke in swiftly. "Maybe you were afraid I might be fallin' in love with *you*," she twitted him, and burst into laughter again.

"I—I had no such expectation," said Peter, stiffening, sure that his dignity was a poor thing.

"Or maybe——," she went on joyfully, "maybe you were afraid *you* might be fallin' in love with *me*." And then as she rose and gathered up her music, tantalizingly, "What *did* you mean, Mr. Nichols?"

He saw that he was losing ground with every word she uttered, but his sense of humor conquered.

"You little pixie!" he cried, dashing for her, with a laugh. "Where have you hidden this streak of impudence all these weeks?" But she eluded him nimbly, running around the table and out of the door before he could catch up with her.

He halted at the doorsill and called to her. She emerged cautiously from behind a bush and made a face at him.

"Beth! Come back!" he entreated. "I've got something to say to you."

"What?" she asked, temporizing.

"I want to talk to you—seriously."

"Good Lord—seriously! You're not goin' to—to take the risk of—of havin' me 'vamp' you, are you?"

"Yes. I'll risk that," he grinned.

But she only broke off a leaf and nibbled at it contemplatively. "Maybe *I* won't risk it. 'I don't want to spoil a single hour,'" she repeated, mocking his dignity, "'by any thought of yours or mine that would lead us away from the music.' Maybe *I'm* in danger." And then, "You know *you're* not so bad lookin' yourself, Mr. Nichols!"

"Stop teasing, Beth."

"I won't."

"I'll make you." He moved a step toward her.

"Maybe I hadn't better come any more," she said quizzically.

"Beth!"

"Suppose I *was* learnin' to love you a little," she went on ironically, "with you scared I might be—and not knowin' how to get out of it. Wouldn't that be terrible! For me, I mean. 'She loved and lost, in seven reels.'"

She was treading on precarious ground, and she must have seen her danger in Peter's face, for as he came toward her she turned and ran down the path, laughing at him. Peter followed in full stride but she ran like a deer and by the time he had reached the creek she was already halfway over the log-jam below the pool. Her laugh still derided him and now, eager to punish her, he leaped after her. But so intent he was on keeping her in sight upon the farther bank that his foot slipped on a tree trunk and he went into the water. A gay peal of laughter echoed in his ears. And he caught a last glimpse of her light frock as it vanished into the underbrush. But he scrambled up the bank after her and darted along the path—lost her in the dusk, and then deep in the woods at one side saw her flitting from tree to tree away from him. But Peter's blood was now warm with the chase—and it was the blood of Peter Nicholaevitch too. Forgotten were the studious hours of patience and toil. Here was a girl who challenged his asceticism—a beautiful young female animal who dared to mock at his self-restraint. She thought that she could get away. But he gained on her. She had stopped laughing at him now.

"Beth! You little devil!" he cried breathlessly, as he caught her. "You little devil, I'll teach you to laugh at me."

"Let me go——"

"No——"

He held her in his arms while she struggled vainly to release herself. Her flushed face was now a little frightened and her large blue eyes stared in dismay at what she saw in his face.

"Let me go?" she whispered. "I didn't mean it——"

But he only held her closer while she struggled, as he kissed her—on the brows, the chin, the cheeks, and as she relaxed in sheer weakness—full on the lips—again—again.

"Do you think I haven't been trying to keep my hands off you all these weeks?" he whispered. "Do you think I haven't wanted you—to teach you what women were meant for? It's for this, Beth—and this. Do you think I haven't seen how lovely you are? Do you think I'm a saint—an anchorite? Well, I'm not. I'll make you love me—love me——"

Something in the reckless tones of his voice—in his very words aroused her to new struggles. "Oh, let me go," she gasped. "I don't love you. I won't. Let me go."

"You shall!"

"No. Let me loose or I—I'll despise you——"

"Beth!"

"I mean it. Let me go."

If a moment ago when she was relaxed in his arms he had thought that he had won her, he had no such notion now, for with a final effort of her strong young arms, she thrust away from him and stood panting and disordered, staring at him as though at one she had never seen before.

"Oh—how I hate you!"

"Beth!"

"I mean it. You—you——," she turned away from him, staring at the torn music on the ground as at a symbol of her disillusionment. Peter saw her look, felt the meaning of it, tried to recall the words he had said to her and failed—but sure that they were a true reflection of what had been in his heart. He had wanted her—then—nothing else had mattered—not duty or his set resolve....

"You mocked at me, Beth," he muttered. "I couldn't stand that——"

"And is *this* the way you punish me? Ah, if you'd only—if you'd only——"

And then with another glance at the torn music, she leaned against the trunk of a tree, sobbing violently.

"Beth——" he whispered, gently, "don't——"

"Go away. Oh, go. Go!"

"I can't. I won't. What did you want me to say to you? That I love you? I do, Beth—I do," he whispered. It was Peter Nichols, not Peter Nicholaevitch, who was whispering now.

"Was this what your teachin' meant?" she flashed at him bitterly. "Was this what you meant when you wanted to pay my way in New York? Oh, how you shame me! Go! Go away from me, please."

"Please don't," he whispered. "You don't understand. I never meant that. I—I love you, Beth. I can't bear to see you cry."

She made a valiant effort to control her heaving shoulders. And then,

"Oh, you—you've spoiled it all. S-spoiled it all, and it was so beautiful."

Had he? Her words sobered him. No, that couldn't be. He cursed his momentary madness, struggling for words to comfort her, but he had known that she had seen the look in his eyes, felt the roughness of his embrace. Love? The love that she had sung to him was not of these. He wanted now to touch her again—gently, to lift up her flushed face, wet like a flower with the fresh dew of her tears, and tell her what love was. But he didn't dare—he couldn't, after what he had said to her. And still she wept over her broken toys—the music—the singing—for they had mattered the most. Very childlike she seemed, very tender and pathetic.

"Beth," he said at last, touching her fingers gently. "Nothing is changed, Beth. It can't be changed, dear. We've got to go on. It means so much to—to us both."

But she paid no attention to the touch of his fingers and turned away, leaving the music at her feet, an act in itself significant.

"Let me go home. Please. Alone. I—I've got to think."

She did not look at him, but Peter obeyed her. There was nothing else to do. There was something in the clear depths of her eyes that had daunted him. And he had meant her harm. Had he? He didn't know. He passed his hand slowly across his eyes and then stood watching her until she had disappeared among the trees. When she had gone he picked up the torn music. It was Massenet's "Elégie."

O doux printemps d'autrefois....Tout est flétrie.

The lines of the torn pieces came together. Spring withered! The joyous songs of birds—silenced! Beth's song? He smiled. No, that couldn't be. He folded the music up and strode off slowly, muttering to himself.

CHAPTER XIV
TWO LETTERS

Peter passed a troublous evening and night—a night of self-revelations. Never that he could remember had he so deeply felt the sting of conscience. He, the Grand Duke Peter Nicholaevitch, in love with this little rustic? Impossible! It was the real Peter, tired of the sham and make-believe of self-restraint and virtue, who had merely kissed a country girl. He was no anchorite, no saint. Why had he tied himself to such a duty from a motive of silly sentimentalism?

He winced at the word. Was it that? Sentimentalism. He had shown her the best side of him—shown it persistently, rather proud of his capacity for self-control, which had ridden even with his temptations. Why should it matter so much to him what this girl thought of him? What had he said to her? Nothing much that he hadn't said to other women. It was the fact that he had said it to Beth that made the difference. The things one might say to other women meant something different to Beth—the things one might do.... He had been a fool and lost his head, handled her roughly, spoken to her wildly, words only intended for gentle moods, softer purposes. Shrewd little Beth, whose wide, blue eyes had seen right down into the depths of his heart. He had been clumsy, if nothing else, and he had always thought that clumsiness was inexcusable. He had a guilty sense that while Beth was still the little lady to her finger tips, born to a natural nobility, he, the Grand Duke Peter, had been the boor, the vulgar proletarian. The look in her eyes had shamed him as the look in his own eyes had shamed her. She had known what his wooing meant, and it hadn't been what she wanted. The mention of love on lips that kissed as his had done was blasphemy.

Yes. He cared what she thought of him—and he vainly cast about for a way in which to justify himself. To make matters worse Beth still believed that this was the payment he exacted for what he had done for her, what he had proposed to do for her, that he measured her favors in terms of value received. What else could she think but that? Every hour of his devotion to her music defamed her.

The situation was intolerable. In the morning he went seeking her at her home. The house was open. No one in Black Rock village locked doors by day or night. Beth was not there. A neighbor said that she had gone early alone into the woods and Peter understood. If she hadn't cared for him she wouldn't have needed to go to the woods to be alone. Of course she didn't appear at the Cabin the next day, and Peter searched for her—fruitlessly. She weighed on his conscience, like a sin unshrived. He had to find her to explain the unexplainable, to tell her what her confidence had meant to him, to recant his blasphemy of her idols in gentleness and repentance.

As he failed to find her, he wrote her a note, asking her forgiveness, and stuck it in the mirror of the old hat-rack in the hall. Many women in Europe and elsewhere, ladies of the great world that Beth had only dreamed about, would have given their ears (since ear puffs were in fashion) to receive such a note from Peter. It was a beautiful note besides—manly, gentle, breathing contrition and self-reproach. Beth merely ignored it. Whatever she thought of it and of Peter she wanted to deliberate a longer while.

And so another music lesson hour passed while Peter sat alone in the Cabin waiting. That night two letters were brought to him. The superscription of one was scrawled in a boyish hand. The other was scented, dainty, of pale lavender, and bore a familiar handwriting and a familiar coronet. In amazement he opened this first. It was from the Princess Galitzin, written in the polyglot of French, English and Russian which she affected.

"CHERE PIERRE," it ran,—in the English, somewhat as follows: "You will no doubt be surprised at hearing from me in far-off America and amazed at the phenomenon of your discovered address at the outlandish place you've chosen for your domicile. It's very simple. In America you have been watched by agents of the so-called government of our wretched country. We know this here in London, because one of *our* agents is also a part of their secret organization. He came upon the report of your doings and knowing that father was interested, detailed the information to us.

"So far as I can learn at the present writing you are in no immediate danger of death, but we do not know here in London how soon the word may be sent forth to 'remove' persons of your importance in the cosmic scheme. It seems that your desire to remain completely in hiding is looked upon with suspicion in Russia as evidence of a possible intention on your part to come to light at the beginnings of a Bourbon movement and proclaim yourself as the leader of a Royalist party. Your uncles and cousins have chosen the line of least resistance in yielding to the inevitable, living in Switzerland, and other spots where their identities are well known.

"I pray, my well remembered and *bel ami*, that the cause of Holy Russia is still and ever present in your heart of hearts and that the thing these devils incarnate fear may one day come to pass. But I pray you to be discreet and watchful, if necessary changing your place of abode to one in which you will enjoy greater security from your enemies. There is at last one heart in London that ever beats fondly in memory of the dear dead days at Galitzin and Zukovo.

"*Helas!* London is dead sea fruit. People are very kind to us. We have everything that the law allows us, but life seems to have lost its charm. I have never quite forgiven you, *mon Pierre*, for your desertion of us at Constantinople, though doubtless your reasons for preserving your incognito were of the best. But it has saddened me to think that you did not deem me worthy of a closer confidence. You are doubtless very much alone and unhappy—also in danger not only from your political enemies, but also from the American natives in the far away woods in which you have been given occupation. I trust, such as it is, that you have taken adequate measures to protect yourself. I know little of America, but I have a longing to go to that splendid country, rugged in its primitive simplicity, in spite of inconveniences of travel and the mass of uncultured beings with whom one must come into contact. Do you think it would be possible for a spoiled creature like me to find a boudoir with a bath—that is, in the provinces, outside of New York?

"It is terrible that you can have no music in your life! I too miss your music, *Pietro mio*, as I miss you. Perhaps one day soon you will see me. I am restless and bored to extinction, with these ramrods of Englishmen who squeeze my rings into my fingers. But if I come I will be discreet toward Peter Nichols. That was a clever invention of yours. It really sounds—quite—American.

"*Garde toi bien, entendez vous? Tout de suite je viendrai. Au revoir.*

"ANASTASIE."

Peter read the letter through twice, amused, astounded and dismayed by turns. His surmise in regard to the stranger with the black mustache had been correct then. The man was a spy of the Russian Soviets. And so instead of having been born immaculate into a new life, as he had hoped—a man without a past, and only a future to be accounted for—he was only the Grand Duke Peter after all. And Anastasie! Why the devil did she want to come nosing about in America, reminding him of all the things that he wanted to forget? The odor of her sachet annoyed him. A bath and boudoir! He realized now that she had always annoyed him with her pretty silly little affectations and her tawdry smatterings of the things that were worth while. He owed her nothing. He had made love to her, of course, because that was what a woman of her type expected from men of his. But there had been no damage done on either side, for he had not believed that she had ever really cared. And now distance, it seemed, had made her heart grow fonder, distance and the romantic circumstances of his exile.

It was kind of her, of course, to let him know of his danger, but only human after all. She could have done no less, having the information. And now she was coming to offer him the charity of her wealth, to tempt him with ease, luxury and London. He would have none of them.

- 167 -

He picked up the other letter with even more curiosity until he read the postmark, and then his interest became intense, for he knew that it was from Jim Coast—Hawk Kennedy. The letter bore the heading, "Antlers Hotel, Colorado Springs."

"DEAR PETE," he read, through the bad spelling, "Here I am back at the 'Springs,' at the 'Antlers,' after a nice trip down Bisbee way, and out along the 'J. and A.' to the mine. It's there all right and they're workin' it yet to beat the cards with half a mountain still to be tapped. I ain't going into particulars—not in a letter, except to tell you that I got what I went for—names, dates and amounts—also met the gents our friend sold out to—nice people. Oh, I'm 'A1' with that outfit, old dear. I'm just writing this to show you I'm on the job and that if you've got an eye to business you'd better consider my proposition. I'll make it worth your while. You can help all right. You did me a good turn that night. I'll give you yours if you'll stand in proper and make McG. do what's right. It ain't what you said it was—it's justice all around. That's all I'm asking—what's right and proper.

"I ain't coming back just yet, not for a month, maybe. I'm living easy and there's a lady here that suits my fancy. So just drop me a line at the above address, letting me know everything's O. K. Remember I'm no piker and I'll fix you up good.

"Your friend,
"JIM."

Peter clenched the paper in his fist and threw it on the floor, frowning angrily at the thought of the man's audacity. But after a while he picked the crumpled note up and straightened it out upon the table, carefully rereading it. Its very touch seemed to soil his fingers, but he studied it for a long while, and then folded it up and put it in his pocket. It was a very careful game that Peter would have to play with Hawk Kennedy, a game that he had no liking for. But if he expected to succeed in protecting McGuire, he would have to outwit Jim Coast—or Hawk Kennedy, as he now thought of him—by playing a game just a little deeper than his own.

Of course he now had the advantage of knowing the whole of McGuire's side of the story, while Kennedy did not believe the old man would have dared to tell. And to hold these cards successfully it would be necessary to continue in Kennedy's mind the belief that Peter did not share McGuire's confidences. It would also be necessary for Peter to cast in his lot, apparently, with Kennedy against McGuire. It was a dirty business at best, but he meant to carry it through if he could, and get the signed agreement from the blackmailer.

Peter seemed to remember an old wallet that Jim Coast had always carried. He had seen it after Coast had taken slips of paper from it and showed them to Peter,—newspaper clippings, notes from inamorata and the like—but of course, never the paper now in question. And if he had carried it all these years, where was it now? In the vault of some bank or trust company probably, and this would make Peter's task difficult, if not impossible.

Peter got up and paced the floor, thinking deeply of all these things in their relation to Beth. And then at last he went out into the night, his footsteps impelled toward the village. After all, the thoughts uppermost in his mind were of Beth herself. Whatever the cost to his pride, he would have to make his peace with her. He knew that now. Why otherwise did his restless feet lead him out into the pasture back of the little post office toward the rear of Mrs. Bergen's house? Yet there he found himself presently, smoking his corncob pipe for comfort, and staring at the solitary light in Tillie Bergen's parlor, which proclaimed its occupant. Mrs. Bergen's house stood at a little distance from its nearest neighbor, and Peter stole slowly through the orchard at the rear toward the open window. It was then that he heard the music for the first time, the "harmonium" wailing softly, while sweet and clear above the accompaniment (worked out painstakingly but lovingly by the girl herself) came Beth's voice singing the "Elégie."

Peter came closer until he was just at the edge of the shadow outside the window. He knew that her back would be turned to him and so he peered around the shutter at her unconscious back. She sang the song through until the end and then after a pause sang it again. Peter had no ear now for the phrasing, for faults in technique, or inaccuracies in enunciation. What he heard was the soul of the singer calling. All that he had taught her in the hours in the Cabin was in her voice—and something more that she had learned elsewhere.... Her voice was richer—deeper, a child's voice no longer, and he knew that she was singing of his mad moment in the woods, which had brought the end of all things that had mattered in her life. It was no girl who sang now, but a woman who had learned the meaning of the song, the plaint of birds once joyous, of woodland flowers once gay—at the memory of a spring that was no more. He had told her that she would sing that song well some day when she learned what it meant. She would never sing it again as she had sung it to-night. All the dross that Peter had worn in the world was stripped from him in that moment, all that was petty and ignoble in his heart driven forth and he stood with bowed head, in shame for what he had been, and in gentleness for this dear creature whose idols he had cast down.

At the end of the second verse, her fingers slipped from the keys and fell to her sides while she bowed her head and sat for a moment immovable. And then her shoulders moved slightly and a tiny smothered sound came from her throat. Suddenly her head bent and she fell forward on her arms upon the muted keys.

Noiselessly he passed over the low windowsill and before she even knew that he was there, fell to his knees beside her.

"Beth," he whispered. "Don't—child—don't!"

She straightened, startled and incredulous at the sight of him, and tried to move away, but he caught one of her hands and with bent head gently laid his lips upon it.

"Don't, Beth—please. I can't bear to see you cry——"

"I—I'm *not* crying," she stammered helplessly, while she winked back her tears, "I—I've just—just got the—the—stomachache."

She tried to laugh—failing dismally in a sob.

"Oh, Beth—don't——" he whispered.

"I—I can't help it—if I—I've got a—a pain," she evaded him.

"But I can," he murmured. "It's in your heart, Beth. I'm sorry for everything. Forgive me."

"There's nothing to forgive."

"Please!"

"There's nothing to forgive," she repeated dully. But she had controlled her voice now and her fingers in his were struggling for release.

"I was a brute, Beth. I'd give everything to have those moments back. I wouldn't hurt you for the world. See—how changed I am——"

She released her fingers and turned slightly away.

"I—I'm changed too, Mr. Nichols," she murmured.

"No. You mustn't be, Beth. And I've got to have you back. You've got to come back to me, Beth."

"Things can't be the same now."

"Yes—just the same——"

"No. Something's gone."

"But if something else has taken its place——"

"Nothing can——"

"Something greater——"

"I don't care for the sample you showed me," she returned quietly.

"I was crazy, Beth. I lost my head. It won't happen again."

"No. I know it won't——"

"You don't understand. It couldn't. I've made a fool of myself. Isn't it enough for me to admit that?"

"I knew it all the time." She was cruel, and from her cruelty he guessed the measure of her pride.

"I've done all I can to atone. I want you to know that I love you. I do, Beth. I love you——"

There was a note in his voice different from that she had heard the other day. His head was bent and he did not hear the little gasp or see the startled look in her eyes, which she controlled before he raised his head. With great deliberateness she answered him.

"Maybe you and I—have a different idea of what love ought to be," she said. But he saw that her reproof was milder.

"I know," he insisted. "You've sung it to me——"

"No—not to you—not love," she said, startled. And then, "You had no right to be listenin'." And then, with a glance at Aunt Tillie's clock, "You have no right to be here now. It's late."

"But I can't go until you understand what I want to do for you. You say that I can't know what love is. It asks nothing and only gives. I swear I wanted to give without thought of a return—until you laughed at me. And then—I wanted to punish you because you wouldn't understand——"

"Yes. You punished me——"

"Forgive me. You shouldn't have laughed at me, Beth. If you knew everything, you'd understand that I'm doing it all without a hope of payment,—just because I've got to."

Her eyes grew larger. "What do you mean?"

"I can't tell you now—but something has happened that will make a great difference to you."

"What?"

"Forgive me. Come to-morrow and perhaps I'll tell you. We've already wasted two days."

"I'm not so sure they've been wasted," said Beth quietly.

"I don't care if you'll only come. Will you, Beth? To-morrow?"

She nodded gravely at last.

"Perhaps," she said. And then, gently, "Good-night, Mr. Nichols."

So Peter kissed her fingers as though she had been his Czarina and went out.

CHAPTER XV
SUPERMAN

Of course Beth Cameron knew nothing of Russia's grand dukes. The only Duke that she had ever met was in the pages of the novel she had read in which the hero was named Algernon. That Duke was of the English variety, proud, crusty, and aged and had only made an unpleasant impression upon her because she had liked Algernon, who had fallen in love with the daughter of the Duke, and the Duke had been very horrid to him in consequence or by reason of that mishap. When she had said to Peter that he reminded her of Algernon she had meant it, and that was really very nice of her, because she thought Algernon all that a self-respecting hero should be. It was true that Peter, though mostly an Englishman, didn't play polo and ride to hounds or swagger around a club and order people about, because he was too poor and was obliged to work for his living.

But he did remind her of Algernon somehow. He had a way with him, as though if there *had* been butlers and valets at Black Rock he *could* have swaggered and ordered them around if he'd had a mind to. He was good looking too. She had noted that even from the very first when she had found him lugging his suitcase down on the road from Pickerel River. Then too he did say things to her, nicer things than any fellow had ever known how to say to her before, and he was much more polite than she had ever believed it possible for any one, to be without seeming queer. But when, eavesdropping at McGuire's, she had heard Peter play the piano, she felt herself conducted into a new world which had nothing at all to do with glass factories and vineyards. Even the sartorial splendor of Miss Peggy McGuire paled into insignificance beside the new visions which the music of Peter Nichols had invoked. He hadn't just lied to her. He *was* a musician. He *could* play. She had never heard anybody bring from a piano sounds like these. And he had said he wanted her to sing for him.

Beth had sung always—just as she had always breathed—but she had never heard any good music except on a talking machine at the boarding house at Glassboro—an old record of Madame Melba's that they played sometimes. But even that song from an opera ("Lay Boheem" they called it), mutilated as it was, had shown her that there was something more wonderful than the popular melodies that the other people liked. Beth's taste for good music, like her taste for nice people, was instinctive. And she had found that in her walk of life the one was about as difficult to find as the other. She had had her awakenings and her disillusionments, with women as well as men, but had emerged from her experiences of two winters in a factory town with her chin high and her heart pure—something of an achievement for one as pretty as Beth.

All in all, she had liked Shad Wells better than any of the men she had met. He was rough, but she had discovered that good manners didn't always mean good hearts or clean minds.

It was this discovery that had made her look askance at Peter Nichols when she had first met him on the road, for he was politer than anybody she had ever met. If her philosophy was to be consistent this new superintendent would need watching. But his music disarmed her and captured her imagination. And then came the incident of the jealous Shad and the extraordinary outcome of Mr. Nichols's championship of her rights. She had witnessed that fight from the shelter of the bushes. It had been dreadful but glorious. Peter's chivalry appealed to her—also his strength. From that moment he was superman.

Then had followed the long wonderful weeks of music at the Cabin, in which she had learned the beginnings of culture and training. Her music-master opened new and beautiful vistas for her, told her of the great musicians and singers that the world had known, described the opera houses of Europe, the brilliant audiences, the splendid ballets, the great orchestras, and promised her that if she worked hard, she might one day become a part of all this. She had learned to believe him now, for she saw that as time went on he was more exacting with her work, more sparing in his praise of her, and she had worked hard—in despair at times, but with a slowly growing confidence in her star of destiny.

And all the while she was wondering why Peter Nichols was doing this for her and what the outcome of it all was to be. He spoke little of the future except to hint vaguely at lessons elsewhere when he had taught her all that he knew. The present it seemed was sufficient for them both. His moods of soberness, of joy, of enthusiasm, were all catching and she followed him blindly, aware of this great new element in her life which was to make the old life difficult, if not impossible. He treated her always with respect, not even touching her arms or waist in passing—an accepted familiarity of men by girls of her social class. Beth understood that it was a consideration due to a delicate situation, the same consideration which had impelled her always to call him Mr. Nichols.

And yet it was this very consideration of Peter's that vexed her. It wasn't an air of superiority, for she couldn't have stood that. It was just discretion, maybe, or something else, she couldn't decide what. But Beth didn't want to be put in a glass case like the wax flowers at home. Her voice was a mere mechanical instrument, as he had taken pains so often to tell her, but he seemed to be making the mistake of thinking *her* a mechanical instrument too. She wasn't. She was very much alive, tingling with vitality, very human under her demure aspect during the singing lessons, and it had bothered her that Peter shouldn't know it. His ignorance, his indifference affronted her. Didn't he see what she looked like? Didn't he see that she might be worth making love to ... just a little, a very little ... once in a while?

The clouds had broken suddenly, almost without warning, when he had talked like a professor—about sentiment—apologized—that was what he had done—*apologized* for not making love to her! Oh!

And then things had happened swiftly—incredible, unbelievable things. The lightning had flashed and it had shown an ugly Mr. Nichols—a different Mr. Nichols from anything that she could have imagined of him. The things he had said to her ... his kisses ... shameful things! A hundred times she had brushed them off like the vision of him from her mind. And still they returned, warm and pulsing to her lips. And still the vision of him returned—remained. He *had* been so nice to her before....

Now Beth sat in the big chair opposite Peter in the Cabin by the log fire (for the evenings were getting cool) while he finished telling her about the death of Ben Cameron, of the murder and of Jonathan K. McGuire's share in the whole terrible affair. It was with some misgivings, even after swearing her to secrecy, that he told her what he had learned through Kennedy and McGuire. And she had listened, wide-eyed. Her father of course was only the shadow of a memory to her, the evil shade in a half-forgotten dream, and therefore it was not grief that she could feel, not even sorrow for one who in life had been so vile, even if his miserable death had been so tragic—only horror and dismay at the thought of the perpetrator of the infamy. And not until Peter had come to the end of the story did she realize what this revelation meant, that the very foundation of McGuire's great fortune was laid upon property which belonged to her.

"Out of all this evil must come some good, Beth," he finished soberly. "That copper mine was yours. McGuire took it and he is going to pay you what he owes."

Beth had already exhausted all the expletives of horror and amazement, and now for a moment this last information staggered her and she stared at him unbelieving.

"Pay me? I can't believe——"

"It was your property by every law of God and man, and I mean that you shall have it." He paused and smiled softly. "You see, Beth, you won't need to depend on me now for your training."

"Oh—then this was what you meant———"

"What I meant when I said that you should owe me nothing—that I———"

"But I *will* owe you—everything. I shall still owe you everything." And then, wonderingly, "And just to think of my livin' here all this time so near the man—and not knowin' about———" Her words trailed off into silent astonishment.

"Yes. And to think of his making his fortune on money that belonged to you! Millions. And he's going to pay you what he got out of the Tarantula mine—every dollar with interest to date."

"But how can you make him do that?" she cried eagerly. "What proof have you got?"

He smiled grimly into the fire as he poked a fallen log into the blaze.

"Blackmail is an ugly word, Beth. But it shouldn't be blackmail, if silence is the price of getting what really belongs to you. McGuire is using your money—and he must give it to you. It's your money—not his. If he won't give it to you of his own free will, he will give it against his will."

"But how can you make him do that?" asked Beth timidly.

"By saving him from Hawk Kennedy. That's my price—and yours."

"But how can you?"

"I don't know. I've got to fight Kennedy with his own weapons—outwit him. And I've thought out a plan———"

"But he's dangerous. You mustn't take any further risks with a man like that for me."

Peter only smiled.

"It will amuse me, Beth. And besides———" He bent forward to tend the fire, his face immediately grave again. "Besides—I think I owe you that, now."

She understood what he meant and thrilled gently. Her joy had come back to her with a rush. All through the music lesson and through the recital of the tale of mystery she had hung breathlessly on his words and watched the changing expression on his features as he talked into the fire. This was *her* Mr. Nichols who was speaking now, her friend and mentor, who wanted her to understand that this was his way of atonement. But she ignored his last remark, to Beth the most important of the entire conversation.

"How—how much will the—the money amount to?" she asked timidly.

Peter laughed.

"Figure it out for yourself. Half a million—six per cent—fifteen years——"

"Half a million dollars——!"

"A million—or more!"

"A million! God-a-mercy!"

Peter recognized one of Aunt Tillie's expressions, Beth's vocabulary being inadequate to the situation.

"But you haven't got it yet," he said.

"And I daren't think of gettin' it. I won't think of it. I'd get my brain so full of things I wanted it would just naturally *bust*. Oh lordy!"

Peter laughed.

"You do want a lot of things, don't you?"

"Of course. A silk waist, a satin skirt, some silk stockings—but most of all, a real sure enough piano," she gasped. And then, as though in reproach of her selfishness, "And I could pay off the mortgage on Aunt Tillie's farm back in the clearing!"

"How much is that?"

"Three thousand dollars. I've already paid off three hundred."

"There ought to be enough for that," said Peter soberly.

"Oh, Mr. Nichols. I hope you don't think I'm an awful fool talkin' this way."

"Not unless you think *I* am."

"But it *is* nice to dream of things sometimes."

"Yes. I do that too. What do you dream of, Beth?"

"Oh, of bein' a great singer, mostly—standin' on a stage with people lookin' up and clappin' their hands at me."

"What else?"

"Oh," she laughed gayly, "I used to dream of marryin' a prince—all girls do. But there ain't any princes now to marry."

"No, that's true," he assented. "The old world hasn't any use for princes now." And then, "But why did you want to marry a prince?" he asked.

"Oh, I don't know. It's just fairy tales. Haven't you ever lived in a fairy tale and loved a princess?"

"Yes, I've lived in a fairy tale, but I've never loved a princess."

"I guess if everybody knew," said Beth with conviction, "the princes in Europe are a pretty bad lot."

"Yes," said Peter slowly, "I guess they are."

She paused a moment, looking into the fire. And then, "Were you ever acquainted with any princes in Europe, Mr. Nichols?"

Peter smiled. "Yes, Beth. I did know one prince rather intimately—rather too intimately."

"Oh. You didn't like him?"

"No, not much. He was an awful rotter. The worst of it was that he had good instincts and when he went wrong, he went wrong in spite of 'em. You see—he was temperamental."

"What's temperamental?"

"Having the devil and God in you both at the same time," muttered Peter after a moment.

"I know," she said. "Satan and God, with God just sittin' back a little to see how far Satan will go."

He smiled at her. "You don't mean that you have temptations too, Beth?"

She ignored his question, her face sober, and went back to her subject.

"I guess your prince wasn't any better or any worse than a lot of other people. Maybe he didn't give God a chance?"

"No. Maybe not," said Peter.

"It seems to me he must have been kind of human, somehow," Beth commented reflectively. "What's become of him now?" she asked, then.

"Oh, he's out of it," replied Peter.

"Dead?"

"Yes. His country has chucked all the nobility out on the dust heap."

"Russia?"

"Yes."

"Did they kill him?"

"They tried to, but couldn't."

"Where is he now?"

"A wanderer on the face of the earth."

"I'm so sorry. It must be terrible to have to eat pork and beans when your stomach's only used to chocolate sundaes."

Peter grinned.

"Some of 'em were glad enough to get off with stomachs to put beans and pork into. Oh, you needn't waste your pity, Beth."

"I don't. I read the papers. I guess they got what they deserved. The workin' people in the world ain't any too keen on buyin' any more diamond tiaras for loafers. I reckon it was about time for a new deal all around without the face cards."

"Perhaps, Beth. But there's always the ten spot to take the deuce."

"I hadn't thought of that," said Beth reflectively. "People aren't really equal— are they? Some apples *are* better than others. I guess," she sighed, "that the real trouble with the world is because there ain't enough friendship in it."

Peter was silent for a moment.

"Yes, that's true," he said, "not enough friendship—not enough love. And it's all on account of money, Beth. There wouldn't have been any European war if some people hadn't wanted property that belonged to somebody else."

"I hope wanting this money won't make me hate anybody or make anybody hate me. I don't want to make Mr. McGuire unhappy or Miss McGuire——"

"You needn't worry," said Peter dryly. "You see, it's your money."

Beth gave a deep sigh.

"I can't help it. I *would* like to have a sport coat and a *cerise* veil like Peggy wears."

"You shall have 'em. What else?"

"Some pretty patent leather shoes with rhinestone buckles——"

"Yes——"

"And a black velvet hat and nice *lingerie*——" (Beth pronounced it lingery).

"Of course. And the piano——"

"Oh, yes. A piano and books—lots of books."

"And a red automobile?"

"Oh, I wouldn't dare wish for that."

"Why not? It's just as easy to wish for an automobile as a piano."

"Yes, I suppose so." She became immediately grave again. "But I can't seem to believe it all. I'm afraid."

"Of what?"

"Of Hawk Kennedy. I feel that he's going to make trouble for us all, Mr. Nichols. I'm afraid. I always seem to feel things before they happen. Any man who could do what he did—murder!"

"There will be some way to get around him."

"But it's dangerous. I don't feel I've got the right to let you do this for me."

"Oh, yes, you have. I'd do it anyhow. It's only justice."

"But suppose he—suppose——"

"What——?"

"He might kill you, too."

Peter laughed. "Not a chance. You see, I wasn't born to die a violent death. If I had been, I'd have been dead months ago."

"Oh—the war, you mean?" she asked soberly.

"Yes—the war. Everything is tame after that. I'm not afraid of Hawk Kennedy."

"But there's danger just the same."

"I hope not. I won't cross that bridge until I come to it."

Beth was silent for a long moment and then with a glance at the clock on the mantel slowly gathered her music, aware of his voice close at her ear.

"And if I do this, Beth,—if I get what belongs to you, will you believe that I have no motive but friendship for you, that I care for you enough to want you to forgive me for what has happened?"

He had caught her fingers in his own but she did not try to release them.

"Oh, don't speak of that—*please*! I want to forget you—that day."

"Can't you forget it more easily by remembering me as I am now, Beth? See. I want you as much now as I did then—just as much, but I cannot have you until you give yourself to me."

What did he mean? She wasn't sure of him. If marriage was what he meant, why didn't he say so? Marriage. It was such an easy word to say. Her fingers struggled in his.

"Please, Mr. Nichols," she gasped.

"You mean that you won't—that you don't care enough——?"

"I—I'm not sure of you——"

"I love you, Beth——"

"You *say* so——"

"I do—better than anything in the world."

"Enough to—enough to...?"

She was weakening fast. She felt her danger in the trembling of her fingers in his. Why didn't he finish her question for her? Marriage. It was such a little word. And yet he evaded it and she saw that he meant to evade it.

"Enough to have you almost in my arms and yet hardly to touch you— enough to have your lips within reach of mine and yet not to take them. Isn't that what you wanted, Beth? Gentleness, tenderness——"

She flung away from him desperately.

"No—no. I want nothing—nothing. Please! You don't want to understand." And then with an effort she found her poise. "Things must be as they are. Nothing else. It's getting late, I must go."

"Beth—Not yet. Just a minute——"

"No."

But she did not go and only stood still, trembling with irresolution. He knew what she wanted him to say. There could be no middle ground for Beth. She must be all to him or nothing. Marriage. It was the Grand Duke Peter Nicholaevitch who had evaded this very moment while Peter Nichols had urged him to it. And it was Peter Nichols who knew that any words spoken of marriage to Beth Cameron would be irrevocable, the Grand Duke Peter (an opportunist) who urged him to utter them, careless of consequences. And there stood Beth adorable in her perplexity, conjuring both of him to speak.

It was Peter Nichols who met the challenge, oblivious of all counsels of pride, culture, vainglory and hypocrisy. This was his mate, a sweeter lady than any he had ever known.

"Beth," he whispered. "I love you. Nothing in the world makes any difference to me but your happiness."

He came to her and caught her in his arms, while she still struggled away from him. "I want you. It doesn't matter who I am or who you are. I want you to——"

Beth suddenly sprung away from him, staring at a figure which stood in the doorway as a strident, highly pitched voice cut in sharply on Peter's confession.

"Oh, excuse *me*! I didn't mean to intrude."

It was Miss Peggy McGuire in her *cerise* veil and her sport suit, with hard eyes somewhat scandalized by what she had seen, for Peter was standing awkwardly, his arms empty of their prize, who had started back in dismay and now stood with difficulty recovering her self-possession. As neither of them spoke Miss McGuire went on cuttingly, as she glanced curiously around the Cabin.

"So this is where you live? I seem to have spoiled your party. And may I ask who——" and her eyes traveled scornfully over Beth's figure, beginning at her shoes and ending at her flushed face—"I think I've seen you before——"

"Miss McGuire," said Peter quietly, "This is Miss Cameron——"

"Oh, yes—the kitchen maid."

"Miss Beth Cameron," insisted Peter frigidly, "who has just done me the honor of promising to marry me."

"Oh! I see——"

Beth stared from one to the other, aware of the meaning of the visitor's manner and of Peter's reply.

"That is not true," she said very quietly, her deep voice vibrant with emotion. "I come here often. Mr. Nichols is teaching me music. I am very proud of his friendship. But I did not promise to marry him."

Peggy McGuire turned on her heel.

"Well, it's almost time you did," she said insultingly.

Peter, now pale and cold with fury, reached the door before her and stood blocking the passageway. "Miss McGuire, I'll trouble you to be more careful in addressing my guests," he said icily.

"Let me pass——"

"In a moment."

"You'd dare——?"

"I would like you to understand that this cabin is mine—while I am in Black Rock. Any guest here comes at my invitation and honors me by accepting my hospitality. But I reserve the privilege of saying who shall come and who shall not. I hope I make myself clear———" And Peter bowed low and then moved aside, indicating the door. "Good-night," he finished.

Miss Peggy McGuire glared at him, red as a young turkey cock, her finishing school training just saving her from a tirade. "Oh, you! We'll see about this———" and dashed past him out of the door and disappeared into the darkness.

Peter followed her with his angry gaze, struggling for his self-control, and at last turned into the room toward Beth, who now stood a smiling image turned into stone.

"Why did you deny what I said, Beth?" he pleaded.

"It wasn't the truth. I never promised to marry you. You never asked me to."

"I *would* have asked you. I ask you now. I *was* asking you when that little fool came in———"

"Maybe you were. Maybe you weren't. Maybe I'm a little hard of hearin'. But I'm not goin' to make *that* an excuse for my bein' here———"

"I don't understand———"

"It's just that I came here because I wanted to come and because you wanted me. People have been talkin'. Let them talk. Let *her* talk———"

"She will. You can be pretty sure of that."

Peter was pacing up and down the room, his hands behind him. "If she'd been a man———" he was muttering. "If she'd only been a man."

Beth watched him a moment, still smiling.

"Oh, I got what she meant—she was just tryin' to insult me."

She laughed. "Seems as if she'd kind of succeeded. I suppose I ought to have scratched her face for her. I think I would have—if she'd just stayed a minute longer. Funny too, because I always used to think she was so sweet."

Peter threw his arms wildly into the air and exploded.

"Sweet! Sweet! *That* girl! Yes, if vinegar is. She'll tear your reputation to shreds."

Beth had stopped smiling now and leaned against the wall, her chin lowered.

"I reckon it serves me right. I hadn't any business to be comin' here—not at night, anyway."

"Oh, Beth," he pleaded, catching her hands. "Why couldn't you have let things be?"

She struggled a little. And then, "Let *her* think I was *engaged* to you when I wasn't?" she gasped.

"But we are, Beth, dear. Say we are, won't you?"

"Not when we're not."

"Beth——!"

"You should have spoken sooner, if you'd really meant it. Oh, I know what it is. I've always known there's a difference between us."

"No—not unless you make it."

"Yes. It was there before I was born. You were brought up in a different kind of life in a different way of thinkin' from mine——"

"What has that got to do with it?"

"Everything. It's not my fault. And maybe I'm a little too proud. But I'm straight——"

"Don't, Beth——" He put his arm around her but she disengaged herself gently.

"No, let me finish. Maybe you wanted me. I guess you did. But not that much—not enough to speak out—and you were too straight to lie to me. I'm thankful for that——"

"But I *have* spoken, Beth," he insisted, taking her by the elbows and holding her so that he could look into her eyes. "I've asked you to—to be my wife. I ask you now. Is that clear?"

Her eyes evaded him and she laughed uneasily.

"Yes, it's clear—and—and your reason for it——"

"I love you——"

"A little, maybe. But I'll marry no man just to save my face—and his."

But he caught her close to him, finding a new joy in his momentous decision. She struggled still, but he would not be denied.

"Yes, you will," he whispered. "You've got to marry me whether you want to or not. You're compromised."

"I don't care."

"Oh, yes, you do. And you love me, Beth."

"I don't love you——"

"You do. And I'm going to marry you whether you want it or not."

"Oh, *are* you?"

"Yes."

"When?"

"Soon."

He kissed her. She didn't resist him. Resistance was useless. He had won.

"Beth, dear," he went on. "I couldn't lie to you. I'm glad you knew that. And I couldn't hurt you. I think I've always loved you—from the first."

"I too—I too," she whispered. "I couldn't help it."

"I think I knew that too——"

"No, no. You couldn't——"

"Yes. It was meant to be. You've given a new meaning to life, torn from its very roots a whole rotten philosophy. Oh, you don't know what I mean—except that nobility is in the mind, beauty in the heart. Nothing else matters."

"No. It doesn't," she sighed. "You see, I—I do believe in you."

"Thank God! But you know nothing of me—nothing of my past——"

"I don't care what your past has been or who you are. You're good enough for me. I'm satisfied——"

He laughed joyously at the terms of her acquiescence.

"Don't you want to know what I've been—who I am——?"

"No. It wouldn't make any difference—not now."

"I'll tell you some day."

"I'll take a chance on that. I'm not afraid."

"And whatever I am—you'll marry me?"

"Yes. Whatever—you—are——"

While he smiled down at her she straightened in his arms and gently released herself, glancing guiltily at the clock.

"I—I must be going now," she whispered.

And so through the quiet forest they went to Black Rock village, hand in hand.

CHAPTER XVI
IDENTIFICATION

The sudden and unexpected arrival of Miss Peggy McGuire upon the scene had been annoying. That young person was, as Peter knew, a soulless little snob and materialist with a mind which would not be slow to put the worst possible construction upon the situation. Of course as matters stood at the close of that extraordinary evening of self-revelations, it did not matter a great deal what Peggy McGuire thought or said or did, for nothing could hurt Beth now. The Grand Duke Peter Nicholaevitch had capitulated and Peter Nichols gloried in his victory over inherited tradition. He had no regrets and he had made his choice, for Beth was what he wanted. She completed him. She was effulgent,—even in homespun. A little tinsel more or less could make no difference in Beth. Those of his own class who would not accept her might go hang for all he cared.

Still Peter had rather that almost any one but Peggy should have come upon the scene, and Beth's frankness had given her a handle for a scandal, if she chose to make one. Beth cared nothing, he knew, for her soul was greater than his, but Peter's anger still smoldered at the words that had been used to Beth.

He did not fear complications with McGuire, nor did he court them, but he knew how this daughter had been brought up, spoiled and pampered to the very limits of McGuire's indulgence and fortune, and he couldn't help holding her up in comparison with Beth, much to Peggy's detriment. For Beth was a lady to her finger tips, born to a natural gentility that put to confusion the mannerisms of the "smart" finishing school which had not succeeded in concealing the strain of a plebeian origin, and Beth's dropped g's and her quaint inversions and locutions were infinitely more pleasing to Peter than Miss Peggy's slang and self-assurance, which reflected the modernity of the fashionable hotel tea-room.

Fortunately, Jonathan K. McGuire, who had returned from the seashore the night before, was not disposed to take his daughter's animadversions too seriously and when Peter announced his engagement to the niece of his housekeeper he made no comment further than to offer his congratulations. He did not even know her name and when McGuire was told that it was Beth Cameron, Peter did not miss his slight start of inquiry. But of course, having only owned his acres of woodland for half a dozen years, he knew little as to the origins of the inhabitants of Black Rock and as Peter said nothing at that moment he asked no questions and only listened to the forester's account of the progress of the work and of the difficulties experienced in attempting to complete the timber-contract. There was no way of improving the labor situation and a visit to the camp proved to him that Peter had done all that could be expected with the poor material at hand. On the way back they stopped at the Cabin and Peter showed him the letter from Hawk Kennedy. And there for a while they sat discussing plans to outwit the enemy and draw his sting.

It was going to be no easy task and could only be accomplished by Peter's apparent compliance with Kennedy's wishes in throwing in his lot with Hawk and simulating an enmity for his employer. McGuire nodded his head and listened soberly. The rest at the seashore had done him good and he was disposed to meet the situation with courage, reflecting Peter's own attitude of confidence and optimism, admitting that his confession to Peter had lifted a weight from his shoulders and given him the spirit to meet the issue, whatever it might be.

"You see," he said at last, "if the worst comes I'm in a pretty bad hole. But it was the shock of meeting Hawk after all these years that took the courage out of me at first. I wasn't quite right in my head for a while. I'd have killed him gladly and gotten away with it perhaps—but I'm glad now that things turned out the way they did. I've got no blood on my hands—that's one thing—whatever I signed. I've been thinking a good deal since I've been away. If I signed that fake confession Hawk Kennedy signed it too. He won't dare to produce it except as a last resort in desperation, to drag me down with him if he fails. We can string him along for a while before he does that and if he falls for your game we may be able to get the paper away from him. You've thought of something, Nichols?" he asked.

"Yes, of several things," said Peter slowly. "I'm going to try diplomacy first. If that doesn't work, then something else more drastic."

McGuire rose at last and took up his hat.

"I don't know how to thank you for what you've done, Nichols," he said awkwardly. "Of course if—if money will repay you for this sort of service, you can count on my doing what you think is right."

Peter rose and walked to the window, looking out.

"I was coming to that, Mr. McGuire," he said gravely.

McGuire paused and laid his hat down again.

"Before you went away," Peter went on, turning slowly toward his employer, "you told me that you had never made any effort to discover the whereabouts of any of the relatives of Ben Cameron. But I inferred from what you said that if you *did* find them, you'd be willing to do your duty. That's true, isn't it?"

McGuire examined him soberly but agreed.

"Yes, that's true. But why do you bring this question up now?"

"I'll explain in a moment. Mr. McGuire, you are said to be a very rich man, how rich I don't know, but I think you'll be willing to admit to me, knowing what I do of your history, that without the 'Tarantula' mine and the large sum it brought you you would never have succeeded in getting to your present position in the world of finance."

"I'll admit that. But I don't see——"

"You will in a minute, sir——"

"Go on."

"If I have been correctly informed, you sold out your copper holdings in Madre Gulch for something like half a million dollars——" Peter paused for McGuire's comment. He made none. But he had sunk into his chair again and was listening intently.

"The interest on half a million dollars, even at six per cent, if compounded, would in fifteen years amount with the principal to a considerable sum."

"Ah, I see what you're getting at——"

"You will admit that what I say is true?"

"Yes——"

"You'll admit also, if you're reasonable, that the money which founded your great fortune was as a matter of fact not yours but Ben Cameron's——?"

"But why speak of him now?" muttered the old man.

"Do you admit this?"

McGuire frowned and then growled, "How can I help admitting it, since you know the facts? But I don't see——"

"Well then, admitting that the 'Tarantula' mine was Ben Cameron's and not yours or Hawk Kennedy's, it seems clear that if any of Ben Cameron's heirs should turn up unexpectedly, they might claim at least a share of what should have been their own."

McGuire had started forward in his chair, his gaze on Peter's face, as the truth was suddenly borne in upon him.

"You mean, Nichols, that——." He paused and gasped as Peter nodded.

"I mean that Ben Cameron's only child, a daughter, lives here at Black Rock—the niece of your housekeeper—Mrs. Bergen——"

"Miss Cameron—My God!" McGuire fell back in his chair, staring at Peter, incapable of further speech.

"Beth Cameron," said Peter gently, "the lady who has done me the honor of promising to become my wife——"

"But how do you know?" gasped McGuire. "There must be some mistake. Are you sure you——" He broke off and then a sly smile curled at the corners of his lips. "You know, Nichols, Cameron is not an unusual name. It's quite possible that you're—er—mistaken."

"No. I'm quite sure there's no mistake. I think the facts can be proved—that is, of course, if you're willing to help to establish this claim and to admit it when established. Otherwise I intend to establish it without your assistance—as an act of justice and of—er—retribution."

McGuire watched his superintendent's face for a while before replying. And then, briefly, "What are the facts on which you base this extraordinary statement?" he asked.

"I'll present those facts when the time comes, Mr. McGuire," said Peter at a venture. "I don't think it will be a difficult matter to identify the murdered man. He wrote home once or twice. He can be traced successfully. But what I would like to know first is what your disposition toward his daughter will be when the proper proofs are presented."

"*If* they're presented," said McGuire.

"Will you answer me?"

"It would seem time enough to answer then. I'll do the right thing."

"Meaning what?"

"Money enough to satisfy her."

"That won't do. She must have what is hers by right. Her price is one million dollars," said Peter quietly.

McGuire started up. "You're dreaming," he gasped.

"It's her money."

"But I developed that mine."

"It was her mine that you developed."

McGuire stopped by the window and turned.

"And if I refuse——?"

"I don't think you will——"

The two men stared at each other, but Peter had the whip hand—or McGuire thought he had, which was quite sufficient.

"Will you help me to perform this act of justice?" Peter went on calmly. "It's the only thing to do, Mr. McGuire. Can't you see that?"

McGuire paced the floor heavily a few times before replying. And then,

"I've got to think this thing over, Nichols. It's all so very sudden—a million dollars. My God! man, you talk of a million as if it grew on the trees." He stopped abruptly before the fireplace and turned to Peter. "And where does Hawk Kennedy come in on this?"

"Beth Cameron's claim comes before his—or yours," said Peter quietly. "Whatever happens to either of you—it's not her fault."

Peter hadn't intended a threat. He was simply stating the principal thought of his mind. But it broke McGuire's front. He leaned upon the armchair and then fell heavily into it, his head buried in his hands.

"I'll do—whatever you say," he groaned at last, "but you've got to get me out of this, Nichols. I've got to have that paper."

Peter poured out a drink of the whisky and silently handed it to his employer.

"Come, Mr. McGuire," he said cheerfully, "we'll do what we can. There'll be a way to outwit Hawk Kennedy."

"I hope to God there is," muttered McGuire helplessly.

"I'll make a bargain with you."

"What?" asked McGuire helplessly.

"If I get the confession from Kennedy, you give Beth Cameron the money I ask for."

"No publicity?"

"None. I give you my word on it."

"Well," muttered the old man, "I guess it's coming to her. I'll see." He paused helplessly. "A million dollars! That's a big sum to get together. A big price—but not too big to clear this load off my conscience."

"Good. I'm glad you see it in this way."

The old man turned shrewdly. "But I've got to have the proofs——"

"Very well. If you're honest in your intentions you'll help me confirm the evidence."

"Yes," said the other slowly. "I'll do what I can."

"Then perhaps you wouldn't mind telling me what Ben Cameron looked like——"

"I've told you as near as I can remember," muttered McGuire.

"Had the murdered man, for instance, lost the little finger of his left hand?" asked Peter, coolly concealing the anxiety which lay behind his question.

But he had his reward, for McGuire shot a quick glance at him, his heavy jowl sagging. And as he didn't reply, Peter urged him triumphantly.

"You promised to help. Will you answer me truthfully? It will save asking a lot of questions."

At last McGuire threw up his hands.

"Yes," he muttered, "that was Ben Cameron. One of his little fingers was missing all right enough."

"Thanks," said Peter, with an air of closing the interview. "If you want this proof that the murdered man was Beth's father, ask Mrs. Bergen."

There was a silence. Peter had won. McGuire gathered up his hat with the mien of a broken man and moved toward the door.

"All right, Nichols. I guess there's no doubt of it. I'll admit the proof's strong enough. It can be further verified, I suppose, but I'd rather no questions were asked. You do your part and I—I'll do mine."

"Very good, sir. You can count on me. If that fake agreement is still in existence, I'll get it for you. If it has been destroyed——"

"I'll have to have proof of that——"

"Won't you leave that in my hands?"

McGuire nodded, shook Peter's hand and wandered out up the path in the direction of Black Rock House.

From the first, Peter had had no doubt that the murdered man was Beth's father, but he had to admit under McGuire's questioning that there might still be a difficulty in tracing the vagrant from the meager history of his peregrinations that Mrs. Bergen had been able to provide. McGuire's attitude in regard to the absent little finger had been really admirable. Peter was thankful for that little finger, and for McGuire's honesty. There was no doubt in his mind now—if any had existed—who Ben Cameron's murderer was. The affair was simplified amazingly. With Beth's claim recognized, Peter could now enter heart and soul into the interesting business of beating Hawk Kennedy at his own game. He would win—he must win, for the pitiful millionaire and for Beth.

And so, jubilantly, he made his way to Black Rock village to fill a very agreeable engagement that he had, to take supper (cooked and served by her own hands) with Miss Beth Cameron. He found that Beth had tried to prevail upon Aunt Tillie to be present but that the arrival of the McGuire family at Black Rock House had definitely prevented the appearance of their chaperon. Peter's appetite, however, suffered little diminution upon that account and he learned that singing was not Beth's only accomplishment. The rolls, as light as feathers and steaming hot, were eloquent of her skill, the chicken was broiled to a turn, the creamed potatoes delicious, and the apple pie of puff-paste provoked memories of the Paris Ritz. Aunt Tillie's best tablecloth and family silver—old, by the looks of it—had been brought into requisition and a bunch of goldenrod and purple asters graced the centerpiece. And above it all presided Beth, her face aflame from the cookstove, gracious and more than lovable in her pride and self-consciousness.

When the supper was finished, Peter helped her to clear away the things and insisted on being allowed to help wash the dishes. But to this Beth demurred for they were of Aunt Tillie's blue colonial china set and not to be trusted to impious hands. But she let Peter sit in the kitchen and watch her (which was quite satisfactory) and even spared him a kiss or two at propitious intervals.

Then when all things had been set to rights they went into the little parlor and sat on the worn Victorian plush-covered sofa. There was much to talk about, matters of grave importance that concerned themselves alone, explanations to be made, hopes to be expressed, and Beth's affair with McGuire to be discussed in all its phases. Peter told her nothing of his rank or station in life, saving that revelation for a later moment. Was not the present all-sufficient? And hadn't Beth told him and didn't she tell him again now that she believed in him and that "no matter what" she loved him and was his, for ever after, Amen. She didn't care who he was, you see.

And when the important business of affirming those vows was concluded again and again, the scarcely less important business of Beth's future was talked over with a calmness which did much credit to Beth's control of the situation. Peter brought out Hawk Kennedy's letter and they read it together, and talked about it, Peter explaining his intention to acquiesce in Hawk's plan. Then Peter told of his conversation with McGuire and of the proof of Ben Cameron's identity which the old man had honestly admitted.

"It looks very much, Beth," said Peter at last, with a smile, "as though you were going to be a very wealthy young woman."

"Oh, Peter," she sighed (the elimination of formal appellations had been accomplished during the earlier stages of the repast), "Oh, Peter, I hope it isn't going to bring us unhappiness."

"Unhappiness! Why, Beth!"

"Oh, I don't know. It seems to me that people with a lot of money always look unhappy wantin' *to want* somethin'."

He laughed.

"The secret of successful wanting is only to want the things you can get."

"That's just the trouble. With a million dollars I'll get so much more than I want. And what then——?"

"You'll have to start all over again."

"No," she said quietly. "I won't. If wantin' things she can't buy makes a girl *hard*, like Peggy McGuire, I think I'd rather be poor."

Peter grew grave again.

"Nothing could ever make you like Peggy McGuire," he said.

"I might be—if I ever get into the habit of thinkin' I was somethin' that I wasn't."

"You'll never be a snob, Beth, no matter how much money you have."

"I hope not," she said with a laugh. "My nose turns up enough already." And then, wistfully, "But I always *did* want a *cerise* veil."

"I've no doubt you'll get it, a *cerise* veil—mauve, green and blue ones too. I'll be having to keep an eye on you when you go to the city."

She eyed him gravely and then, "I don't like to hear you talk like that."

But he kept to his topic for the mere delight of hearing her replies.

"But then you might see somebody you liked better than me."

She smiled at him gently. "If I'd 'a' thought that I wouldn't 'a' picked you out in the first place."

"Then you did pick me out. When?"

"H-m. Wouldn't you like to know!"

"Yes. At the Cabin?"

"No——"

"At McGuire's——?"

"No-o. Before that——"

"When——"

She blushed very prettily and laughed.

"Down Pickerel River road."

"Did you, Beth?"

"Yes. I liked your looks. You *do* smile like you meant it, Peter. I said to myself that anybody that could bow from the middle like you was good enough for me."

"Now you're making fun of me."

"Oh, no. I'm not. You see, dear, you've really lived up to that bow!"

"I hope," said Peter gently, "I hope I always will."

"I'm not worryin'. And I'm glad I knew you loved me before you knew about the money."

"You did know, then——"

"Yes. What bothered me was your findin' it so hard to tell me so."

Peter was more awkward and self-conscious at that moment than he could ever remember having been in his life. Her frankness shamed him—made it seem difficult for him ever to tell her the real reasons for his hesitation. What chance would the exercise of inherited tradition have in the judgment of this girl who dealt instinctively and intimately with the qualities of the mind and heart, and only with them?

"I—I was not good enough for you," he muttered.

She put her fingers over his lips. And when he kissed them—took them away and gave him her lips.

"I'll hear no more of *that*, Peter Nichols," she whispered. "You're good enough for me——"

Altogether, it may be said that the evening was a success at every angle from which Peter chose to view it. And he made his way back to the Cabin through the deep forest along the path that Beth had worn, the path to his heart past all the fictitious barriers that custom had built about him. The meddlesome world was not. Here was the *novaya jezn* that his people had craved and shouted for. He had found it. New life—happiness—with a mate ... his woman—soon to be his wife—whether Beth Nichols or the Grand Duchess Elizabeth...? There was no title of nobility that could make Beth's heart more noble, no pride of lineage that could give her a higher place than that which she already held in his heart.

His blood surging, he ran along the log at the crossing and up the path to the Cabin, where a surprise awaited him. For he found the lamp lighted, and, seated complacently in Peter's easy chair, stockinged feet toward the blaze of a fresh log, a bottle at his elbow, was Hawk Kennedy.

CHAPTER XVII
PETER BECOMES A CONSPIRATOR

Peter entered and stood by the door, startled from his rhapsody by the appearance of the intruder, who had made himself quite at home, regardless of the fact that the final words of their last meeting had given no promise of a friendship which would make his air of easy familiarity acceptable to Peter, whose first impulse moved him to anger, fortunately controlled as he quickly remembered how much hung upon the assumption of an amicable relationship with McGuire's arch enemy. Peter hadn't replied to Hawk's letter which had indicated that some weeks might elapse before Black Rock received another of his visitations. The speculations in Peter's mind as to the change in his visitor's plans and the possible causes for them may have been marked in his face, for Hawk grinned at him amiably and rose and offered his hand with an air of assurance.

"Wondering why I dropped in on you so unexpected-like? Let's say that I got tired of staring at the lonely grandeur of Pike's Peak, *mon gars*, or that the lady who gave me the pleasure of her society skipped for Denver with a younger man, or that the high altitude played Billy-be-damned with my nerves, and you'll have excuse enough. But the fact is, Pete, I *was* a bit nervous at being so long away from the center of financial operations, and thought I'd better come right on and talk to you."

"I got your letter," said Peter calmly, "I hadn't answered it yet——"

"I thought it better to come for my answer."

"I've been thinking it over——"

"Good. It will be worth thinkin' over. You'll bless the day Jim Coast ran athwart your course."

"You seem to be taking a good deal for granted."

"I do. I always do. Until the present opportunity it was about the only thing I got a chance to take. You wouldn't of done me a good turn that night, if you hadn't been O.K. Will you have a drink of your own? It's good stuff— ten years in the wood, I see by the label, and I'm glad to get it, for whisky is scarcer than hen's teeth between this and the Rockies."

As Peter nodded he poured out the drinks and settled down in Peter's chair with the air of one very much at home.

"Well, Pete, what's yer answer to be?" he said at last. "You weren't any too polite when I left here. But I didn't think you'd turn me down altogether.

And you're straight. I know that. I've been countin' on your sense of justice. How would *you* like to be treated the way *I* was treated by Mike McGuire?"

"I wouldn't like it."

"You just bet you wouldn't. You wouldn't stand for it, *you* wouldn't. I've got justice on my side and I've got the law—if I choose to use it—but I'd rather win this case as man to man—without its getting into the newspapers. That wouldn't matter much to a poor man like me, but it would make a heap of difference to a man who stands where McGuire does."

"That's true."

"Yes. And he knows it. He hasn't got a leg to stand on." Kennedy paused and looked Peter over coolly. Peter had been studying the situation critically, playing his game with some care, willing to placate his visitor and yet taking pains not to be too eager to gain his confidence. So he carefully lighted his cigarette while he debated his course of action.

"What makes you think that I'm in a different mood now from when you left here?"

"Haven't I told you? Because I believe that you know that right's right and wrong's wrong."

"But I told you that I didn't want to have anything to do with the case."

"True for you. But you will when I've finished talking to you."

"Will I?"

"You will if you're not a fool, which you ain't. I always said you had somethin' between your ears besides ivory. You don't like to stay poor any more than anybody else. You don't have to. A good half of McGuire's money is mine. If it hadn't been for me helpin' to smell that copper out he'd of been out there grub-stakin' yet an' that's a fact. But I'm not goin' to be too hard on him. I'm no hog. I'm goin' to let him down easy. What's a million more or less to him? It might pinch him a little here and there sellin' out securities he had a fancy for, but in a year or so he'd have it all back and more, the way he works. Oh, I know. I've found out a bit since I've been away. And he'll come across all right, when he hears what I've got to say to him."

"Why don't you go to him direct?" asked Peter.

"And have him barricadin' the house and shootin' promiscuous at me from the windows? Not on your life. I know what I'm about. This thing has got to be done quiet. There's no use stirring up a dirty scandal to hurt his reputation for honest dealin' in New York. Even as it is, the story has got around about the mystery of Black Rock. No use makin' talk. That's why I want you. You stand ace high with the old man. He'll listen to you and we'll work the game all right and proper."

"But suppose he won't listen to me."

"Then we'll put the screws on."

"What screws?"

Hawk Kennedy closed one eye and squinted the other at Peter quizzically.

"I'll tell you that all in good time. But first I've got to know how you stand in the matter."

Peter judicially examined the ash of his cigarette. "He ought to do the right thing," he said slowly.

"He will—never you fear. But can I count on *you*, Pete?"

"What do you want me to do?" asked Peter after a moment.

"Oh, now we're talkin'. But wait a minute. We won't go so fast. Are you with me sure enough—hope I may die—cross my heart?"

"If you'll make it worth my while," said Peter cautiously.

"A hundred thousand. How's that?"

"It sounds all right. But I can't see what I can do that you couldn't do yourself."

"Don't you? Well, you don't know all this story. There's some of it you haven't heard. Maybe it's that will convince you you're makin' no mistake——"

"Well—I'm listening."

A shrewd look came into Kennedy's face—a narrowing of the eyelids, a drawing of the muscles at the mouth, as he searched Peter's face with a sharp glance.

"If you play me false, Pete, I'll have your heart's blood," he said.

Peter only laughed at him.

"I'm not easily scared. Save the melodrama for McGuire. If you can do without me—go ahead. Play your hand alone. Don't tell me anything. I don't want to know."

The bluff worked, for Kennedy relaxed at once.

"Oh, you're a cool hand. I reckon you think I need you or I wouldn't be here. Well, that's so. I do need you. And I'm goin' to tell you the truth—even if it gives away my hand."

"Suit yourself," said Peter, indifferently.

He watched his old "bunkie" pour out another drink of the whisky, and a definite plan of action took shape in his mind. If he could only get Kennedy drunk enough.... The whisky bottle was almost empty—so Peter got up, went to his cupboard and brought forth another one.

"Good old Pete!" said Hawk. "Seems like July the first didn't make much difference to you."

"A present from Mr. McGuire," Peter explained.

"Well, here's to his fat bank account. May it soon be ours." And he drank copiously. Peter filled his own glass but when the opportunity offered poured most of it into the slop-bowl just behind him.

"I'm goin' to tell you, Pete, about me and McGuire—about how we got that mine. It ain't a pretty story. I told you some of it but not the real part—nobody but Mike McGuire and I know that—and he wouldn't tell if it was the last thing he said on earth."

"Oh," said Peter, "something crooked, eh?"

Kennedy laid his bony fingers along Peter's arm while his voice sank to an impressive whisper.

"Crooked as Hell, Pete—crooked as Hell. You wouldn't think Mike McGuire was a murderer—would you?"

"A murderer——!"

Kennedy nodded. "We took that mine—stole it from the poor guy who had staked out his claim. Mike killed him——"

"You don't mean——?"

"Yes, sir. Killed him—stuck him in the ribs with a knife when he wasn't lookin'. What do you think of that?"

"McGuire—a murderer——!"

"Sure. Nice sort of a boss you've got! And he could swing for it if I didn't hold my tongue."

"This is serious——"

"You bet it is—if he don't come across. Now I guess you know why he was so cut up when I showed up around here. I've got it on him all right."

"Can you prove it?"

Kennedy rubbed his chin for a moment.

"I could but I don't want to. You see—Pete——" He paused again and blinked pensively at his glass. "Well, you see—in a manner of speakin'—he's got it on me too."

And Peter listened while his villainous companion related the well known tale of the terrible compact between the two men in which both of them had agreed in writing to share the guilt of the crime, carefully omitting to state the compulsion as used upon McGuire. Hawk Kennedy lied. If Peter had ever needed any further proof of the honesty of his employer he read it in the shifting eye and uncertain verbiage of his guest, whose tongue now wagged loosely while he talked of the two papers, one of which was in McGuire's possession, the other in his own. Hawk was no pleasant companion for an evening's entertainment. From the interesting adventurer of the *Bermudian,* Jim Coast had been slowly changing under Peter's eyes into a personality more formidable and sinister. And the drink seemed to be bringing into importance potentialities for evil at which Peter had only guessed. That he meant to fight to the last ditch for the money was clear, and if the worst came would even confess, dragging McGuire down among the ruins of both their lives. In his drunken condition it would have been ridiculously easy for Peter to have overpowered him, but he was not sure to what end that would lead.

"You say there were two papers," said Peter. "Where are they?"

"McGuire's got his—here at Black Rock," muttered Hawk.

"How do you know that?" asked Peter with interest.

"Where would he keep it?" sneered Hawk. "In his business papers for 'zecutors to look over?"

"And where's yours?" asked Peter.

He hoped for some motion of Kennedy's fingers to betray its whereabouts, but the man only poured out another drink and leered at Peter unpleasantly.

"That'sh *my* business," he said with a sneer.

"Oh. Is it? I thought I was to have a hand in this."

Kennedy grinned.

"Y'are. Your job is t' get other paper from McGuire's safe. And then we'll have fortune in—hic—nutshell."

The man wasn't as drunk as he seemed. Peter shrugged.

"I see. I've got to turn burglar to join your little criminal society. Suppose I refuse?"

"Y' won't. Why, Pete, it ought to be easiest job in world. A few dropsh in glass when you're talkin' business and he'd never know it happened. Then we 'beat it,' y'understand, 'n' write lettersh—nice lettersh. One of 'em to that swell daughter of his. That would do the business, *pronto*."

"Yes, it might," admitted Peter ruminatively.

"Sure it will—but we'll give him chance. Are y' on?" he asked.

Peter was silent for a moment. And then,

"I don't see why you want that paper of McGuire's," he said. "They're exactly alike, you say—both incriminating. And if you've got your paper handy——
"

Peter paused but Kennedy was in the act of swallowing another glass of whisky and he didn't stop to answer the half-formulated query. He gave a gasp of satisfaction and then shrugged.

"No use, Pete," he said huskily. "I said I had paper and I *have* paper handy, but I've got to have McGuire's paper too. I ain't got money and spotless rep'tation like Mike McGuire but I don't want paper like that floatin' roun' universh with *my* name signed to it."

"I don't blame you," said Peter dryly.

Hawk Kennedy was talking thickly now and spilled the whisky in trying to pour out a new glassful.

"Goo' whisky this—goo' ole whisky, Pete. Goo' ole Peter. Say, you'll get pater, Peep—I mean Peter pape—Oh H—— Paper. *You* know."

"I'll have to think about it, Jim."

"Can't think when yer drunk, Pete," he muttered with an expiring grin. "To-morr'. 'Nother drink an' then we'll go sleep. Don't mind my sleepin' here, Pete. Nice plache shleep. Goo' old shleep...."

Peter paused in the act of pouring out another drink for him and then at a sound from Kennedy set the bottle down again. The man suddenly sprawled sideways in the chair, his head back, snoring heavily. Peter watched him for a moment, sure that he couldn't be shamming and then looked around the disordered room. Hawk's overcoat and hat lay on the bed. On tiptoe Peter got up and examined them carefully, watching the man in the chair intently the while. Hawk stirred but did not awaken. Peter searched the overcoat inch by inch. There was nothing in the pockets, but a tin of tobacco and a Philadelphia newspaper. So Peter restored the articles and then hung the hat and coat on the nails behind the door. Hawk Kennedy did not move. He was dead drunk.

The repulsive task of searching the recumbent figure now lay before him. But the game had been worth the candle. If the fateful confession was anywhere in Hawk's clothing Peter meant to find it and yet even now he hesitated. He put the whisky bottle away, cleared up the mess and then bodily picked his visitor up and carried him to the bed. Hawk muttered something in his sleep but fell prone and immediately was snoring stertorously. Then Peter went through his pockets methodically, removing an automatic pistol from his trousers, and examining all his papers carefully by the light of the lamp-a hotel bill receipted, some letters in a woman's hand, a few newspaper clippings bearing on the copper market, a pocketbook containing bills of large denomination, some soiled business cards of representatives of commercial houses, a notebook containing addresses and small accounts, a pass book of a Philadelphia bank, the address of which Peter noted. And that was all. Exhausting every resource Peter went over the lining of his coat and vest, inch by inch, even examined his underwear and his shoes and stockings. From the skin out, Hawk Kennedy had now no secrets from Peter. The incriminating confession was not on Hawk Kennedy's clothing.

At last Peter gave up the search and went out into the air, and lighted his corncob pipe, puzzled at his failure. And yet, was it a failure after all? Hawk had eluded every attempt to discuss his copy of the confession. He had it "handy," he had said. A safe deposit box at the Philadelphia bank of which Peter had made record would be handy, but somehow Peter thought the chances were much against Kennedy's having put it there. Men of his type usually carry everything they possess about their persons. Peter remembered the ragged wallet of the *Bermudian*. What if after all these years of hardship the paper had been worn so that it was entirely illegible, or indeed that in Kennedy's many wanderings it had been lost? Either of these theories was plausible, but none provoked a decision. So after awhile Peter went indoors and opening all the windows and doors to cleanse the air, sat in the big chair and bundling himself in a blanket fell asleep.

CHAPTER XVIII
FACE TO FACE

We are told, alas, that at the highest moment of our expectations the gods conspire to our undoing, and therefore that it is wise to take our joys a little sadly, that we may not fall too far. But Beth, being wholesome of mind and body and an optimist by choice, was not disposed to question the completeness of her contentment or look for any dangers which might threaten its continuance. And so when Peter went home through the forest, she took her kerosene lamp to her room, there to smile at her joyous countenance in the mirror and to assure herself that never since the beginning of the world had there been a girl more glad that she had been born. All the clouds that had hung about her since that evening in the woods had been miraculously rolled away and she knew again as she had known before that Peter Nichols was the one man in all the world for her.

Their evening together was a wonderful thing to contemplate, and she lay in bed, her eyes wide open, staring toward the window, beyond which in a dark mass against the starlit sky she could see the familiar pines, through which was the path to Peter's cabin. The stars twinkled jovially with assurance that the night could not be long and that beyond the night were to-morrows still more wonderful than to-day. And praying gently that all might be well with them both, she fell asleep, not even to dream.

Early morning found her brisk at her work around the house, cleansing and polishing, finishing to her satisfaction the tasks which Peter's impatience had forbidden the night before. All of Aunt Tillie's blue china set was carefully restored to its shelves, the napery folded away, the shiny pots hung upon their hooks and the kitchen carefully mopped. Then, with a towel wrapped about her head (for such was the custom of the country), she attacked the dining-room and parlor with broom and dust-cloth, singing *arpeggios* to remind herself that everything was right with the world.

It was upon the plush-covered sofa where she and Peter had sat the night before that Beth's orderly eye espied a square of paper just upon the point of disappearing in the crease between the seat and back of Aunt Tillie's most cherished article of furniture and of course she pounced upon it with the intention of destroying it at the cookstove. But when she drew it forth, she found that it was an envelope, heliotrope in color, that it bore Peter's name in a feminine handwriting, and that it had a strange delicate odor with which Beth was unfamiliar. She held it in her hand and looked at the writing, then turned it over and over, now holding it more gingerly by the tip ends of her fingers. Then she sniffed at it again. It was a queer perfume—strange—like violet mixed with some kind of spice.

She put her broom aside and walked to the window, her brow puckered, and scrutinized the postmark. "London!" Of course—London was in England where Peter had once lived. And Peter had drawn the letter from his pocket last night with some other papers when he had shown her the communication from "Hawk" Kennedy. It was lucky that she had found it, for it might have slipped down behind the plush covering, and so have been definitely lost. Of course Peter had friends in London and of course they should wish to write to him, but for the first time it seemed curious to Beth that in all their conversations Peter had never volunteered any information as to the life that he had lived before he had come to Black Rock. She remembered now that she had told him that whatever his past had been and whoever he was, he was good enough for her. But the heliotrope envelope with the feminine handwriting and the strange odor immediately suggested queries along lines of investigation which had never before entered her thoughts. Who was the lady of the delicate script and the strange perfume? What was her relationship to Peter? And upon what topic was she writing to him?

Beth slipped the note about a quarter of an inch out of its envelope until she could just see a line of the writing and then quickly thrust it in again, put the envelope on the mantel above the "parlor heater" and resolutely went on with her sweeping. From time to time she stopped her work and looked at it just to be sure that it was still there and at last took it up in her fingers again, a prey to a more lively curiosity than any she had ever known. She put the envelope down again and turning her back to it went into the kitchen. Of course Peter would tell her who this lady was if she asked him. And there was no doubt at all that it *was* a lady who had written the letter, some one familiar with a delicate mode of existence and given to refinements which had been denied to Beth. It was this delicacy and refinement, this flowing inscription written with such careless ease and grace which challenged Beth's rusticity. She would have liked to ask Peter about the lady at once. But Peter would not be at the Cabin at this early hour of the morning, nor would Beth be able to see him until late this afternoon—perhaps not until to-night. Meanwhile, the note upon the mantel was burning its way into her consciousness. It was endued with a personality feminine, insidious and persuasive. No ladies of London affecting heliotrope envelopes had any business writing scented notes to Peter now. He was Beth's particular property....

When she went up to the second floor of the cottage a few minutes later she took the heliotrope letter with her and put it on her bureau, propped against the pincushion, while she went on with her work. And then, all her duties for the morning finished, she sat down in her rocking chair by the window, the envelope in her idle fingers, a victim of temptation. She looked out at the pine woods, her gaze afar, her guilty fingers slipping the letter out of its covering an inch, two inches. And then Beth opened Peter's heliotrope note and read it. At least, she read as much of it as she could understand,—the parts that were written in English—with growing amazement and incertitude. A good deal of the English part even was Greek to her, but she could understand enough to know that a mystery of some sort hung about the letter and about Peter, that he was apparently a person of some importance to the heliotrope lady who addressed him in affectionate terms and with the utmost freedom. Beth had learned in the French ballads which Peter had taught her that *ami* meant friend and that *bel* meant beautiful. And as the whole of the paragraph containing those words was written in English, Beth had little difficulty in understanding it. What had Peter to do with the cause of Holy Russia? And what was this danger to him from hidden enemies, which could make necessary this discretion and watchfulness in Black Rock? And the last sentence of all danced before Beth's eyes as though it had been written in letters of fire. "There is at least one heart in London that ever beats fondly in memory of the dear dead days at Galitzin and Zukovo."

What right had the heliotrope lady's heart to beat fondly in memory of dear dead days with Peter Nichols at Galitzin or Zukovo or anywhere else? Who was she? Was she young? Was she beautiful? And what right had Peter given her to address him in terms of such affection? Anastasie!

And now for the first time in her life, though to all outward appearance calm, Beth felt the pangs of jealousy. This letter, most of it in the queer-looking script (probably Russian) that she could not even read, in its strange references in English to things beyond her knowledge, seemed suddenly to erect a barrier between her and Peter that could never be passed, or even to indicate a barrier between them that had always existed without her knowledge. And if all of the parts of the letter that she could not understand contained sentiments like the English part that she *could* understand, it was a very terrible letter indeed and indicated that this heliotrope woman (she was no longer "lady" now) had claims upon Peter's heart which came long before Beth's. And if this Anastasie—other women too....

Beth read the letter again and then slipped it back into its envelope, while she gazed out of the window at the pines, a frown at her brows and two tiny lines curving downward at the corners of her lips. She was very unhappy. But she was angry too—angry at the heliotrope woman, angry at Peter and angrier still at herself. In that moment she forgot that she had taken Peter Nichols without reference to what he was or had been. She had told him that only the future mattered and now she knew that the past was beginning to matter very much indeed.

After a while she got up, and took the heliotrope letter to the bureau where she wrote upon the envelope rather viciously with a soft lead pencil, "You left *this* last night. You'd better go back to Anastasie." Then she slipped the letter into her waist and with an air of decision went down the stairs (the ominous parentheses still around her mouth), and made her way with rapid footsteps toward the path through the forest which led toward Peter's cabin.

Beth was primitive, highly honorable by instinct if not by precept, but a creature of impulse, very much in love, who read by intuition the intrusion of what seemed a very real danger to her happiness. If her conscience warned her that she was transgressing the rules of polite procedure, something stronger than a sense of propriety urged her on to read, something stronger than mere curiosity—the impulse of self-preservation, the impulse to preserve that which was stronger even than self—the love of Peter Nichols.

The scrawl that she had written upon the envelope was eloquent of her point of view, at once a taunt, a renunciation and a confession. "You left *this* last night. You'd better go back to Anastasie!"

It was the intention of carrying the letter to Peter's cabin and there leaving it in a conspicuous position that now led her rapidly down the path through the woods. Gone were the tender memories of the night before. If this woman had had claims upon Peter Nichols's heart at the two places with the Russian names, she had the same claims upon them now. Beth's love and her pride waged a battle within her as she approached the Cabin. She remembered that Peter had told her last night that he would have a long day at the lumber camp, but as she crossed the log-jam she found herself hoping that by some chance she would find Peter still at home, where, with a fine dignity (which she mentally rehearsed) she would demand explanation, and listening, grant forgiveness. Or else ... she didn't like to think of the alternative.

But instead of Peter, at the Cabin door in the early morning sunlight she found a strange man, sitting in a chair in the portico, smoking one of Peter's cigarettes, and apparently much at home. The appearance of the stranger was for a moment disconcerting, but Beth approached the familiar doorway, her head high, the heliotrope letter burning her fingers. She had intended to walk in at the door of the Cabin, place the letter in a conspicuous position where Peter could not fail to see it, and then return to her home and haughtily await Peter's arrival. But the presence of this man, a stranger in Black Rock, making free of Peter's habitation, evidently with Peter's knowledge and consent, made her pause in a moment of uncertainty.

At her approach the man in the chair had risen and she saw that he was tall—almost as tall as Peter, that he had a hooked nose and displayed a set of irregular teeth when he smiled—which he did, not unpleasantly. There was something about him which repelled her yet fascinated at the same time.

"Mr. Nichols has gone out?" Beth asked, for something to say.

"Yes, Miss," said the stranger, blinking at her with his bleary eyes. "Mr. Nichols is down at the lumber camp—won't be back until night, I reckon. Anythin' I can do for ye?"

"No, I——?" Beth hesitated. "I just wanted to see him—to leave somethin' for him."

"I guess he'll be right sorry to miss you. Who shall I say called?"

"Oh, it doesn't matter," said Beth, turning away. But she was now aware of a strange curiosity as to this person who sat with such an air of well-being in Peter's chair and spoke with such an air of proprietorship. The insistence of her own personal affair with Peter had driven from her mind all thoughts of the other matters suggested in the letter, of the possible dangers to Peter even here in Black Rock and the mysterious references to Holy Russia. This man who stood in Peter's portico, whoever he was, was not a Russian, she could see that at a glance and read it in his accents, but she was equally certain from his general character that he could be no friend of Peter's and that his business here was not of Peter's choosing.

"If ye'd like to wait a while——"

He offered her the chair, but Beth did not accept it.

"Ye don't happen to be Miss Peggy McGuire, do ye?" asked the stranger curiously.

"No," replied the girl. "My name is Beth Cameron."

"Beth——?"

"Cameron," she finished firmly.

"Oh——"

The stranger seemed to be examining her with a glowing interest, but his look was clouded.

Beth had decided that until Peter came explaining she had no further possible interest either in him or his affairs, but in spite of this she found her lips suddenly asking,

"Are you a friend of Mr. Nichols's?"

The man in the portico grinned somberly.

"Yes. I guess I am—an old friend—before he came to America."

"Oh!" said Beth quietly. "You've known him a long time then?"

"Ye might say so. We were buddies together."

"Then you knew him in—in London?"

The man grinned. "Can't say I did. Not in London. Why do you ask?"

"Oh, I just wanted to know."

The gaze of the stranger upon her was disquieting. His eyes seemed to be smoldering like embers just ready to blaze. She knew that she ought to be returning and yet she didn't want to go leaving her object unaccomplished, the dignity of her plan having already been greatly disturbed. And so she hesitated, curiosity at war with discretion.

"Would you mind telling me your name?" she asked timidly.

The man shrugged a shoulder and glanced away from her. "I reckon my name wouldn't mean much to you."

"Oh—I'm sorry. Perhaps I shouldn't have asked?"

The stranger put his hands into his coat pockets and stared down at Beth with a strange intrusive kind of smile.

"You and Pete seem kind of thick, don't ye?" he muttered.

"Pete!"

"Pete Nichols. That's his name, ain't it? Kind of thick, I'd say. I can't blame him though——"

"You're mistaken," said Beth with dignity, "there's nothin' between Peter Nichols and me." And turning heel, Beth took a step away.

"There! Put my foot in it, didn't I? I'm sorry. Don't go yet. I want to ask ye something."

Beth paused and found that the stranger had come out from the portico and still stood beside her. And as her look inquired fearlessly,

"It's about your name, Miss," he muttered, and then with an effort spoke the word savagely, as though it had been wrenched from him by an effort of will, "Cameron——? Your name's Cameron?"

"Yes," said Beth, in some inquietude.

"Common name in some parts—Cameron—not so common in others—not in Jersey anyway——"

"I didn't know——"

"Is yer father livin'?" he snapped.

"No—dead. Many years ago. Out West."

"Tsch!" he breathed, the air whistling between his teeth, "Out West, ye say—out West?"

He stood in front of Beth now, his arms akimbo, his head bent forward under the stress of some excitement. Beth drew away from him, but he came forward after her, his gaze still seeking hers.

"Yes—out West," said Beth haltingly.

"Where?" he gasped.

"I don't know——"

"Was his name—was his name—Ben Cameron?" He shot the question at her with a strange fury, catching meanwhile at her arm.

"Let me go——," she commanded. "You're hurtin' me."

"Was it——?"

"Yes. Let me go."

The stranger's grip on her arm suddenly relaxed and while she watched his face in curiosity the glow in his eyes suddenly flickered out, his gaze shifting from side to side as he seemed to shrink away from her. From timidity at his roughness she found new courage in her curiosity at his strange behavior. What had this stranger to do with Ben Cameron?

"What did you want to know for?" she asked him.

But his bent brows were frowning at the path at his feet. He tried to laugh—and the sound of the dry cackle had little mirth in it.

"No matter. I—I thought it might be. I guess ye'd better go—I guess ye'd better." And with that he sank heavily in Peter's chair again.

But Beth still stood and stared at him, aware of the sudden change in his attitude toward her. What did it all mean? What were Peter's relations with this creature who behaved so strangely at the mention of her name? Why did he speak of Ben Cameron? Who was he? Who——?

The feeling of which she had at first been conscious, at the man's evil leering smile which repelled her suddenly culminated in a pang of intuition. This man ... It must be ... Hawk Kennedy—the man who ... She stared at him with a new horror in the growing pallor of her face and Hawk Kennedy saw the look. It was as though some devilish psychological contrivance had suddenly hooked their two consciousnesses to the same thought. Both saw the same picture—the sand, the rocks, the blazing sun and a dead man lying with a knife in his back.... And Beth continued staring as though in a kind of horrible fascination. And when her lips moved she spoke as though impelled by a force beyond her own volition.

"You—you're Hawk Kennedy," she said tensely, "the man who killed my father."

"It's a lie," he gasped, springing to his feet. "Who told you that?"

"I—I guessed it——"

"Who told ye about Hawk Kennedy? Who told ye about him?"

"No one——"

"Ye didn't dream it. Ye can't dream a name," he said tensely. "Pete told ye—he lied to ye."

"He didn't."

But he had caught her by the wrist again and dragged her into the Cabin. She was thoroughly frightened now—too frightened even to cry out—too terrified at the sudden revelation of this man who for some days had been a kind of evil spirit in the background of her happiness. He was not like what she had thought he was, but he embodied an idea that was sinister and terrible. And while she wondered what he was going to do next, he pushed her into the armchair, locked the door and put the key into his pocket.

"Now we can talk," he muttered grimly. "No chance of bein' disturbed—Pete ain't due for hours yet. So he's been tellin' *you* lies about me. Has he? Sayin' *I* done it. By G—, I'm beginnin' to see...."

He leered at her horribly, and Beth seemed frozen into her chair. The courage that had been hers a moment ago when he had shrunk away from her had fled before the fury of his questions and the violence of his touch. She was intimidated for the first time in her life and yet she tried to meet his eyes, which burned wildly, shifting from side to side like those of a caged beast. In her terror she could not tell what dauntless instinct had urged her unless it was Ben Cameron's soul in agony that had cried out through her lips. And now she had not only betrayed Peter—but herself....

"I'm beginnin' to see. You and Pete—playin' both ends against the middle, with McGuire comin' down somethin' very handsome for a weddin' present and leavin' me out in the cold. Very pretty! But it ain't goin' to work out just that way—not that way at all."

All of this he muttered in a wildly casual kind of a way, at no one in particular, as his gaze flitted from one object in the room to another, always passing over Beth almost impersonally. But in a moment she saw his gaze concentrate upon her with sudden eagerness.

"He told ye I done it, did he? Well, I didn't," he cried in a strident voice. "I didn't do it. It was McGuire and I'll prove it, all right. McGuire. Pete can't fix *that* on me—even if he wanted to. But he told *you* or ye wouldn't of spoke like ye did. I guess maybe ye wouldn't of said so much if Pete had been here. But ye let the cat slip out of the bag all right. You and Pete—and maybe McGuire's with ye too—all against me. Is that so?... Can't yer speak, girl? Must ye sit there just starin' at me with yer big eyes? What are ye lookin' at? Are ye dumb?"

"No, I'm not dumb," gasped Beth, struggling for her courage, aware all the while of the physical threat in the man's very presence.

"Speak then. Tell me the truth. Pete said it was your money McGuire took—your money McGuire's got to make good to ye? Ain't that the truth?"

"I won't answer."

"Oh, yes, ye will. You'll answer all right. I'm not goin' to trifle. What did ye come here to see Pete about? What's that letter ye came to give him? Give it to me!"

Beth clutched the heliotrope note to her bosom but Hawk Kennedy caught at her hands and tried to tear it away from her. It needed only this new act of physical violence to give Beth the courage of despair. She sprang to her feet eluding him but he caught her before she reached the window. She struck at him with her fists but he tore the letter away from her and hurled her toward the bed over which she fell breathless. There was no use trying to fight this man.... There was a cruelty in his touch which spoke of nameless things.... And so she lay motionless, nursing her injured wrists, trying desperately to think what she must do.

Meanwhile, watching her keenly from the tail of his eye, Hawk Kennedy was reading the heliotrope letter, spelling out the English word by word. Fascinated, Beth saw the frown of curiosity deepen to interest and then to puzzled absorption.

"Interestin'—very," she heard him mutter at last, as he glanced toward the bed. "Holy Russia. H——! What's this mean, girl? Who *is* Peter Nichols? Answer me."

"I—I don't know," she said.

"Yes, ye do. Where did ye get this letter?"

"He left it at—at my house last night."

"Oh! *Your* house! Where?"

"In the village."

"I see. An' this scrawl on the envelope—you wrote it——"

Beth couldn't reply. He was dragging her through the very depths of humiliation.

At her silence his lips curved in ugly amusement.

"Anastasie!" he muttered. "Some queen that—with her purple paper an' all. And ye don't know who she is? Or who Pete is? Answer me!"

"I—I don't know," she whispered. "I—I don't, really."

"H-m! Well, he ain't what he's seemed to be, that's sure. He ain't what he's seemed to be to you and he ain't what he's seemed to be to me. But whoever he is he can't put anything over on *me*. We'll see about this."

Beth straightened and sat up, watching him pace the floor in deep thought. There might be a chance that she could escape by the window. But when she started up he ordered her back roughly and she soon saw that this was impossible.

At last he stopped walking up and down and stared at her, his eyes narrowed to mere slits, his brows drawn ominously together. It seemed that he had reached a decision.

"You behave yourself an' do what I tell ye an' ye won't be hurt," he growled.

"Wh-what are you goin' to do?" she gasped.

"Nothin' much. Ye're just goin' with me—that's all."

"W-where?"

"That's my business. Oh, ye needn't be scared of any love makin'. I'm not on that lay this trip."

He went to the drawer of Peter's bureau and took out some handkerchiefs.

"But ye'd better be scared if ye don't do what I tell ye. Here. Stand up!"

Beth shrank away from, him, but he caught her by the wrists and held her.

"Ye're not to make a noise, d'ye hear? I can't take the chance."

And while she still struggled desperately, he fastened her wrists together behind her. Then he thrust one of Peter's handkerchiefs in her mouth and securely gagged her. He wasn't any too gentle with her but even in her terror she found herself thanking God that it was only abduction that he planned.

Hawk Kennedy went to the window and peered out up the path, then he opened the door and looked around. After a moment he came in quickly.

"Come," he muttered, "it's time we were off."

He caught her by the arm and helped her to her feet, pushing her out of the door and into the underbrush at the corner of the cabin. Her feet lagged, her knees were weak, but the grasp on her shoulder warned her of cruelties she had not dreamed of and so she stumbled on—on into the depths of the forest, Hawk Kennedy's hard hand urging her on to greater speed.

CHAPTER XIX
YAKIMOV REVEALS HIMSELF

It was with some misgivings that Peter left his cabin, leaving Hawk Kennedy there to sleep off the effects of his potations, but the situation at the lumber camp was so hazardous that his presence was urgently required. Hawk had awakened early, very early, and very thirsty, but Peter had told him that there was no more whisky and threatened to throw over the whole affair if he didn't sober up and behave himself. And so, having exacted a promise from Hawk Kennedy to leave the Cabin when he had had his sleep out, Peter had gotten the "flivver" from McGuire's garage (as was his custom) and driven rapidly down toward the camp.

He had almost reached the conclusion that the copy of the partnership agreement which Hawk had held as a threat over McGuire had ceased to exist—that it had been lost, effaced or destroyed. But he wanted to be more certain of this before he came out into the open, showed his hand and McGuire's and defied the blackmailer to do his worst. He felt pretty sure now from his own knowledge of the man that, desperate though he was in his intention to gain a fortune by this expedient, he was absolutely powerless to do evil without the signature of McGuire. The question as to whether or not he would make a disagreeable publicity of the whole affair was important to McGuire and had to be avoided if possible, for Peter had given his promise to bring the affair to a quiet conclusion.

Until he could have a further talk with McGuire, he meant to lead Hawk Kennedy on to further confidences and with this end in view and with the further purpose of getting him away from the Cabin, had promised to meet him late that afternoon at a fork of the road to the lumber camp, the other prong of which led to a settlement of several shanties where Hawk had managed to get a lodging on the previous night and on several other occasions. In his talk with the ex-waiter he learned that on his previous visits the man had made a careful survey of the property and knew his way about almost as well as Peter did. It appeared that he also knew something of Peter's problems at the lumber camp and the difficulties the superintendent had already encountered in getting his sawed lumber to the railroad and in completing his fire-towers. Indeed, these difficulties seemed only to have begun again, and it was with great regret that Peter was obliged to forego the opportunity of seeing Beth that day, perhaps even that evening. But he had told her nothing of his troubles the night before, not wishing to cloud a day so fair for them both.

The facts were these: Flynn and Jacobi, the men he had dismissed, had appeared again at the camp in his absence, bent on fomenting trouble, and Shad Wells, already inflamed against the superintendent, had fallen an easy prey to their machinations. Accidents were always happening at the sawmills, accidents to machinery and implements culminating at last in the blowing out of a tube of one of the boilers. It was this misfortune that had held the work up for several days until a spare boiler could be installed. Peter tried to find out how these accidents had happened, but each line of investigation led up a blind alley. Jesse Brown, his foreman, seemed to be loyal, but he was easy-going and weak. With many of his own friends among the workers both at the camp and mills he tried to hold his job by carrying water on both shoulders and the consequences were inevitable. He moved along the line of least resistance and the trouble grew. Peter saw his weakness and would have picked another man to supersede him, but there was no other available. The truth was that though the men's wages were high for the kind of work that they were doing, the discontent that they had brought with them was in the air. The evening papers brought word of trouble in every direction, the threatened railroad and steel strikes and the prospect of a coalless winter when the miners went out as they threatened to do on the first of November.

At first Peter had thought that individually many of the men liked him. He had done what he could for their comfort and paid them the highest price justifiable, but gradually he found that his influence was being undermined and that the good-natured lagging which Peter had at first tried to tolerate had turned to loafing on the job, and finally to overt acts of rebellion. More men had been sent away and others with even less conscience had taken their places. Some of them had enunciated Bolshevist doctrines as wild as any of Flynn's or Jacobi's. Jonathan K. McGuire stood as a type which represented the hierarchy of wealth and was therefore their hereditary enemy. Peter in a quiet talk at the bunk-house one night had told them that once Jonathan K. McGuire had been as poor, if not poorer, than any one of them. But even as he spoke he had felt that his words had made no impression. It was what McGuire was *now* that mattered, they told him. All this land, all this lumber, was the people's, and they'd get it too in time. With great earnestness, born of a personal experience of which they could not dream, Peter pointed out to them what had happened and was now happening in Russia and painted a harrowing picture of helplessness and starvation, but they smoked their pipes in silence and answered him not at all. They were not to be reasoned with. If the Soviet came to America they were willing to try it. They would try anything once.

But Shad Wells was "canny" and Peter had never succeeded in tracing any of the accidents or any of the dissensions directly to his door. Without evidence against him Peter did not think it wise to send him out of camp, for many of the men were friendly to Shad and his dismissal was sure to mean an upheaval of sorts. Peter knew that Shad hated him for what had happened at the Cabin but that in his heart he feared to come out into the open where a repetition of his undoing in public might destroy his influence forever. So to Peter's face he was sullenly obedient, taking care to give the appearance of carrying out his orders, while as soon as Peter's back was turned he laughed, loafed and encouraged others to do the same.

And for the last week Peter had not liked the looks of things. At the lumber camp the work was almost at a standstill, and the sawmills were silent. Jesse Brown had told him that Flynn and Jacobi had been at the bunk-house and that the men had voted him down when the foreman had tried to send them away. It was clear that some radical step would have to be taken at once to restore discipline or Peter's authority and usefulness as superintendent would be only a matter of hours.

It was of all of these things that Peter thought as he bumped his way in the "flivver" over the corduroy road through the swampy land which led to the lower reserve, and as he neared the scene of these material difficulties all thought of Hawk Kennedy passed from his mind. There was the other danger too that had been one of the many subjects of the letter of Anastasie Galitzin, for Peter had no doubt now that the foreigner with the dark mustache who had followed him down from New York and who some weeks ago had been sent out of the camp was no other than the agent of the Soviets, who had forwarded to London the information as to his whereabouts. Peter had not seen this man since the day of his dismissal, but he suspected that he was in the plot with Flynn, Jacobi and perhaps Shad Wells to make mischief in the lumber camp.

The opportunity that Peter sought to bring matters to a focus was not long in coming, for when he reached the sawmills, which had resumed desultory operations, he found Flynn and Jacobi, the "Reds," calmly seated in the office, smoking and talking with Shad Wells. Peter had left his "flivver" up the road and his sudden entrance was a surprise. The men got up sullenly and would have slouched out of the door but Peter closed it, put his back to it, and faced them. He was cold with anger and held himself in with difficulty, but he had taken their measure and meant to bring on a crisis, which would settle their status and his own, once and for all time.

"What are you doing here?" he began shortly, eying Flynn.

The Irishman stuck his hands into his pockets and shrugged impudently.

"That's my business," he muttered.

"H-m. You two men were discharged because you were incompetent, because you were getting money you didn't earn and because you were trying to persuade others to be as worthless and useless as yourselves. You were ordered off the property——"

"Ye can't keep us off——"

"I'll come to that in a moment. What I want to say to you now is this," said Peter, planting his barbs with the coolness of a matador baiting his bull. "Some men go wrong because they've been badly advised, some because they can't think straight, others because they'd rather go wrong than right. Some of you 'Reds' believe in what you preach, that the world can be made over and all the money and the land divided up in a new deal. You two don't. You don't believe in anything except getting a living without working for it—and trying to make honest men do the same. You, Jacobi, are only a fool—a cowardly fool at that—who hides behind the coat-tails of a man stronger than you——"

"Look-a here, Mister——"

"Yes, Flynn's your master, but he isn't mine. And he isn't the master of any man on this job while I'm superintendent——"

"We'll see about that," said Flynn with a chuckle.

"Yes, we will. Very soon. *Now*, as a matter of fact——"

"How?"

"By proving which is the better man—you or me——"

"Oh, it's a fight ye mean?"

"Exactly."

The Irishman leered at him cunningly.

"I'm too old a bird to be caught wit' that stuff—puttin' you wit' the right on yer side. We're afther sheddin' no blood here, Misther Nichols. We're on this job for peace an' justice fer all."

"Then you're afraid to fight?"

"No. But I'm not a-goin' to——"

"Not if I tell you you're a sneak, a liar and a coward——"

Flynn's jaw worked and his glance passed from Jacobi to Wells.

"I'll make ye eat them names backwards one day, Misther Nichols—but not now—I'm here for a bigger cause. Stand away from the door."

"In a moment. But first let me tell you this, and Shad Wells too. You're going out of this door and out of this camp,—all three of you. And if any one of you shows himself inside the limits of this property he'll have to take the consequences."

"Meanin' what?" asked Wells.

"Meaning *me*," said Peter, "and after me, the law. Now go."

He stood aside and swung the door open with one hand, but he didn't take his eyes from them.

They laughed in his face, but they obeyed him, filing out into the open, and strolled away.

Peter had hoped to coax a fight out of Flynn, thinking that the Irish blood in him couldn't resist his taunts and challenge. But Flynn had been too clever for him. A defeat for Flynn meant loss of prestige, a victory possible prosecution. Either way he had nothing to gain. Perhaps he was just a coward like Jacobi or a beaten bully like Shad. Whatever he was Flynn seemed very sure of himself and Peter, though apparently master of the situation for the present, was conscious of a sense of defeat. He knew as Flynn did that no matter what forces he called to his aid, it was practically impossible to keep trespassers off a property of this size, and that, after all, the success of his logging operations remained with the men themselves.

But he breathed more freely now that he had made his decision with regard to Shad Wells. He spent a large part of the morning going over the mills, getting the men together and giving them a little talk, then went up to the camp in search of Jesse Brown. The news of his encounter with Shad and the "Reds" had preceded him and he saw that trouble was brewing. Jesse Brown wagged his head in a deprecating way and tried to side-step the entire situation. But Peter had reached a point where he was tired of equivocation.

"I say, Jesse," he said at last, "you've let things get into a pretty bad mess down here."

"I'm a peaceable man, Mr. Nichols," said Jesse. "I've tried to steer this camp along easy-like, 'til this bit of woods is cleared up and here you go stirrin' up a hornet's nest about our ears."

Peter frowned. "You know as well as I do that the men are doing just as they please. At the rate they're going they wouldn't have this section finished by Christmas. I'm paying them for work they don't do and you know it. I put you in here to see that McGuire gets what he's paying for. You haven't done it."

"I've done the best I could," muttered Jesse.

"That isn't the best I want. You knew Flynn and Jacobi were back in camp yesterday. Why didn't you tell me so?"

"I can't do nothin'. They've got friends here."

"And haven't you got friends here too? I sent those men out of camp. If they're here again I'll find the power to arrest them."

"I'd advise you not to try that."

"Why?"

"They're stronger than you think."

"I'll take my chances on that. But I want to know where you stand. Are you with me or against me?"

"Well," said Jesse, rubbing his head dubiously, "I'll do what I can."

"All right. We'll make a fresh start. Round up all hands. I'm going to talk to them at dinner time."

Jesse glanced at him, shrugged and went out and Peter went into the office where he spent the intervening time going over the books. It was there that one of the clerks, a man named Brierly, brought forth from the drawer of his desk a small pamphlet which he had picked up yesterday in the bunk-house. Peter opened and read it. It was a copy of the new manifest of the Union of Russian Workers and though written in English, gave every mark of origin in the Lenin-Trotzky regime and was cleverly written in catch phrases meant to trap the ignorant. It proposed to destroy the churches and erect in their stead places of amusement for the working people. He read at random. "Beyond the blood-covered barricades, beyond all terrors of civil war, there already shines for us the magnificent, beautiful form of man, without a God, without a master, and full of authority." Fine doctrine this! The pamphlet derided the law and the state, and urged the complete destruction of private ownership. It predicted the coming of the revolution in a few weeks, naming the day, of a general strike of all industries which would paralyze all the functions of commerce. It was Bolshevik in ideal, Bolshevik in inspiration and it opened Peter's eyes as to the venality of the gentleman with the black mustache. Brierly also told him that whisky had been smuggled into the camp the night before and that a fire in the woods had luckily been put out before it had become menacing. Brierly was a discharged soldier who had learned something of the value of obedience and made no effort to conceal his anxiety and his sympathies. He voiced the opinion that either Flynn or Jacobi had brought in the liquor. Peter frowned. Jesse Brown had said nothing of this. The inference was obvious.

At the dinner-shed, Peter was to be made aware immediately of the difficulty of the task that confronted him, for dour looks met him on all sides. There were a few men who sat near him whom he thought he might count on at a venture, but they were very few and their positions difficult. Some of the men still showed the effects of their drink and hurled epithets about the room, obviously meant for Peter's ear, but he sat through the meal patiently and then got to his feet and demanded their attention.

As he began he was interrupted by hoots and cat-calls but he waited calmly for silence and seeing that they couldn't ruffle him by buffoonery they desisted after a moment.

"Men, I'm not going to take much of your time," he said. "A short while ago I came down here and talked to you. Some of you seemed to be friendly toward me and those are the men I want to talk to now. The others don't matter."

"Oh, don't they?" came a gruff voice from a crowd near the door. And another, "We'll see about that."

Peter tried to find the speakers with his gaze for a moment and then went on imperturbably. "I'm going to talk to you in plain English, because some things have happened in this camp that are going to make trouble for everybody, trouble for me, trouble for McGuire, but more trouble for you."

"That's what we're lookin' for—trouble——," cried the same voice, and Peter now identified it as Flynn's, for the agitator had come back and stolen in unawares.

"Ah, it's you, Flynn," said Peter easily. "You've come back." And then to the crowd, "I don't think Flynn is likely to be disappointed if he's looking for trouble," he said dryly. "Trouble is one of the few things in this world a man can find if he looks for it."

"Aye, mon, an' without lookin' for it," laughed a broad-chested Scot at Peter's table.

"That's right. I met Flynn a while ago over in the office. I made him an offer. I said I'd fight him fair just man to man, for our opinions. He refused. I also told him he was a coward, a sneak and a liar. But he wouldn't fight—because he's what I said he was."

"I'll show ye, Misther——," shouted Flynn, "but I ain't ready yet."

"You'll be ready when this meeting is over. And one of us is going out of this camp feet first."

"We'll see about that."

"One of us will. And I think I'll do the seeing."

A laugh went up around Peter, drowned immediately by a chorus of jeers from the rear of the room.

But Peter managed to be heard again.

"Well, *I* didn't come on this job looking for trouble," he went on coolly. "I wanted to help you chaps in any way I could." ("The Hell you did.") "Yes, I did what I could for your comfort. I raised your wages and I didn't ask more than an honest day's work from any one of you. Some of you have stuck to your jobs like men, in spite of the talk you've heard all about you, and I thank you. You others," he cried, toward the rear of the room, "I've tried to meet in a friendly spirit where I could, but some of you don't want friendship——" ("Not with you, we don't.") "Nor with any one else——" Peter shouted back defiantly. "You don't know what friendship means, or you wouldn't try to make discontent and trouble for everybody, when you're all getting a good wage and good living conditions." ("That ain't enough!")

Peter calmly disregarded the interruptions and went on. "Perhaps you fellows think I don't know what socialism means. I do. To the true socialist, socialism is nothing else but Christianity. It's just friendship, that's all. He believes in helping the needy and the weak. He believes in defending his own life and happiness and the happiness of others." ("That's true—that's right.") "And he believes that the world can be led and guided by a great brotherhood of humanity seeking just laws and equality for all men." (Conflicting cries of "That's not enough!" and "Let him speak!") "But I know what anarchy means too, because less than six months ago I was in Russia and I saw the hellish thing at work. I saw men turn and kill their neighbors because the neighbors had more than they had; I saw a whole people starving, women with children at the breast, men raging, ready to fly at one another's throats from hunger, from anger, from fear of what was coming next. That is what anarchy means."

"What you say is a lie," came a clear voice in English, with a slight accent. A man had risen at the rear of the room and stood facing Peter. He was not very tall and he was not in working clothes, but Peter recognized him at once as the man with the dark mustache, the mysterious stranger who had followed him to Black Rock. Peter set his jaw and shrugged. He was aware now of all the forces with which he had to deal.

"What does anarchy mean, then?" he asked coolly.

"You know what it means," said the man, pointing an accusing finger at Peter. "It means only the end of all autocracy whether of money or of power, the destruction of class distinction and making the working classes the masters of all general wealth which they alone produce and to which they alone are entitled."

A roar of approval went up from the rear of the room and cries of, "Go it, Bolsche," and "Give him Hell, Yakimov."

Peter waited until some order was restored, but he knew now that this type of man was more to be feared than Flynn or any other professional agitator of the I. W. W. When they had first come face to face, this Russian had feigned ignorance of English, but now his clearly enunciated phrases, though unpolished, indicated a perfect command of the language, and of his subject. That he should choose this time to come out into the open showed that he was more sure of himself and of his audience than Peter liked. And Peter had no humor to match phrases with him. Whatever his own beliefs since he had come to America, one fact stood clear: That he was employed to get this work done and that Yakimov, Flynn and others were trying to prevent it. It was to be no contest of philosophies but of personalities and Peter met the issue without hesitation.

"You are a communist then and not a socialist," said Peter, "one who believes in everybody sharing alike whether he works for it or not—or an anarchist who believes in the destruction of everything. You're an agent of the Union of Russian Workers, aren't you?"

"And what if I am——?"

"Oh, nothing, except that you have no place in a nation like the United States, which was founded and dedicated to an ideal, higher than any you can ever know——"

"An ideal—with money as its God——"

"And what's your God, Yakimov?"

"Liberty——"

"License! You want to inflame—pillage—destroy—And what then?"

"You shall see——"

"What I saw in Russia—no wages for any one, no harvests, factories idle, blood—starvation—if that's what you like, why did you leave there, Yakimov?"

The man stood tense for a second and then spoke with a clearness heard in every corner of the room.

"I came for another reason than yours. I came to spread the gospel of labor triumphant. *You* came because——" Here the Russian leaned forward, shaking his fist, his eyes suddenly inflamed and hissing his words in a fury. "*You* came because you believed in serfs and human slavery—because your own land spewed you out from a sick stomach, because you were one of the rotting sores in its inside—that had made Russia the dying nation that she was; because it was time that your country and my country cleansed herself from such as you. That's why you came. And we'll let these men judge which of us they want to lead them here."

The nature of the attack was so unexpected that Peter was taken for a moment off his guard. A dead silence had fallen upon the room as the auditors realized that a game was being played here that was not on the cards. Peter felt the myriads of eyes staring at him, and beyond them had a vision of a prostrate figure in the corner of a courtyard, the blood reddening his blouse under the falling knout. They were all Michael Kuprins, these foreigners who stared at him, all the grievances born of centuries of oppression. And as Peter did not speak at once, Yakimov pursued his advantage.

"I did not come here to tell who this man is," he shouted, "this man who tells you what liberty is. But you ought to know. It's your right. You know why Russia rose and threw off the yoke of bondage of centuries. It was because this man before you who calls himself Peter Nichols and others like him bound the people to work for him by terrible laws, taxed them, starved them, beat them, killed them, that he and others like him might buy jewels for their mistresses and live in luxury and ease, on the sweat of the labor of the people. And he asks me why I came to America! It was for a moment such as this that I was sent here to find him out that I might meet him face to face and confront him with his crimes—and those of his father—against humanity."

Yakimov paused suddenly in his furious tirade for lack of breath and in the deathly silence of the room, there was a sudden stir as a rich brogue queried anxiously of nobody in particular:

"Who in Hell *is* he, then?"

"I'll tell you who he is," the Russian went on, getting his breath. "He's one of the last of a race of tyrants and oppressors, the worst the world has ever known—in Russia the downtrodden. He fled to America to hide until the storm had blown over, hoping to return and take his place again at the head of a new government of the Democrats and the Bourgeoisie—the Grand Duke Peter Nicholaevitch!"

The uproar that filled the room for a moment made speech impossible. But every eye was turned on Peter now, some in incredulity, some in malevolence, and some in awe. He saw that it was now useless to deny his identity even if he had wished to do so, and so he stood squarely on his feet, staring at Yakimov, who still leaned forward menacingly, shrieking above the tumult, finally making himself heard.

"And this is the man who dares to talk to you about a brotherhood of humanity, just laws and equality among men! This tyrant and son of tyrants, this representative of a political system that you and men like you have overthrown for all time. Is this the man you'll take your orders from? Or from the Union of Russian Workers which hates and kills all oppressors who stand in the way of the rights and liberties of the workers of the world!"

A roar of negation went up from the rear of the room, and an ominous murmur spread from man to man. Only those grouped around Peter, some Americans, the Scot, Brierly, the ex-soldier, Jesse Brown, and one or two of the Italians remained silent, but whether in awe of Peter or of his position could not be determined. But Peter still stood, his hands in his pockets, firm of jaw and unruffled. It has been said that Peter had a commanding air when he chose and when he slowly raised a hand for silence the uncouth "Reds" at the rear of the room obeyed him, the menacing growl sinking to a mere murmur. But he waited until perfect silence was restored. And then quietly,

"What this man has said is true," he announced calmly. "I *am* Peter Nicholaevitch. I came to America as you have come—to make my way. What does it matter who my fathers were? I am not responsible for what my fathers did before me. I am only responsible for what I am—myself. If this man in whom you put your trust would speak the truth, he would tell you that I tried to bring peace and brotherhood into the part of Russia where I lived——"

"He lies——"

"I speak the truth. There people knew that I was their friend. They came to me for advice. I helped them——"

"Then why did they burn down your castle?" broke in Yakimov triumphantly.

"Because people such as you from the Soviet came among honest and peaceful men, trying to make them as mad as you—I came from Russia to find new life, work, peace and happiness. I came to build. You came to destroy. And I intend to build and you shall not destroy. If the madness of Russia comes to Black Rock it will be because mad dogs come foaming at the mouth and making others mad——"

A savage cry went up and a glass came hurtling at Peter's head, but it missed him and crashed against the wall behind him. That crash of glass liberated the pent-up forces in the hearts of these men, for in a moment the place was in a furious uproar, the men aligning themselves in two camps, that of Peter and his friends much the smaller.

Peter retreated a pace or two as a shot was fired from a revolver, but the Scot and Brierly and two of the Americans joined him and met the first onslaught bravely. The handful of men was forced back against the wall by sheer weight of numbers, but they struck out manfully with their fists, with chairs, and with their feet, with any object that came to hand, and men went down with bleeding heads. Peter was armed but he did not wish to kill any one—his idea being to make a successful retreat to the office, where the telephone would put him in touch with May's Landing and reinforcements. Yakimov stood at the edge of the crowd, waving a revolver, when a well-aimed missile from the hand of the Scot sent him sprawling to the floor among the benches.

Peter and his crowd had fought their way to the door, when Flynn and Jacobi who had led a group of men by the other door, fell on them from the rear. Between the two groups their position was hopeless but Peter fought his way out into the open, dodging a blow from Jacobi and using the terrible *savate* in Flynn's stomach, just as Shad Wells rushed at him from one side. Peter saw the blow coming from a broken axhandle—but he had no time to avoid it. Instinctively he ducked his head and threw up his left arm, but the bludgeon descended and Peter fell, remembering nothing more.

CHAPTER XX
THE RUSSIAN PAYS

When Peter came back to consciousness, he found himself lying in the shelter of the underbrush alone. And while he attempted to gather his scattered wits together a figure came creeping through the bushes toward him. It was Brierly, the clerk, carrying a hatful of water which he had procured from the neighboring rivulet. Brierly had a lump on his forehead about the size of a silver dollar, and his disheveled appearance gave evidence of an active part in the mêlée.

"What's happened?" asked Peter slowly, starting up as memory came back to him.

But Brierly didn't answer at once.

"Here, drink this. I don't think you're badly hurt——"

"No. Just dazed a bit," muttered Peter, and let Brierly minister to him for a moment.

"You see, there were too many for us," Brierly explained. "We made a pretty good fight of it at that, but they buried us by sheer weight of numbers. Yours isn't the only bruised head, though. Yakimov got his early in the game—and Jacobi. And gee! but that was a 'beaut' you handed Flynn—right in the solar plexus with your heel. The *savate*—wasn't it? I saw a Frenchy pull that in a dive in Bordeaux. I reckon Flynn won't be doin' much agitatin' for a while—except in his stommick."

"How did I get here?" asked Peter.

"I hauled you into the bush as soon as I got a chance—in the confusion—and gradually, got you back in here. But I think they're lookin' for us, so we'd better get a move on soon as you're fit enough."

"Where's Jesse?"

"Beat it, I reckon. Haven't seen him."

"I see." And then, "Brierly, I'm obliged to you. I'll try to make it up to you for this."

"You needn't bother. I'm for you. You can't let a lot of roughnecks put it over on you like this."

"No—I can't—I can't," muttered Peter.

"I wish we had a bunch of the boys I was with over in France down here. There's a few up in May's Landing who'd clean this lot up in no time."

"I wish we had them." Peter straightened with some difficulty and rose to a sitting posture as the thought came to him. "I've got to get to the 'phone, Brierly."

"No. I wouldn't advise that—not here. Those roughnecks are between us and the office—in the office too, I reckon, by this time. It wouldn't be safe. Who were you goin' to 'phone to?"

"May's Landing—the Sheriff. I'm going to see this thing through."

"Righto! And I'm with you to a fare-ye-well. But it's got to be managed different. They'll beat you to death if you show up now. It was Yakimov that shot at you. He's after you. You were armed. It's a wonder you didn't shoot him down." And then, with some hesitation, "Say, Mr. Nichols. You ain't really the Grand Duke Peter, are you?"

Peter smiled. "What's left of him—I am. This man Yakimov is an agent of Trotzky."

Brierly whistled softly between his teeth. "I reckon *they* want to get you, don't they?"

Peter nodded. "But they won't—not yet."

They held a brief council of war and in a moment on hands and knees were making their way through the underbrush in the general direction of Black Rock. Behind them they heard rough laughter and an occasional outburst of song which proclaimed that new supplies of whisky had been unearthed and that the anarchy which Yakimov so much desired now prevailed. After a while, Peter managed to get to his feet and moved on at a greater speed. He had only been stunned by Shad's blow—a part of the force of which he had caught on his arm. The arm was still numb and his head thumped, but as he went on in the cool air his brain cleared and he found it possible to plan with some definiteness. Brierly knew the sheriff at May's Landing. There was nothing his friends would rather do than to be sworn in as deputies for a job like this. He had thought it a wonder that Peter hadn't called the Sheriff in before.

"I thought I could manage the situation alone, Brierly," said Peter quietly, "but it's got the best of me."

The way was long to Black Rock—at least eight miles by the way they took— and it was almost six o'clock when, they reached McGuire's. They knew that with the "flivver" in the possession of the outlaws it was quite possible that some of the ringleaders of the disturbance might have preceded them, and so they kept under cover until near the house, when they quickly emerged from the bushes and made their way to the kitchen door, entering without knocking.

An unpleasant surprise awaited them here, for in the kitchen, securely gagged and bound to a chair, they found McGuire's valet, Stryker.

It took only a moment to release the man and to get the gag out of his mouth, when he began sputtering and pointing toward the door into the house.

"Hawk—Hawk Kennedy!" the amazed Peter made out.

And after staring at the man in a moment of bewilderment, Peter drew out his revolver and dashed through the house, keyed up at once to new adventure, the eager Brierly at his heels. They went up the stairs and to the door of McGuire's own room, where they stood for a moment aghast at the disorder and havoc before them.

Papers and books were scattered everywhere upon the floor, chairs were overturned, and the door of the safe was ajar. At first he saw no one, but when Peter entered the room he heard a sound from the corner beyond the table, a sound halfway between a gasp and a groan, and there he found his employer, Jonathan K. McGuire, doubled up on the floor, bound and trussed like his valet and quite as helpless. It was evident that the long awaited terror had come to Black Rock.

But if he was dismayed and frightened it seemed that McGuire was uninjured and when he was released he was lifted to his feet and a chair, into which he sank speechless for a moment of rehabilitation. There was no need to question him as to what had happened in this room, for the evidences of Hawk's visit and its purpose were all too evident. Without a word to McGuire, Peter found the telephone in the hall, called for May's Landing, then turning the instrument over to Brierly, with instructions as to what he was to do, returned to McGuire's room and closed the door behind him.

"Well, sir," he said briefly. "I see he's come."

"My God, yes," gasped McGuire. "And you know what he came for—he got it, Nichols. He got it."

"That proves that he *had* lost the duplicate," said Peter quietly. "How did it all happen?"

The old man drew a trembling hand across his brow.

"He took me off my guard—all of us. I don't know. It only happened half an hour ago. Where's Stryker?"

"He was tied to a chair in the kitchen. We let him loose. He's outside somewhere."

"And Mrs. Bergen and Sarah?"

"I don't know, sir."

Peter went to the door and called Stryker and that bewildered person appeared at the foot of the steps with Mrs. Bergen and Sarah who had been locked in the cellar. Peter called them up and they all began screaming their tale at once. But at last Peter got at the facts. Hawk Kennedy had come suddenly into the kitchen where the two women were and, brandishing a revolver, commanding silence, threatening death if they made a sound. He had surprised the valet in the lower hall and had marched him back into the kitchen, where he had bound him to a chair with a clothes-line and then gagged him.

McGuire waved the trio out of the room when their story was told, and signaled to Peter to close the door again, when he took up his interrupted tale.

"I was at the window, looking out, Nichols. I didn't expect him for a couple of weeks anyway. I'd just about gotten my nerve back. But he got the drop on me, Nichols. How he ever got into the room without my hearin' him! I must have been in a trance. His shoes were off. The first thing I know is a voice close at my ear and a gun in my ribs. I turned quick—but my gun was in the table drawer. His face was close to mine and I knew he meant business. If I'd 'a' moved he'd 'a' killed me. So I put my hands up. There wasn't anything else to do. I thought I'd play for time but he caught my glance toward the door and only laughed.

"'There ain't anybody comin', Mike,' he says. 'It's just you an' me.' I asked him what he wanted and he grinned. 'You know,' he says. And with his left hand he brought out a rope he had stuffed in his pocket. 'I'll fix *you* first. Then we'll talk,' he says. He was cool like he always was. He caught a slip noose around my wrists before I knew it, twisted the rope around me and threw me over on the floor. I tell you that man is the devil himself."

"What then?"

"He made me give up the keys to the drawers in the safe—it was open just like it is now. I wouldn't speak at first but he kicked me and then put the gun at my head. I still hoped some one would come. I gave in at last. He found it. My God!" The old man aroused himself with an effort and rose to his feet. "But we've got to catch him—just you and I. He can't have gone far. We've got the right to shoot him now—to shoot on sight——"

"Yes—yes. I'm getting the Sheriff at May's Landing now——"

"The Sheriff!" The Irishman's small eyes stared and then became alive in sudden comprehension. "Not the Sheriff, Nichols. I won't have him."

"You've got to—at once." And then rapidly Peter gave an account of what had happened at the logging camp. But it seemed to have no effect upon McGuire, who listened with glassy eyes. He was obsessed with the other—the graver danger.

"We'll keep this thing quiet if you like—the real meaning of this visit, and we've got to pick up his trail. But we can't let those men at the camp have the run of the place. They'll be looting this house next." And then, as McGuire seemed to agree, Peter went to the door and found Brierly still on the 'phone. He was talking to the Sheriff and had told the whole story. The Sheriff had already heard something about the Black Rock camp trouble and would be ready to move in an hour.

"Tell him to move fast and to come to McGuire's first," said Peter. "And you'll be here to show him the way."

Brierly nodded and finished the message, while Peter returned to McGuire.

"What else did Kennedy say?" Peter asked him.

"He asked a lot of questions—about you and Beth Cameron—about the money—about what I'd promised you. He's the very devil, I tell you. He knows everything. He said he'd 'get' you and that he'd 'get' Beth Cameron."

Peter caught McGuire fiercely by the shoulder. "What did you say? Are you sure?"

With all of his other troubles Peter had forgotten Beth and now thought guiltily of the possible danger to which she might have been subjected.

How could Hawk have found out about Beth Cameron?

"What I told you," muttered McGuire wearily, "he said he'd 'get' her——"

Sick with anxiety, Peter flung away from his protesting employer and made for the door, rushing past the astonished Brierly in the hall, down the stairs and out at a run over the bridge and through the village to the Bergen house. The door was open and he rushed in, calling Beth's name. There was no response. Now desperate and fearing the worst, he ran from room to room, downstairs and up. There were signs of her—a towel on a chair, a broom leaning against a door upstairs, the neatly made beds, the orderly kitchen, giving evidence of the morning cleaning, but no supper cooking on the stove, the fire of which had burned to cinders. She had not been here for a long while—since early morning possibly. But where had she gone—where? Hawk Kennedy would hardly have dared to come here—to the village— hardly have succeeded in enticing her away from this house, surrounded by neighbors—still less have succeeded in carrying her off without their knowledge. He rushed out into the road and questioned. No one seemed to have seen her. The eagerness and suppressed anxiety of Peter's manner quickly drew a crowd which felt the contagion of his excitement. A man joined the group. Yes. He had seen Beth in the morning early. She was hurrying down the path which led into the pines. He had not seen her since.

Peter glanced at him just once more to be sure that he was speaking the truth and then, without a thought as to the impression he had created in the minds of the villagers, set off running through the path toward his cabin.

Fool that he had been! To leave Beth unguarded—unwarned even—with Hawk within a quarter of a mile of her. Why had he not seen the hand of fate in Beth's presence here at Black Rock near McGuire, the man who had wronged her father—the hand of fate, which with unerring definiteness was guiding the principals in this sordid tragedy together from the ends of the earth for a reckoning? And what was this reckoning to be? McGuire had already fallen a victim to the man's devilish skill and audacity. And Beth—— ? What match was she for a clever desperate rogue who balked at nothing? How had he learned of Beth's existence and how, knowing of it, had he managed to beguile her away from the village? Peter was beginning to believe with McGuire that Hawk Kennedy was indeed in league with the devil.

Peter was not now aware of any pain or even of bodily fatigue, for there was no room in his mind for any thought of self. Scarcely conscious of his new exertions, he ran across the log-jam below the pool and up the path to the Cabin. What he expected to find there he did not know, but it seemed clear that Beth had come this way in the morning and if not to the Cabin, where else? Hawk had been here when she had come into the woodland path. That was enough. As he reached the turn in the path, he saw that the door of the Cabin was open and when he rushed in, prepared for anything, he saw that the room was unoccupied. He stood aghast for a moment, trying to adjust his mind to take in logically the evidence he found there—the overturned chair, the blankets dragging on the floor by the bed, the broken water pitcher, the opened bureau drawers, the torn bits of linen—parts of his own handkerchiefs—upon the floor—all visible signs' of a commotion, perhaps of a struggle, that had taken place. And then under the table he espied a square of heliotrope paper. He picked it up quickly and took it to the light of the window. It was the envelope of the letter he had received from Anastasie Galitzin. And what was this——? A scrawl in Beth's hand, "You left *this* last night. You'd better go back to Anastasie."

Bewildered for a moment, Peter stared at the forceful characters of the handwriting, written hurriedly in a scrawl of lead pencil, and then the probable sequence of events came to him with a rush. She had opened the note of Anastasie Galitzin and read it. What had it said? He had forgotten details. But there were phrases that might have been misconstrued. And Beth———. He could see her now coming up the path, her head high, seeking explanations—and meeting Hawk!

But where was the letter itself? He searched for it without success. Hawk! The answer to all of his questions was in the personality of the man as Peter knew him. The bits of torn linen and Beth's own handkerchief, which he found in the corner of the bed against the wall, crumpled into a ball and still moist with her tears, were mute but eloquent evidences of her suffering and torture in the presence of this man who had not been too delicate in the means by which he had accomplished her subjugation.

Peter raged up and down the floor of the Cabin like a caged animal. What must he do—which way turn? That Hawk had gagged and bound her was obvious. But what then? He rushed outside and examined the shrubbery around the Cabin. There was nothing to indicate the direction in which he had taken her—and the forest at his very elbow stretched for miles in all directions, a hiding place that had served other guilty ones before Hawk— the New Jersey pines that he had learned to love, now wrapped in a conspiracy of silence. It would be dusk very soon. A search of the pine barrens at night would be hopeless. Besides, Hawk had had the whole of the morning and most of the afternoon in which to carry out his purpose.... What was that purpose? Where had he taken Beth? Where had he left her when he had returned to Black Rock House to rob McGuire? Or had he...? Impossible! Even Hawk wouldn't have dared.... Peter clenched his fists in agony and rage at the terrible thoughts that came swarming into his brain, driving out all reason.

His Highness had suffered greatly the last few years of his life, the physical pain of wounds received in battle, the mental pain of falling hopes, of fallen pride, of disillusionment, but he could not remember any pain that had seemed to matter like the anguish of the present moment. The other sufferings were those of the Grand Duke Peter Nicholaevitch, material sufferings born of his high estate. But this present suffering was primitive. It wrenched at the very fibers of the heart, for the love that he had found was a finer thing than had ever happened in his life, a love which asked nothing and only craved the joy of giving. And this woman—this mate that he had chosen out of all the women that he had known in the world...!

Hawk Kennedy would have fared badly if Peter could have had him within arm's reach at that moment. But after a time, as Peter went into the Cabin, he grew calmer, and pacing the floor for a while, began to think more lucidly. Less than an hour ago Hawk Kennedy had been at Black Rock House giving Jonathan McGuire and Stryker their unpleasant half-hour. He wouldn't have dared to return and accomplish what he had done after a deed so terrible as that which had entered Peter's thoughts. He was still a human being and Beth.... He couldn't have killed Beth out of hand. The thought was monstrous—even of Hawk.

He had taken her somewhere—to one of his hiding-places in the woods, and proposed keeping her, the legal heir of Ben Cameron, for ransom, as a part of his plot to win his share of the McGuire fortune. He had stolen the telltale agreement too and now held all the cards—all of them.

Peter paused standing by the window seat, looking out at the leaves falling in the rising wind, his mind already resolved on a plan. He was about to turn toward the telephone, when he noted a commotion in the bushes opposite his window. A flash of fire almost at the same moment, a crash of broken glass, and the hair on his head twitched violently.

Instinctively Peter dropped to the floor.

Close shooting! His scalp stung uncomfortably—but aside from that he knew that he was not hurt. A fraction of an inch lower——

Hawk——! His first impulse had been to rush to the door—but the events of the day had taught him caution and so he crouched, drawing his revolver. Too much depended upon his existence at the present moment to take a chance in the open with a hidden enemy—especially if that enemy were Hawk Kennedy. He listened intently. No sound. Then the breaking of a twig and the sibilance of whispering voices—two of them—perhaps more. And still Peter did not move. His quick thinking had done him a service. It was clear that the men outside had decided that the shot had taken effect.

And now, instead of creeping to the doorway, Peter settled back upon the floor again, prostrate, but in such a position that his eyes and his revolver commanded the entrance to the Cabin. He waited. It was a nerve-racking business but the thought of all that depended upon his safety steadied him into a preternatural calm like that which falls at the presence of death. Death was imminent here for some one. It lurked just outside. It lurked in the finger that Peter held against the trigger. And Peter meant that the adventure should end at the doorway.

Presently he heard a gentle shuffling of feet outside and the whisper again, this time quite distinctly, "You got him, I reckon."

Whose voice was that? Not Hawk Kennedy's ... Peter lowered his head to his arm and closed his eyes, watching the door-jamb through his eyelashes, his revolver hidden but its muzzle in line. A bulky shadow on the step, a foot and then a head cautiously protruded—that of Shad Wells, followed immediately by another, swathed in a bandage which only partially concealed the dark eyes and beard of Yakimov the Russian. It took considerable exercise of will on Peter's part to remain quiescent with the stare of those four eyes upon him, especially when he noted the weapon in the fingers of the Russian. But he waited until the two men got into the room.

"There he is. You got him, Yakimov," said Shad with a laugh.

"Perhaps——" Peter heard, "but I'll make sure of it——"

Yakimov's pistol rose slowly, halfway to the level of his eyes. But it was never fired, for Peter's revolver flashed fire, twice—three times, and Yakimov with a sudden wide stare at vacancy pitched forward and crashed down. The surprise was complete, for a fourth shot went into the right arm of Shad Wells, which ruined his shot and sent his weapon clattering to the floor.

Peter had taken Shad's measure once before and the memory of the blow from the axhandle earlier in the day did nothing to soften Peter's intent. The quick command as he scrambled to his feet and the sight of the imminent weapon caused Shad suddenly to forget everything but the desire, whatever else happened, not to die as Yakimov had done. And so he put his hands up—staggering back against the wall. Peter, with his weapon still covering Shad, put his fingers over Yakimov's heart. The man was dead. Then he rose soberly and faced Shad.

"I ought to kill you like the dog that you are," he said tensely, "but I want to question you first. Stand over by the bed."

Shad obeyed and Peter, watching him closely, picked up his weapon and Yakimov's and examined them carefully, putting one in his pocket and laying the other beside him on the mantel. But all the fight was out of Shad, who stood stupidly while Peter bound his wrists behind him. The man was badly hurt, but it was no time for Peter to be playing the good Samaritan.

"So much for keeping bad company," said Peter coolly. "You'll find more of the same sort in the lock-up at May's Landing."

"You daresn't send me there," muttered Shad, with a feeble attempt at bravado.

"Won't I? You'll see—for attempted murder. The Sheriff is on his way here now. Have you anything to say?"

Shad was silent, eying the dead man.

"Oh, very well," said Peter. He closed and locked the door and, keeping the man covered with his revolver, moved to the telephone and got McGuire at Black Rock House, telling him in a few phrases what had happened.

"Yes, Yakimov the Russian—I shot him.... Yes.... I killed him. It was to save my own life.... Shad Wells.... A prisoner. Send Brierly with a car down here at once. Hawk has been here too and has met Beth Cameron ... God knows. He has taken her away with him somewhere—abducted her.... Yes ... Yes ... I've got to find her. Yes, *Beth*—can't you understand?... She came here to bring me a letter ... I found it. Hawk was here early this morning.... I know it. He bound her with some of my handkerchiefs ... No, there's no doubt of it—none at all.... I can't stand here talking. Send Brierly at once. Understand?"

And Peter hung up the receiver and turned toward Shad, who was leaning forward toward him, his face pale, his mouth agape at what he had heard. But Peter, unaware of the sudden transformation in his prisoner, only glanced at him and bending over began a search of the pockets of the dead man, when Shad's voice cut the silence——

"You—you say——," he stammered chokingly, "you say B-Beth has been abducted, Mister—Beth Cameron?"

Peter straightened, his eyes searching the lumberman's face.

"Yes. To-day—this morning," he answered crisply. "What of it? Do you know anything——?"

"Hawk Kennedy took her?" the man faltered. "Are you sure?"

Peter sprang up, his eyes blazing with eagerness.

"What do you know of Hawk Kennedy?" he cried. And then, as Shad seemed suddenly to have been stricken dumb, Peter seized him by the shoulder and shook him. "Speak! Do you know Hawk Kennedy?"

"Yes," said Shad in a bewildered way. "I do—but Beth——"

"He's taken her away—don't you understand?"

"W-Why?"

"God knows," said Peter wildly. "It's part of a plot—against McGuire—to get money. Do you know where he is? Do you know where he's gone with her? Speak, man! Or must I——?"

"I know him. I've seen him——," muttered Shad with a hang-dog air.

"To-day?"

"No."

Peter gasped in disappointment, but still questioned quickly.

"Where did you see him?"

"Down near the camp. He came back again yesterday. He'd been away——"

"Yes, yes, I know. What did he say?"

"Oh, he was very peart—swaggered around like he owned the place and talked about a lot of money he was goin' to have. An' how he was——"

"Do you know where he took Beth Cameron?" broke in Peter again.

"No. I don't—My God—*him!*"

"Yes, *him*. You know what it means. He'd kill her if he dared."

"Would he? My God! Mister. You can't let——"

"No. No." And then, sharply, "Speak up, Wells, and I'll set you free. Do you know where he could have taken her?"

"I'm not sure, but maybe——"

"Where——?"

"He stayed down at the Forks——"

"Yes. But he wouldn't have dared to take her there——"

"No. That's so. Maybe——"

"Where?"

"Some other place——"

"Of course. Was there any other place that he knew about?"

"Yes, there was. But when he first came he rode down on a horse from Hammonton."

"Yes, yes. Go on. And later——"

"He used to come around the camp for food. It was when you first came on the job. But he bought it and paid for it."

"I don't care about that. Where was he hiding?"

"Back in the woods. He used to sleep in the old tool house down by the cedar swamp."

Peter was now on edge with excitement.

"Do you think he'd be likely to take Beth there?"

"How should I know? Maybe he took her to Hammonton or Egg Harbor."

"No. He wouldn't have had time. Where's this tool house?"

"About half a mile from the mills."

"Could you show me the way?"

"I reckon I could——," Shad Wells sank into a chair and bent his head. "My God! Mister. If I'd only 'a' known! If you'd only let me help you—I can't stand thinkin' of anythin' happenin' to Beth—you an' me—we ain't got along, an' maybe you've got the upper hand of me, but——"

"We've got to forget that now," put in Peter quickly, and taking out his hasp knife he cut the cords that bound Shad's wrists. "Just to show you that I mean what I say." And then, soberly, "You know these woods. Help me to find Beth Cameron and I'll make no charge against you. Is that a bargain?"

"Yes, Mister."

Peter glanced at his face and at the blood dripping from his finger ends. The man was suffering much pain but he hadn't whimpered.

"All right. Take off your coat and I'll tie your arm up first."

Silently Shad rose and obeyed while Peter got water and washed the wound, a clean one right through the muscles of the forearm. But no bones were broken and Peter bandaged it skillfully. Shad clenched his jaws during the washing of the wound but he said nothing more. Peter knew that the man still hated him but he knew also that Shad was now powerless to do him any injury, and that there was a tie to bind them now into this strange alliance. As Peter finished the bandaging and was improvising a sling for the wounded arm, Shad crumpled side-long upon the edge of the bed, his face ghastly, and would have fallen to the floor if Peter hadn't held him upright, and half carried him to the armchair. Then Peter unlocked a cupboard and brought forth whisky, giving Shad half a tumblerful and in a moment the man began to revive. So Peter poured another glass and slowly Shad pulled himself together.

"Perhaps you're not up to it——," Peter began.

But Shad wagged his head with some determination.

"Yes, I—I'm up to it all right. I've got to go, Mister. We'll find her if she's in these woods——"

"Bully for you. Feeling better now?"

Shad nodded and then raised his head, staring with a frown out of the window by the piano. Peter had been so absorbed in his task of setting the man to rights that he had not noticed the dull glow that had risen in the southern sky. And following Shad's glance he turned his head and looked out of the window. At first he thought it might be the afterglow of the sunset until a word from Shad aroused him to the real significance of the light.

"Fire!" gasped the lumberman.

"Fire!" echoed Peter, aghast.

"They've set the woods afire, Mister," muttered Shad helplessly.

At the same moment the telephone from the house began jangling furiously. It was McGuire, who had made the same discovery.

"Yes," replied Peter to the hysterical questions. "It's the lumber camp. They've broken loose and set the woods afire. You've got to get all the men you can together and rush them down there. Where's Brierly? On the way? Oh, all right. Good. He'll take me down and I'll send him back.... Yes. I've got a clew to Hawk ... I don't know, but I'm going to try it. I'm taking Shad Wells with me ... The old tool house by the cedar swamp. Brierly will know. Send the men on in relays when they come—with shovels and sacks.... What did you say?... What?... Oh, 'D——n the woods.'... All right. I'll get the paper if I can ... Yes. It's my affair as much as yours now.... Yes.... Good-by."

Peter hung up the receiver and turned to Shad, who had risen, his arm in the sling, just as Brierly came running up the path to the door.

CHAPTER XXI
THE INFERNO

The way through the woods was long, but Beth stumbled on, urged by the rough tone and strong hand of her captor. She knew the woods well, better than Hawk, but she had never ventured so far into the forest as he led her. She felt very certain that he knew even less than she of the way he was taking, and that his object in avoiding the roads and paths which led to the southward was to keep her hidden from the eyes of any persons that might be met on the paths between Black Rock and the lumber camp. But after a while she began to think that he knew with more or less definiteness the general direction in which they were moving, for he stopped from time to time to look at the sun and get his bearings. And then with a gruff word he would move on again, always to the south and east, and she knew that he had already decided upon their destination. With her hands still bound behind her, progress through the underbrush was difficult, for the branches stung her like whip-lashes, and thorn-bushes caught at her arms and tore her flimsy frock to shreds. The gag in her mouth made breathing painful, but Hawk seemed to be unaware of her sufferings or purposely oblivious of them, for he hardly glanced at her and said no word except to urge her on to greater exertion.

When they approached the road which he wanted to cross, he warned her with an oath to remain where he left her and went forward to investigate, after which he returned and hurried her across into the thicket upon the other side. And it was not until they were securely hidden again far from the sight of any possible passers-by that he untied the bonds at her wrists and took the gag from her mouth. But she knew more than ever that she was completely in his power.

He was sinister. He typified terror, physical and mental—and behind the threat of his very presence lay the gruesome vision of sand and sun and the bearded man lying with the knife in his back. She tried to summon her native courage to combat her fears, to believe that the situation in which she found herself was not so evil as she imagined it—and that soon Hawk Kennedy would have a change of heart and give her a chance to speak in her own behalf. But he silenced her gruffly whenever she addressed him and she gave up at last, in fear of bringing his wrath upon her. She could see that he was deeply intent upon his object to get her away from Black Rock where none could find her. And what then?

In a wild impulse—a moment of desperation, she broke away from him and ran, but he caught her easily, for by this time she was very tired. Again, she thought of a struggle with him hand to hand, but he read her mind and drew a pistol, pushing her on ahead of him as before, threatening bodily injury. By this time she had learned to believe him capable of any cruelty. But she thanked God that the dangers that threatened were only those which could come from a brutal enemy and in his very brutality she even found refuge from the other and more terrible alternative of his amiability. As Hawk had said, he wasn't "on that lay this trip."

But what his ultimate purpose was she had no means of determining. She knew that he was totally without scruple and had thought in her first moments of terror that he meant to take her far back into the woods—and there kill her as he had done her father, thus again destroying all claim. But as the moments passed and she saw that he had some definite objective, the feeble remnants of her courage gathered strength. Her attempt to escape had failed, of course, but his tolerance gave her a hope that he did not dare to do the dreadful violence of which she had thought.

For hours—it seemed—they went through underbrush and swamp-land, stopping from time to time at Hawk's command while he listened and got their bearings. Beth had never been in this part of the woods, but she had an idea, from the crossing of the road and the character of the trees, that they were now somewhere in the Lower Reserve and not very far from the lumber camp. It was there that Peter Nichols was. Her heart leaped at the thought of his nearness. All memory of the heliotrope envelope and of its contents seemed to have been wiped from her consciousness by the rough usage of this enemy to them both. It seemed to matter very little now who this woman was that Peter had known. She belonged to a mysterious and unhappy past—for he had hinted at that—which had nothing to do with the revelation that Beth had read in his eyes as to the meaning of the wonderful present for them both. She knew now that he could have explained, if she had given him the chance. Instead of which she had rushed heedlessly to misfortune, the victim of a childish pride, plunging them both into this disaster. That pride was a pitiful thing now, like her disordered hair and her bedraggled frock, which flapped its ribbons, soaked and muddy, about her knees.

But as long as she was still alive and in no immediate danger, she tried to hope for some incident which would send Peter back to Black Rock earlier than Hawk had expected, where, at the Cabin, he would guess the truth as to her meeting with Hawk and what had followed. But how could he guess all that? The difficulty dismayed her, He would hunt for her of course as soon as he learned of her disappearance, but clever as he was there seemed no way in which he could solve the mystery of her flight, still less, having guessed Hawk Kennedy's purpose, follow any trail through the wilderness by which her captor had led her.

Even in the apparent hopelessness of her situation, she had not reached the point of actual despair. Youth and her customary belief in all that was good in the world sustained her. Something would happen—something *must* happen.... As she trudged along, she prayed with her whole heart, like David, to be delivered from the hand of the oppressor.

That prayer comforted her and gave her strength and so when they came out at the edge of the swamp some moments later she obeyed his instructions more hopefully. There was a path along the edge of the water which presently led into the heart of the woods again, and there almost before she was aware of it she found herself facing a small wooden house or shanty which seemed in a fairly good state of preservation.

Silently, Hawk Kennedy unfastened the hasp which held the door, and gruffly ordered her to go inside. Wondering, she obeyed him. But her captor now acted with a celerity which while it gave her new fears, set other fears at rest, for he took the handkerchiefs from his pockets and gagged and bound her arms and wrists again, pushing her down on a pile of sacking which had served some one for a bed, tying her feet and knees with ropes that were there so that she could neither move nor make a sound.

There for a moment he stood, staring down at her with a grim kind of humor, born of his successful flight.

"Some kid, by G——! I'm kinder sorry—d—— if I ain't. But ye hadn't any business bein' who ye are. I believe I'd rather kill ye outright than hurt ye any more—that I would. Maybe I won't have to do either. Understand? But I got somethin' to do first. It ain't any child's play an' I ain't got much time to spare. Be a good kid an' lie quiet an' go to sleep and I'll be back after a while an' set ye free. Understand?"

Beth nodded helplessly, for it was the only thing that she could do and with relief watched his evil shape darken the doorway out of which he went, carefully closing the door and fastening the hasp on the outside. Then she heard the crunch of his footsteps in the dry leaves behind the Cabin. They moved rapidly and in a few moments she heard them no more.

Lying on her side, her head pillowed on the bagging, it did not seem at first as though she were uncomfortable, and her eyes, wide open, peered around her prison. There was a small window unglazed and by the light which came from it she could see some axhandles piled in one corner of the hut, several cross-cut saws on a box at one side, a few picks and a shovel or two. It must be a tool house used for the storage of extra implements and she remembered dimly that Shad had once spoken of the cutting that had been begun down by the swamp and abandoned for a better location. This then was where Hawk Kennedy had taken her and she knew that it was a spot little visited nowadays except by hunters, and at some distance from the scene of present logging operations, toward the spur of the railroad. It was here perhaps that Hawk Kennedy had hidden while making his earlier investigations of Black Rock while he ripened his plot against Mr. McGuire. There were several empty bottles upon the floor, a moldy crust of bread, and a broken water-pitcher which confirmed the surmise.

She realized that Hawk had planned well. It seemed hardly possible to hope for a chance passer-by in this deserted spot. And even if she heard the sound of guns or even heard footsteps in the leaves, what chance had she of making known her whereabouts? But she strained her ears, listening, only to hear the twittering of the birds, the chattering of squirrels and the moaning of the wind in the tree tops. How near was freedom and yet how difficult of attainment! She wriggled gently in her bonds but each motion seemed to make them tighter, until they began to cut more and more cruelly into her tender flesh. She tried by twisting her hands and bending her body to touch the knots at her knees but her elbows were fastened securely and she couldn't reach them. And at last she gave up the attempt, half stifled from her exertions and suffering acutely. Then she lay quiet, sobbing gently to herself, trying to find a comfortable posture, and wondering what was to be the end of it all.

Hours passed in which the scampering of the four-footed things grew less and less and the birds ceased their chirping. Only the moaning of the wind continued, high in the tree tops. Once or twice she thought she plainly heard footsteps near by and renewed her efforts to free herself, but desisted again when she learned that it was only the sound of the flying leaves dancing against the outside walls of her prison.

She thought of all the things that had happened in her brief and uneventful life, but most she thought of Peter Nichols, and all that his visit to Black Rock had meant to her. And even in her physical discomfort and mental anguish found herself hoping against hope that something would yet happen to balk the sinister plans of Hawk Kennedy, whatever they were. She could not believe that happiness such as hers had been could come to such a dreadful end so soon. But what was Hawk Kennedy's mission now? Where had he gone unless to Black Rock again? And what would he be doing there? Was revenge his motive now, stronger since her revelation of her parentage? And was it Peter that he was going to...? Her cry was muffled in the bandage. He had gone back to Black Rock to lie in wait for Peter—to kill him perhaps. Sobbing anew she struggled again with her bonds, until at last she lay back relaxed and exhausted, and prayed with all her might to the God that had always been her guide.

And after a while she grew calm again, refreshed and strengthened by her faith. No harm would befall Peter. No further harm would come to her. Evil such as Hawk's was powerless against her prayers. Already he had done her a great injury. The God of her faith would keep her scatheless until Peter, the man she loved, came to save her. She was as sure of this now as though she could see him coming, vengeance in his hand, with long strides through the forest to her hiding-place. And so, after a while, exhausted from her efforts, she fell into a doze.

When she awoke from troubled dreams it was with a sense of suffocation. She had stirred in her sleep and the thongs had cut more deeply into the flesh at her knees, causing her pain. Below the knees she was numb from the constant pressure, but she moved her toes up and down and her limbs tingled painfully as the constricted blood flowed into her extremities. How long she had lain there she did not know, but the interior of the shed seemed to have grown quite dark, as though a storm were rising outside. The wind was still blowing, and above the moaning of the pines she could hear the continuous rustle of the leaves and the creaking of moving branches. She managed with an effort to turn her head toward the window, where through the dark leaves of the overshadowing trees she could catch glimpses of the sky, which seemed to have turned to a pinkish purple, like the afterglow of a sunset. Was it possible that she could have slept so long? In the turning of her head it seemed that the bandage over her mouth had become loosened and as she tried the experiment again, the handkerchief slipped down around her neck. In a moment she had gotten rid of the wad of linen in her mouth. At least she could breathe freely now and moisten her parching lips. This boon seemed almost in answer to her prayers. And if one bandage could come loose by God's help, why not another?

And so cheerfully and with a persistence which took no thought of the pain she was inflicting upon herself, she began working her hands to and fro behind her until she fancied that the pressure on her wrists was not so great as before. With an effort she managed to wriggle over against the wall and so to straighten into a sitting posture.

It was then that she suddenly raised her head and sniffed at the air from the small window above her through which a slender wisp of smoke came curling. Smoke! The smell of burning brush, familiar to her, and yet back here in the woods, unless from a well tended camp-fire, fraught with perilous meaning. She glanced out of the small opening again. The purple had grown redder, a dull crimson shot with streaks of blue—smoke everywhere, endless streamers and tortuous billows sweeping down on the wings of the wind.

Fire in the woods! She knew the meaning of that. And the reddish purple was not the sunset but the glow of mighty flames near by, a "crown" fire in the pines! From the volume of smoke, increasing with every moment, it seemed that the old tool house in which she was imprisoned must be directly in the path of the flames. Now thoroughly aware of her possible fate if she could not release herself she strained her ears, listening, and now heard distinctly above the sounds nearer at hand a distant crackling roar and the thud of heavy branches falling. The interior of the cabin had now grown even dimmer—to a dark redness—and the smoke came billowing in at the window almost stifling her with its acrid fumes. Outside the window, when she struggled for freedom, she caught a glimpse of sparks, flying like meteors past the dim rectangle of her vision, small ones, larger ones, and then flaming brands which must set fire to whatsoever they touched.

She was half mad now with terror. She tried to think calmly, because she knew that unless a miracle happened she would die alone here—the most horrible of all deaths. And then her eye caught the gleam of something upon the tool chest in the shadows beyond—the teeth of the cross-cut saw!

If she could reach it! She fell over purposely on the sacking and with great difficulty wriggled slowly toward it, inch by inch. Could she reach it with her wrists? With an effort she squirmed to the chest and straightened, her back against it, as she had done against the wall, and then turning, in spite of the increased pressure of her thongs, managed in some way to get to her knees, feeling for the teeth of the saw with her fingers behind her. It was not very sharp, but if she could direct it between her wrists it would do.

In her new thrill of hope, she was hardly conscious of the suffocating smoke which now filled the cabin, stinging her eyes so that she could hardly see, or of the heat which with her exertions had sent the perspiration streaming down her face. For now, balancing herself with great care, she moved her tortured arms, half numb with pain, up and down against the rusty edges. A sharp pain and she bit her lips,—readjusting herself to her task. But she felt the saw cutting into the rope—one strand, another, and in a moment her hands were released.

In her joy of the achievement, she toppled over on the floor, but managed to release her elbows. Now, panting with her exertions and moving her arms quickly to restore the circulation, she felt for the knots at her knees and ankles and in a moment her limbs were free. But she had not reckoned with the effects of their long period of inactivity, for when she tried to get to her feet she found that her limbs were powerless. But she moved her knees up and down, suffering keenly as the blood took up its course, and after a time managed to scramble to her feet, and stagger to the opening in the wall.

It seemed that all the forest was now a mass of flaming brands and that the roar of the flames was at her very ears. It was stiflingly hot too and in one corner of the cabin there was a tiny bright spot and a curl of smoke. Had her liberty come too late? She was not even free yet, for the hole in the wall of the building was no larger than a single pane of glass and the door of the shanty was fastened by the hasp on the outside.

There was no time now to hesitate unless she wished to be burned alive. With an effort she threw herself against the door—again and again, but it would not yield. Despairing and blinded by smoke, she staggered to the box hunting an ax, when her fingers met the handle of the friendly saw. It was heavy but she knew how to use it, and set it at the hole in the wall, drawing it back and forth. The wood was dead and she felt it yield to the strong teeth of the tool, so that she struggled on, the width of the board; then cut again, at the upper edge of the aperture, and in a moment the board fell away.

She was not a moment too soon, for as she crawled through the opening and fell exhausted on the outside, one end of the building suddenly caught fire, blazing fiercely. The sparks were all around her and her skirt caught fire in the flaming leaves into which she had fallen, but she put it out with her blistered hands and rose to her feet. A figure was coming toward her, bent, its hand before its eyes. She could not make out who it was, but as she turned to run Hawk Kennedy espied her.

"Ho there, kid! Got loose, hey? Just in time. Did ye think I was goin' to let ye be burned to death?"

———————————

With Brierly leading them to the machine and listening to Peter's story as they went, Peter made his way across the foot of the lawn to the road where the machine was waiting for them. As they climbed into it, the glow to the south had turned a lurid red, staining the dusky sky to the zenith. Brierly drove and for precaution's sake Peter sat in the tonneau with Shad. But the lumberman, if he had ever been considered formidable even in his own estimation, showed no evidence of any self-confidence. Peter had given him signs of mettle which were not to be denied and like all bullies Shad knew that he was beaten. The one vestige of his decency,—his honorable affection for Beth, which had blinded him to reason and all sense of duty, was now dedicated to the task of saving her. And though the dull hatred of Peter still burned in his breast, the instinct of self-preservation, and the chance of retrieving himself at the last, made it necessary for him to put his pride in his pocket and accept the inevitable.

"Ye'll keep yer word, Mister?" he inquired of Peter, after a moment. "I didn't have nothin' to do with settin' them woods afire. Ye'll get me out o' this scrape?"

"Yes," said Peter shortly. "I will."

But he watched him nevertheless.

The ex-soldier drove the car at a furious pace over the rough road, rejoicing in the open cut-out and the rush of the wind past his ears. He had been, for a time, a chauffeur of a staff car on the other side, and the present conditions were full of promise of the kind of excitement that appealed to his youthful spirit. Shad shouted instructions over his shoulder but Brierly only nodded and sent the car on over the corduroy to which they had come, with the throttle wide. Night had nearly fallen but the road was a crimson track picked out with long pencilings of shadow. The wind was still tossing the tree tops and leaves and twigs cut sharply across their faces. There was no mistaking the danger to the whole of the Lower Reserve unless the wind fell—a "crown" fire after two weeks of drought was not a subject for jest.

But Peter was not thinking of the damage to McGuire's property. He roared questions eagerly at Wells as to the location of the cabin with reference to the probable course of the flames. The man only shook his head dubiously, but it was plain that he was considering that danger. As they neared the fire they could see the flames clearly now, beyond the pines just before them, which were etched in deeply bitten lines, every quivering frond in silhouette against the glare.

As the car neared the "Forks," Shad directed Brierly to take the turn to the left—away from the main road to camp, and they swung into a sandy road, the wind at their backs, their way for a time almost parallel to the course of the flames. They passed the small settlement of the "Forks," the few denizens of which were standing beside the road, their few household goods packed in barrows and carts, undecided whether or not the red terror would come their way. The flames were clearly visible now, leaping skyward like devils freed from Hell, and so hot was the fire and so high the wind that whole branches were carried high into the air and flaming fell beyond into the cool dark to kindle new destruction. Anything that lay to leeward of the holocaust was doomed. Peter furiously questioned Wells again, but he only shook his head while he anxiously watched the flames as the road converged toward them. But as the road swung to the left Shad shouted and held up his hand and Brierly brought the car to a stop.

"This is the nearest point, I guess, Mister. From here on to Cranberry town the road runs to the left of Cedar Swamp."

"Where's the cabin?" queried Peter anxiously.

"In yonder, not far from the edge of the swamp," Shad replied with a frown. "Looks like the fire's pretty near there."

"Come on, then," said Peter quickly. "Brierly, you go back to Black Rock and bring the men here. Follow in. We'll be on the lookout for you."

And leaving Brierly to turn the car, he started off with Shad Wells into the underbrush. His heart sank as he saw how furiously the fire was raging and how near it seemed to be. But Shad needed no urging now and led the way with a long stride, Peter following closely. The woods were not so heavy here and the forest was now as bright as at midday, and so they made rapid progress, coming out at the end of some minutes at the edge of the swamp, whose burnished pools sullenly reflected the fiery heavens. There they found a path and proceeded more quickly. To Peter's anxious questions Shad shook his head and only peered before him, forgetting his own suffering in the dreadful danger to which the girl they sought might be subjected. A terrible thought had come into Peter's mind in the last few moments—that it was Hawk Kennedy who had set fire to the woods after imprisoning Beth in a cabin in the path of the flames. This was his vengeance, terrible in its simplicity—for a lighted match in the dry leaves would do the trick, and incendiarism in the woods was difficult to trace. A vengeance fatal in its effectiveness, for such a fire would tell no tales. Peter found himself hoping that it was not to the old tool cabin that Beth had been taken—that she was even far away from this inferno that lay before him. The glare was already hot on his face and stray breezes which blew toward him from time to time showed that the wind might be veering to the eastward, in which case all the woods which they now traversed would soon be afire.

But to the credit of Shad Wells it may be said that he did not hesitate, for when he reached a point in the path where it turned closely along the edge of the swamp, he plunged boldly into the woods, directly toward the flames, and Peter, even more eager than he, ran ahead, peering to right and left for signs of the cabin which now could not be far away. The roar and the crackling were now ominously near and the flames seemed to be all about them, while the tree tops seemed to be filled with flaming brands. Sparks and live cinders fell upon them and the hot breath of the wind blistered them with its heat.

Suddenly the panting Shad grasped Peter sharply by the arm with his uninjured hand.

"The cabin! My God! It's burning now——Quick, Mister—or——"

Peter sprang forward through the flaming leaves. He seemed to be in the very midst of the flames. Blinded and suffocated by the smoke, Peter plunged forward and reached the cabin. One end and side of it was blazing furiously but he dashed around the lower end of it, seeking the door. It was open and already aflame. The hut was empty. He ran out again, blinded by the smoke and the glare. Was it a fool's errand? And had he and Shad only entrapped themselves to no good end? To the right of him the fire roared and with his back to the glare his eyes eagerly sought the shadows down the wind. Vague shapes of gnarled branches and pallid tree trunks, spectral bushes quivering before the advancing demon, some of them already alight. Safety lay only in this one direction—for Beth, if she had been there, for Shad——Peter suddenly remembered the lumberman and turned to his left to look, when suddenly he espied a figure moving away from him and ran after it, calling. He realized immediately that his hoarse cry was lost in the inferno of the flames, but he ran more rapidly, beating out the embers which had ignited the sleeve of his shirt.

He saw the figure clearly now, but it was not Shad—for Shad had been in his shirt sleeves. This figure wore a coat and stumbled away half bent, one arm over its head, pushing something—some one ahead of it. Peter drew his revolver, leaping the burning leaves and calling aloud.

He saw the figures ahead of him halt and turn as they heard his voice and the glare behind him shone full upon them, the face of the man agape with inflamed surprise—Hawk Kennedy's, and the other, wide-eyed as at the sight of an apparition—Beth's.

Only thirty paces separated them when Hawk Kennedy fired. Peter heard Beth's scream and saw her strike at the man's arm, but furiously he swung her in front of him and fired again. But her struggles and the uncertain light sent the bullet wide. Peter did not dare to shoot for the man was using her as a shield, but he did not hesitate and ran in, trusting to luck and Beth's struggles. One bullet struck him somewhere as Beth seemed to stumble and crumple to the ground, but he went on unspent and catapulted into his man with a rush that sent them both sprawling into the smoldering foliage. Blinded by the smoke, but mad with fury, Peter struck and clutched, and Hawk's last shot went upward for Peter wrenched his wrist and then struck him full on the head with his own weapon.

He felt the man relax and slip down into the dust and smoke, where he lay motionless.

Peter drew himself up to arm's length, wondering at the feebleness of his muscles and the trouble with his breathing.

"Beth!" he gasped, frantically, searching the smoking ground for her.

"Peter—thank God!" Her voice was just at his ear and an arm went around his neck.

"Beth! Beth! You've got to get out of this."

"Come, Peter—there's time——"

Just then a branch crashed down just beside them, showering them with sparks.

"Come, Peter—come!" she cried.

He struggled up with an effort, one hand clutching at his breast.

"Go, Beth!" he gasped. "For God's sake, go!"

Beth stared at him for one short terrible moment as she realized what had happened to him.

"Peter! You—you're——"

"I—I think I'm hurt—a little—it isn't much."

He swayed but she caught him and put an arm around one shoulder, clutching it with the other hand.

"Lean on me," she muttered. "I'm strong enough——"

"No—go, Beth——"

But she put her strength under him and began walking while he staggered on beside her. Sparks and fiery brands rained down upon them, blistering and burning, the hot breath of the furnace drove their breath poisoned back into their lungs and scorched their bodies, but still they remained upright—and by a miracle still moved on.

"To the left," Peter heard dimly, "the swamp is close by."

He obeyed her, more dead than alive, and by sheer effort of will kept his feet moving, paced to hers. He seemed to be walking as though in a red fever, on leaden feet, carrying a body that had no weight or substance.

But after a while his feet too seemed to grow lighter and he felt himself falling through space. But her arms were still about him.

"Peter," he heard her voice in agony, "only a few yards further——"

With a last remaining effort he struggled and then his feet stumbling, toppled forward and sank into something soft, something deliciously cool and soothing. He felt a hand tugging at him, but he had no pain now, no weakness—only the perfect happiness of a body that, seeking rest, has found it.

After a while he revived at the sound of a voice at his ear. Water was splashing over his face and he struggled up.

"No—keep down," he heard Beth's voice saying. "We're safe, Peter—the wind is changing——"

"And you, Beth——?"

"All right, dear. A little patience——"

The voice trembled, but there was a world of faith in it. After all that had happened, it was impossible that further disaster should follow now.

"Y-you're all right?" he gasped weakly.

"Yes. Yes. Lie still for a while."

And so they half lay, half crouched in the mud and water, while the inferno swept over them, passing to the south. His head was on her breast and against his ear he could feel her heart beating bravely, a message of strength and cheer. From time to time her wet fingers brushed his hair with water and then, as he seemed to be sinking into a dream again, he felt lips light as thistle-down upon his brows.

Death such as this, he thought, was very pleasant.

And then later he was aroused by a shrill clear call.... Then saw lights flashing.... Heard men's voices.... Felt himself carried in strong arms ... but all the while there were soft fingers in his own.

CHAPTER XXII
RETRIBUTION

When they lifted him into the automobile and Beth got in beside him, his fingers moved in her own.

"Beth," she heard him whisper.

"Peter—I'm here."

"Thank God. And—and Shad——? He—he was with me——"

"He's asking for Shad," she repeated to Brierly, unaware that her cousin, like his Biblical namesake, had come scatheless through the fiery furnace. But some one heard the question and replied:

"Shad's here, Miss. He's all right——"

"Oh," gasped Peter. "And there's something else——"

"No, no—we must go. Your wound——"

But he insisted. "I—I'm all—right. Something else,—Beth—some one must get—paper—blue envelope—Hawk Ken——"

His words ended in a gasp and he sank back in her arms.

Beth was frightened at the sudden collapse and the look in his face, but she knew that his injunction was important. And keeping her courage she called Shad Wells to the side of the car and gave quick directions. There was a note of appeal in her voice and Shad listened, his gaze over his shoulder in the direction she indicated.

"If he ain't burned to a crisp by now——"

"Go, Shad—please! And if you can get to him bring the papers in his pocket to me."

He met her gaze and smiled.

"I reckon I'll get to him if anybody can."

"Oh, thanks, Shad—thanks——" she muttered, as the lumberman turned, followed by one of the others, and silently moved toward the flames.

And in a moment the car was on its way to Black Rock, Brierly driving carefully over the rough road. That was a terrible ride for Beth. She supported the wounded man against her shoulder, her gaze on his pallid face. Her poor blistered arm was about his waist, but she had no thought for her own suffering. Every ounce of strength that remained to her was given to holding Peter close to her so that he would not slip down, every ounce of faith in her soul given to combat with the fears that assailed her. It seemed to Beth that if the Faith that had brought her through this day and out of that furnace were still strong enough she could combat even the Death that rode with them. And so she prayed again, holding him closely. But he was so cold and inert. She put her hand over his heart and a tiny pulsation answered as though to reassure her. Her hand came away dry, for the wound was not near his heart. She thanked God for that. She found it high up on the right side just below the collar bone and held her fingers there, pressing them tightly. If this blood were life and she could keep it within him she would do it. But he was so pale....

Brierly drove to Black Rock House instinctively. Here were beds, servants and the telephone. He sounded his horn as they came up the driveway and an excited group came out upon the porch. But Beth saw only McGuire.

"Mr. Nichols has been shot, Mr. McGuire—he's dangerously hurt," she appealed. "He's got to have a doctor—at once."

"Who—who shot him?"

"Hawk Kennedy."

"And he—Hawk——?"

"He's dead, I think."

She heard McGuire's sudden gasp and saw Aunt Tillie come running.

"He's got to be put to bed—Aunt Tillie," she pleaded.

"Of course," said McGuire, finding his voice suddenly, "Of course—at once. The blue room, Mrs. Bergen. We'll carry him up. Send Stryker."

And Aunt Tillie ran indoors.

Peter was still quite unconscious, but between them they managed to get him upstairs.

McGuire seemed now galvanized into activity and while the others cut Peter's coat away and found the wound he got Hammonton and a doctor on the 'phone. It was twelve miles away but he promised to be at Black Rock House inside half an hour.

"Twenty minutes and you won't regret it. Drive like Hell. It's a matter of life or death."

Meanwhile, Aunt Tillie, with anxious glances at Beth, had brought absorbent cotton, clean linen, a basin of water and a sponge, and Stryker and Brierly washed the wound, while McGuire rushed for his bottle and managed to force some whisky and water between Peter's teeth. The bullet they found had gone through the body and had come out at the back, shattering the shoulder-blade. But the hemorrhage had almost ceased and the wounded man's heart was still beating faintly.

"It's the blood he's lost," muttered Brierly sagely.

"He'll come around all right. You can't kill a man as game as that."

Beth clung to the arms of the chair in which they had placed her. "You think—he—he'll live?"

"Sure he will. I've seen 'em worse'n that——"

She sank back into her chair, exhausted. She had never fainted in her life and she wasn't going to begin. But now that all that they could do had been done for Peter, they turned their attention to Beth. She had not known how much she needed it. Her hair was singed, her wrists were raw and bleeding, and her arms, half naked, were red and blistered. Her dress, soaked with mud and water, was partly torn or burned away.

"She must be put to bed here, Mrs. Bergen," said McGuire. "She'll need the doctor too."

Beth protested and would not leave the room until the doctor came. But McGuire, who seemed—and somewhat justly—to have complete faith in the efficacy of his own remedy, gave her some of the whisky and water to drink, while Aunt Tillie washed her face and rubbed vaseline upon her arms, crooning over her all the while in the comforting way of women of her kind, to the end that Beth felt the pain of her body lessen.

It was not until the doctor arrived with a businesslike air and made his examination, pronouncing Peter's condition serious but not necessarily fatal, that the tension at Beth's heart relaxed.

"He—he'll get well, Doctor?" she asked timidly.

"I think so," he said with a smile, "but we've got to have absolute quiet now. I'd like some one here to help me——"

"If you'd only let me——"

But she read refusal in his eyes as he looked at her critically, and saw him choose Stryker.

"You're to be put to bed at once," he said dryly. "You'll need attention too, I'm thinking."

And so Beth, with McGuire's arm supporting and Aunt Tillie's arm around her, was led to the room adjoining,—the pink room of Miss Peggy McGuire. McGuire closed the door and questioned her eagerly.

"You say Hawk Kennedy was killed——?"

"I think so—or—or burned," said Beth, now quivering in the reaction of all that she had experienced. "I—I sent Shad Wells to see. We left him lying there. We just had time to get away. The fire was all around. We got to the swamp—into the water—but he——" She put her face into her hands, trembling with the recollection. "It was horrible. I can't talk about it."

Aunt Tillie glared at McGuire, but he still questioned uneasily.

"You—you saw nothing of a blue envelope, a paper——"

With an effort Beth lowered her hands and replied:

"No—Peter—Mr. Nichols thought of it. Shad Wells will bring it—if it isn't burned."

"Oh, I see——"

"But what you can't see," broke in Aunt Tillie with spirit, "is that the poor child ain't fit to answer any more questions to-night. And she shan't."

"Er—no—of course," said McGuire, and went out.

If it had been an eventful day for Peter and Beth, the night was to prove eventful for McGuire, for not content to wait the arrival of Shad Wells, he took his courage in his hands and with Brierly drove at once to the scene of the disaster. The wind had died and a gentle rain began to fall, but the fire was burning fiercely.

The other matter in McGuire's thoughts was so much the more important to him that he had given little thought to the damage to his property. His forests might all be burned down for all that he cared.

At the spot to which Beth and Peter had been carried he met Shad and the party of men that had been looking for Hawk Kennedy, but the place where the fight had taken place was still a mass of fallen trees and branches all flaming hotly and it was impossible for any one to get within several hundred yards of it.

There seemed little doubt as to the fate of his enemy. Jonathan K. McGuire stood at the edge of the burned area, peering into the glowing embers. His look was grim but there was no smile of triumph at his lips. In his moments of madness he had often wished Hawk Kennedy dead, but never had he wished him such a death as this. He questioned Shad sharply as to his share in the adventure, satisfying himself at last that the man had told a true story, and then, noting his wounded arm, sent him back with Brierly in the car to Black Rock House for medical treatment with orders to send the chauffeur with the limousine.

The rain was now falling fast, but Jonathan K. McGuire did not seem to be aware of it. His gaze was on the forest, on that of the burning area nearest him where the fire still flamed the hottest, beneath the embers of which lay the one dreadful secret of his life. Even where he stood the heat was intense, but he did not seem to be aware of it, nor did he follow the others when they retreated to a more comfortable spot. No one knew why he waited or of what he was thinking, unless of the damage to the Reserve and what the loss in money meant to him. They could not guess that pity and fear waged their war in his heart—pity that any man should die such a death—fear that the man he thought of should not die it.

But as the hours lengthened and there was no report brought to him of any injured man, being found in the forest near by, he seemed to know that Peter Nichols had not struck for Beth in vain.

When the limousine came, he sent the other watchers home, and got into it, sitting in solitary grandeur in his wet clothing, peering out of the window. The glow of the flames grew dimmer and died at last with the first pale light to the eastward which announced the coming of the dawn. A light drizzle was still falling when it grew light enough to see. McGuire got down and without awakening the sleeping chauffeur went forth into the spectral woods. He knew where the old tool cabin had stood and, from the description Wells had given him, had gained a general idea of where the fight had taken place— two hundred yards from the edge of the swamp where Nichols and the Cameron girl had been found, and nearly in a line with the biggest of the swamp-maples, the trunk of which still stood, a melancholy skeleton of its former grandeur.

The ground was still hot under the mud and cinders, but not painfully so, and he was not aware of any discomfort. Clouds of steam rose and among them he moved like the ghost of a sin, bent, eager, searching with heavy eyes for what he hoped and what he feared to find. The old tool house had disappeared, but he saw a heap of ashes and among them the shapes of saws and iron picks and shovels. But he passed them by, making a straight line to the eastward and keeping his gaze upon the charred and blackened earth, missing nothing to right and left, fallen branches, heaps of rubbish, mounds of earth.

Suddenly startled, McGuire halted and stood for a long moment.... Then, his hand before his eyes he turned away and slowly made his way back to his automobile. But there was no triumph in his eyes. A power greater than his own had avenged Ben Cameron.

His vigil was over—his nightly vigil—the vigil of years. He made his way to his car and, awakening his chauffeur, told him to drive to Black Rock House. But when he reached home, the set look that his face had worn for so many weeks had disappeared. And in its place among the relaxed muscles which showed his years, sat the benignity of a new resolution.

It was broad daylight when he quietly knocked at the door of the room in which the injured man lay. The doctor came to the door. It seemed that all immediate danger of a further collapse had passed for the heart was stronger and unless there was a setback Peter Nichols had an excellent chance of recovery. McGuire himself offered to watch beside the bed; but the doctor explained that a trained nurse was already on the way from Philadelphia and would arrive at any moment. So McGuire went to his own room and, sinking into his armchair, slept for the first time in many weeks at peace, smiling his benignant smile.

Beth awoke in the pink room of Miss Peggy McGuire in which she had been put to bed. She lay for a moment still stupefied, her brain struggling against the effects of the sleeping potion that the doctor had given her and then slowly straightened to a sitting posture, regarding in bewilderment the embroidered night-robe which she wore and the flowered pink hangings at the windows. She couldn't at first understand the pain at her head and other aches and pains which seemed to come mysteriously into being. But she heard a familiar voice at her ear and saw the anxious face of Aunt Tillie, who rose from the chair at her bedside.

"Aunt Tillie!" she whispered.

"It's all right, dearie," said the old woman. "You're to lie quite still until the doctor sees you———"

"The doctor———? Oh, I—I remember———" And then with a sudden awakening to full consciousness—"Peter!" she gasped.

"He's better, dearie."

"But what does the doctor say?"

"He's doin' as well as possible———"

"Will he get well?"

"Yes, yes. The doctor is very hopeful."

"You're sure?"

"Yes. He's sleepin' now—quiet—ye'd better just lie back again."

"But I want to go to him, Aunt Tillie. I want to."

"No. Ye can't, dearie—not now."

And so by dint of reassurance and persuasion, Aunt Tillie prevailed upon the girl to lie back upon her pillows and after a while she slept again.

But Beth was no weakling and when the doctor came into her room some time later, the effects of her potion wearing away, she awoke to full consciousness. He saw the imploring question in her eyes, before he took her pulse and answered it with a quick smile.

"He's all right. Heart coming on nicely——"

"Will h-he live?" she gasped.

"He'll be a fool if he doesn't."

"What——?"

"I'd be, if I knew there was a girl like you in the next room with that kind of look in her eyes asking for me."

But his remark went over Beth's head.

"He's better?"

"Yes. Conscious too. But he'll have to be kept quiet."

"D-did he speak of me?"

The doctor was taking her pulse and put on a professional air which hid his inward smiles and provoked a repetition of her question.

"D-did he?" she repeated softly.

"Oh, yes," he said with a laugh. "He won't talk of anything else. I had to give him a hypodermic to make him stop."

Beth was silent for a moment. And then timidly——

"What did he say?"

"Oh, just that you saved his life, that's all."

"Nothing else?"

"Oh, yes. Now that I come to think of it, he did."

"What?"

"That he wanted to see you."

"Oh! And can I——?"

The doctor snapped his watch and relinquished her wrist with a smile.

"If everything goes well—to-morrow—for two minutes—just two minutes, you understand."

"Not until to-morrow?" she asked ruefully.

"You ought to be glad to see him alive at all. He had a narrow shave of it. An inch or two lower——" And then with a smile, "But he's going to get well, I promise you that."

"Oh, thanks," said Beth gratefully.

"Don't worry. And if you behave yourself I'll let you get up after lunch." He gave some directions to Mrs. Bergen as to the treatment of Beth's blistered arms, and went out.

So in spite of the pain that she still suffered, Beth was content. At least she was content until Aunt Tillie brought her Miss Peggy McGuire's silver hand-mirror and she saw the reflection of her once beautiful self.

"Aunt Tillie!" she gasped. "I'm a sight."

"Maybe—but that's a sight better than bein' burned to death," said the old lady, soberly.

"My hair——!"

"It's only frizzled. They say that's good for the hair," she said cheerfully.

"Oh, well," sighed Beth as she laid the mirror down beside her. "I guess I ought to be glad I'm alive after——"

And then with an uncontrollable shudder, she asked, "And—and—*him?*"

"Dead," said Aunt Tillie with unction. "Burned to a crisp."

Beth gasped but said nothing more. She didn't want to think of yesterday, but she couldn't help it—the horrors that she had passed through—the fate that might have been in store for her, if—Peter hadn't found her in time!

Beth relaxed in comfort while Aunt Tillie bathed and anointed her, brushed out the hair that was "frizzled," refreshing and restoring her patient, so that after lunch she got up and put on the clothing that had been brought from her home. Her arms were swathed in bandages from wrists to shoulders but the pain was much less, so, when McGuire knocked at the door and asked if he might see her, she was sitting in a chair by the window and greeted him with a smile.

He entered timidly and awkwardly, rubbing his fingers uncomfortably against the palms of his hands.

"They tell me you're feelin' better, Miss Cameron," he said soberly. "I—I'd like to talk to you for a moment," and with a glance at Aunt Tillie, "alone if you don't mind."

Aunt Tillie gathered up some bandages and grudgingly departed.

McGuire came forward slowly and sank into a chair beside Beth's, laying his hand timidly on hers.

"I thank God nothing happened to you, child, and I hope you believe me when I say it," he began in an uncertain voice.

"Oh, yes, sir, I do."

"Because the only thing that matters to me now is setting myself straight with you and Mr. Nichols."

He paused in a difficulty of speech and then went on.

"He—Mr. Nichols has told you everything———?"

Beth wagged her head like a solemn child and then laid her other hand on his.

"Oh, I'm so sorry for you," she said.

"You mustn't say that," he muttered. "I—I've done you a great wrong—not trying to find out about Ben Cameron—not trying to find *you*. But I've suffered for it, Miss———" And then eagerly———"You don't mind my calling you Beth, do you?"

"No, Mr. McGuire."

"I ought to have told what happened. I ought to have tried to find out if Ben Cameron had any kin. I did wrong. But I've paid for it. I've never had a happy hour since I claimed that mine that didn't belong to me. I've made a lot of money but what I did has been hanging over me for years making an old man of me before my time———"

"Oh, please don't be unhappy any more———"

"Let me talk Miss—Beth. I've got to tell you. It'll make me feel a lot easier." Beth smoothed his hand reassuringly and he clasped hers eagerly as though in gratitude. "I never was much good when I was a lad, Beth, and I never could get along even after I got married. It wasn't in me somehow. I was pretty straight as young fellows go but nothing went right for me. I was a failure. And then———"

He paused a moment with bent head but Beth didn't speak. It was all very painful to her.

"Hawk Kennedy killed your father. But I was a crook too. I left Hawk there without water to die. It was a horrible thing to do—even after what he'd done to me. My God! Maybe I didn't suffer for that! I was glad when I learned Hawk didn't die, even though I knew from that time that he'd be hanging over me like a curse. He did for years and years. I knew he'd turn up some day, I tried to forget, but I couldn't. The sight of him was always with me."

"How terrible!" whispered Beth.

"But from that moment everything I did went well. Money came fast. I wasn't a bad business man, but even a bad business man could have put *that* deal through. I sold out the mine. I've got the figures and I'm going to show them to you, because they're yours to see. With the money I made some good investments. That money made more money and more besides. Making money got to be my passion. It was the only thing I cared for—except my girls—and it was the only thing that made me forget."

"Please don't think you've got to tell me any more."

"Yes, I want to. I don't know how much I'm worth to-day." And then in a confidential whisper—"I couldn't tell within half a million or so, but I guess it ain't far short of ten millions, Beth. You're the only person in the world outside the Treasury Department that knows how much I'm worth. I'm telling you. I've never told anybody—not even Peggy. And the reason I'm telling you is because, you've got to know, because I can't sleep sound yet, until I straighten this thing out with you. It didn't take much persuading for Mr. Nichols to show me what I had to do when he'd found out, because everything I've got comes from money I took from you. And I'm going to give you what belongs to you, the full amount I got for that mine with interest to date. It's not mine. It's yours and you're a rich girl, Beth——"

"I won't know what to do with all that money, Mr. McGuire," said Beth in an awed voice.

"Oh, yes, you will. I've been thinking it all out. It's a deed by gift. We'll have to have a consideration to make it binding. We may have to put in the facts that I've been—er—only a sort of trustee of the proceeds of the 'Tarantula' mine. I've got a good lawyer. He'll know what to do—how to fix it."

"I—I'm sure I'm very grateful."

"You needn't be." He paused and laid his hand over hers again. "But if it's all the same to you, I'd rather not have much talk about it—just what's said in the deed—to explain."

"I'll say nothin' you don't want said."

"I knew you wouldn't. Until the papers are drawn I'd rather you wouldn't speak of it."

"I won't."

"You're a good girl. I—I'd like to see you happy. If money will make you happy, I'm glad I can help."

"You've been very kind, Mr. McGuire—and generous. I can't seem to think about all that money. It's just like a fairy tale."

"And you forgive me—for what I did——? You forgive me, Beth?"

"Yes, I do, Mr. McGuire. Don't say anythin' more about it—please!"

The old man bent his head and kissed her hand and then with a great sigh of relief straightened and rose.

"Thank God!" he said quietly. And bidding her good-by he walked from the room.

CHAPTER XXIII
A VISITOR

The two minutes permitted by the doctor had come and gone. There had been much to say with too little time to say it in. For Beth, admonished that the patient must be kept quiet, and torn between joy at Peter's promised recovery and pity for his pale face, could only look at him and murmur soothing phrases, while Peter merely smiled and held her hand. But that, it seemed, was enough, for Beth read in his eyes that what had happened had merely set an enduring seal upon the affection of both of them.

With the promise that she could see him again on the morrow, Beth went back to her room. She had wanted to return to the village, but McGuire had insisted upon her staying where she was under the care of the doctor until what they were pleased to call the shock to her system had yielded to medical treatment. Beth said nothing. She was already herself and quite able to take up her life just where she had left it, but she agreed to stay in McGuire's house. It seemed to make him happier when she acquiesced in his wishes. Besides, it was nice to be waited on and to be next to the room where the convalescent was.

But the revelation as to Peter's identity could not be long delayed. Brierly had brought the tale back from the lumber camp, and the village was all agog with excitement. But Beth had seen no one but Mr. McGuire and Aunt Tillie, and Peter had requested that no one should tell her but himself. And so in a day or so when Beth went into Peter's room she found him with a color in his cheeks, and wearing a quizzical smile.

"I thought you were never coming, Beth," he said.

"I came as soon as they'd let me, Peter. Do you feel stronger?"

"Every hour. Better when you're here. And you?"

"Oh, I'm all right."

He looked at her with his head on one side.

"Do you think you could stand hearing something very terrible about me, Beth?"

She glanced at him anxiously and then a smile of perfect faith responded to his. She knew that he was getting well now, because this was a touch of his old humor.

"H-m. I guess so. I don't believe it can be so *very* terrible, Peter."

"It is—*very* terrible, Beth."

But the pressure of his fingers was reassuring.

"I'm listenin'," she said.

"Well, you know, you told me once that you'd marry me no matter what I'd been——"

"Yes. I meant that, Peter. I mean it now. It's what you are——"

Peter Nichols chuckled. It was his last chuckle as Peter Nichols.

"Well, I'm not what you thought I was. I've been acting under false colors— under false pretenses. My name isn't Peter Nichols. It's Peter Nicholaevitch——"

"Then you *are* all Russian!" she said.

Peter shook his head.

"No. Only half of me. But I used to live in Russia—at a place called Zukovo. The thing I wanted to tell you was that they fired me out because they didn't want me there."

"You! How dared they! I'd like to give them a piece of my mind," said Beth indignantly.

"It wouldn't have done any good. I tried to do that."

"And wouldn't they listen?"

"No. They burned my—my house and tried to shoot me."

"Oh! How could they!" And then, gently, "Oh, Peter. You *have* had troubles, haven't you?"

"I don't mind. If I hadn't had them, I wouldn't have come here and I wouldn't have found you."

"So after all, I ought to be glad they did fire you out," she said gently.

"But aren't you curious to know *why* they did?"

"I am, if you want to tell me, but even if it was bad, I don't care *what* you did, Peter."

He took her fingers to his lips.

"It wasn't so very bad after all, Beth. It wasn't so much what I did as what my—er—my family had done that made them angry."

"Well, *you* weren't responsible for what your kin-folks did."

Peter laughed softly.

"*They* seemed to think so. My—er—my kin-folks were mixed up in politics in Russia and one of my cousins had a pretty big job—too big a job for *him* and that's the truth." A cloud passed for a moment over Peter's face and he looked away.

"But what did *his* job have to do with *you?*" she asked.

"Well, you see, we were all mixed up with him, just by being related—at least that's what the people thought. And so when my cousin did a lot of things the people thought he oughtn't to do and didn't do a lot of other things that they thought he *ought* to have done, they believed that I was just the same sort of man that he was."

"How unjust, Peter!"

He smiled at the ceiling.

"I thought so. I told them what I thought. I did what I could to straighten things out and to help them, but they wouldn't listen. Instead they burned my—my house down and I had to run away."

"How terrible for you!" And then, after a pause, "Was it a pretty house, Peter?"

"Yes," he replied slowly, "it was. A very pretty house—in the midst of a forest, with great pines all about it. I wish they hadn't burned that house, Beth, because I loved it."

"Poor dear! I'm *so* sorry."

"I thought you would be, because it was a big house, with pictures, books, music——"

"All burned! Land's sakes alive!"

"And a wonderful grand piano."

"Oh, Peter!" And then with a flash of joy, "But you're goin' to have another grand piano just like it soon."

"Am I? Who's going to give it to me?"

"*I* am," said Beth quietly. "And another house and pictures and books and music."

He read her expression eagerly.

"Mr. McGuire has told you?" he asked.

She nodded. "You knew?"

"Yes," he replied. "He told me yesterday."

"Isn't it wonderful?" she whispered. And then went on rapidly, "So you see, Peter, maybe I can be some good to you after all."

He pressed her fingers, enjoying her happiness.

"I can hardly believe it's true," she gasped, "but it must be, because Mr. McGuire had his lawyer here yesterday talkin' about it——"

"Yes. It's true. I think he's pretty happy to get all that off his conscience. You're a rich girl, Beth." And then, with a slow smile, "That was one of the reasons why I wanted to talk with you about who *I* was. You see, I thought that now that you're going to have all this money, you might want to change your mind about marrying a forester chap who—who just wants to try to show the trees how to grow."

"Peter! Don't make fun of me. *Please.* And you hurt me so!" she reproached him. "You know I'll never want to change my mind ever, *ever*—even if I had all the money in the world."

He laughed, drew her face down to his and whispered, "Beth, dear. I knew you wouldn't want to—but I just wanted to hear you say it."

"Well, I *have* said it. And I don't want you ever to say such a thing again. As if I cared for anythin'—anythin' but *you*."

He kissed her on the lips and she straightened.

"I wanted to hear you say *that* too," he said with a laugh.

And then, after a silence which they both improved by gazing at each other mutely, "But you don't seem very curious about who I am."

Beth pressed his fingers confidently. What he was to *her* mattered a great deal—and she realized that nothing else did. But she knew that something was required of her. And so, "Oh, yes. Indeed I am, Peter,—awfully curious," she said politely.

"Well, you know, Beth, I'm not really so poor as I seem to be. I've got a lot of securities in a bank in Russia, because nobody knew where they were and so they couldn't take them."

"And they would have taken your money too?"

"Yes. When this cousin of mine—his name was Nicholas—when Nicholas was killed——"

"They killed him! Who?"

"The Bolsheviki—they killed Nicholas and his whole family—his wife, son and four daughters———"

"Peter!" Beth started up and stared at him in startled bewilderment, as she remembered the talks she had had with him about the Russian Revolution. "Nicholas———!" she gasped. "His wife—son—daughters. He had the same name as—as the Czar—!" And as her gaze met his again she seemed to guess.... "Peter!" she gasped. "What—what do you mean?"

"I mean that it was the Little Father—the Czar—who was my cousin, Beth."

She stared at Peter in awe and a kind of fear of this new element in their relations.

"And—and you———? You're———?"

"I'm just Peter Nichols———," he said with a laugh.

"But over there———"

"I'm nothing. They chucked us all out, the Bolsheviki—every last one of us that had a handle to his name."

"A handle———?"

"Yes. I used to be Grand Duke Peter Nicholaevitch of Zukovo and Galitzin———"

"G-Grand Duke Peter!" she whispered in a daze. And then, "Oh—how—how *could* you?" she gasped.

Peter laughed.

"I couldn't help it, Beth. I was born that—way. But you *will* forgive me, won't you?"

"Forgive———? Oh—it—it makes such a difference to find—you're not *you*—but somebody else———"

"No. I *am*—*me*. I'm not anybody else. But I had to tell you—sometime. You don't think any the less of me, do you, Beth?"

"I—I don't know *what* to think. I'm so—you're so———"

"What?"

"Grand—and I'm———"

Peter caught her hands and made her look at him.

"You're the only woman in the world I've ever wanted—the only one—and you've promised me you'd marry me—you've promised, Beth."

Her fingers moved gently in his and her gaze, wide-eyed, sought his.

"And it won't make any difference——?"

"No, Beth. Why should you think that?"

"I—I was afraid—it might," she gasped. And then for a while Peter held her hands, whispering, while Beth, still abashed, answered in monosyllables, nodding from time to time.

Later the nurse entered, her glance on her wrist-watch.

"Time's up," she said. And Beth rose as one in a dream and moved slowly around the foot of the bed to the door.

Jonathan K. McGuire had been as much astonished as Beth at the revelation of Peter's identity, and the service that Peter had rendered him made him more than anxious to show his appreciation by doing everything he could for the wounded man's comfort and happiness. He visited the bedside daily and told Peter of his conversation with Beth, and of the plans that he was making for her future—which now, it seemed, was Peter's future also. Peter told him something of his own history and how he had met Jim Coast on the *Bermudian*. Then McGuire related the story of the suppression of the outbreak at the lumber camp by the Sheriff and men from May's Landing, and the arrest of Flynn and Jacobi on charges of assault and incendiarism. Some of the men were to be deported as dangerous "Reds." Brierly had been temporarily put in charge at the Mills and Jesse Brown, now much chastened, was helping McGuire to restore order. Shad Wells was technically under arrest, for the coroner had "viewed" the body of the Russian Committeeman before it had been removed by his friends and buried, and taken the testimony. But McGuire had given bail and arranged for a hearing both as to the shooting of and the death of Hawk Kennedy, when Peter was well enough to go to May's Landing.

The death of Hawk had produced a remarkable change in the character and personality of the owner of the Black Rock Reserve. His back was straighter, his look more direct, and he entered with avidity into the business of bringing order out of the chaos that had resulted from the riot. His word carried some weight, his money more, and with the completion of his arrangements with Beth Cameron, he drew again the breath of a free man.

But of all this he had said nothing to Peggy, his daughter. He had neither written to her nor telephoned, for he had no desire that she should know more than the obvious facts as to the death of Hawk Kennedy, for conflicting reports would lead to questions. Since she had suspected nothing, it was needless to bring that horror to her notice, now that the threat had passed.

McGuire was a little afraid of his colorful daughter. She talked too much and it had been decided that nobody, except the lawyer, Peter, Beth and Mrs. Bergen should know the source of Beth's sudden and unexpected inheritance. The girl had merely fallen heir to the estate of her father, who had died many years before, not leaving any record of this daughter, who had at last been found. All of which was the truth, so far as it went, and was enough of a story to tell Peggy when he should see her.

But Jonathan McGuire found himself somewhat disturbed when he learned one morning over the telephone that Peggy McGuire and a guest were on their way to Black Rock House for the week-end. The message came from the clerk of the hotel, and since Peggy and her friend had already started from New York, he knew of no way to intercept them. There was nothing to do but make the best of the situation. Peter had the best guest room, but Beth had decided the day before to return to the cottage, which was greatly in need of her attention. And so McGuire informed Mrs. Bergen of the impending visit and gave orders that Miss Peggy's room and a room in the wing should be prepared for the newcomers.

Beth had no wish to meet Peggy McGuire in this house after the scene with Peter in the Cabin, when the young lady had last visited Black Rock, for that encounter had given Beth glimpses of the kind of thoughts beneath the pretty toques and *cerise* veils that had once been the apple of her admiring eyes. But as luck would have it, as Beth finished her afternoon's visit to Peter's bedside and hurried down to get away to the village before the visitors arrived, Miss Peggy's low runabout roared up to the portico. Beth's first impulse was to draw back and go out through the kitchen, but the glances of the two girls met, Peggy's in instant recognition. And so Beth tilted her chin and walked down the steps just beside the machine, aware of an elegantly attired lady with a doll-like prettiness who sat beside Peggy, oblivious of the sharp invisible daggers which shot from eye to eye.

"*You* here!" said Peggy, with an insulting shrug.

Beth merely went her way. But no feminine adept of the art of give and take could have showed a more perfect example of studied indifference than Beth did. It was quite true that her cheeks burned as she went down the drive and that she wished that Peter were well out of the house so long as Peggy was in it.

But Peggy McGuire could know nothing of Beth's feelings and cared not at all what she thought or felt. Peggy McGuire was too much concerned with the importance of the visitor that she had brought with her, the first live princess that she had succeeded in bringing into captivity. But Anastasie Galitzin had not missed the little by-play and inquired with some amusement as to the very pretty girl who had come out of the house.

"Oh—the housekeeper's niece," replied Peggy, in her boarding school French. "I don't like her. I thought she'd gone. She's been having a *petite affaire* with our new forester and superintendent."

Anastasie Galitzin, who was in the act of descending from the machine, remained poised for a moment, as it were, in midair, staring at her hostess.

"Ah!" she said. "*Vraiment!*"

By this time the noise of the motor had brought Stryker and the downstairs maid from the house, and in the confusion of carrying the luggage indoors, the conversation terminated. It was not until Peggy's noisy greetings to her father in the hallway were concluded and the introduction of her new guest accomplished that Jonathan McGuire was permitted to tell her in a few words the history of the past week, and of the injury to the superintendent, who lay upstairs in the room of the guest of honor.

"H-m," sniffed Peggy, "I don't see why you had to bring him *here!*"

"It's a long story, Peg," said McGuire calmly. "I'll tell you presently. Of course the Princess is very welcome, but I couldn't let him be taken anywhere but here, after he'd behaved so fine all through the rioting."

"Well, it seems to me," Peggy began, when the voice of her guest cut in rather sharply.

"*Pierre!*" gasped Anastasie sharply, and then, in her pretty broken English, "You say, Monsieur, it is he—Pe-ter Nichols—who 'as been badly 'urt?"

"Yes, ma'am, pretty bad—shot through the breast——"

"*Sainte Vierge!*"

"But he's getting on all right now. He'll be sitting up in a day or so, the doctor says. Did you know him, ma'am?"

Anastasie Galitzin made no reply, and only stared at her host, breathing with some difficulty. Peggy, who had been watching her startled face, found herself intensely curious. But as she would have questioned, the Princess recovered herself with an effort.

"No—yes, Monsieur. It—it is nothing. But if you please—I should like to go at once to my room."

And Peggy and her father, both of them much mystified, led the way up the stairs and to the room that had been prepared in the wing of the house, Stryker following with the bag and dressing case.

At the door of the room the Princess begged Peggy to excuse her, pleading weariness, and so the astonished and curious hostess was forced to relinquish her latest social conquest and seek her own room, there to meditate upon the extraordinary thing that had happened. Why was Anastasie Galitzin so perturbed at learning of the wounds of Peter Nichols? What did it all mean? Had she known him somewhere in the past—in England—in Russia? What was he to her?

But in a moment Jonathan McGuire joined her and revealed the identity of his mysterious forester and superintendent. At first Peggy was incredulous, then listened while her father told a story, half true, half fictitious, which had been carefully planned to answer all the requirements of the situation. And unaware of the cyclonic disturbances he was causing in the breast of his only child, he told her of Beth and Peter, and of the evidences of their devotion each to the other in spite of their difference in station. Peggy's small soul squirmed during the recital, but she only listened and said nothing. She realized that in a situation such as this mere words on her part would be superfluous. The Grand Duke Peter Nicholaevitch! Here at Black Rock! Her pop's superintendent! And she had not known. She had even insulted him. It was hideous!

And the Princess? The deep emotion that she had shown on hearing of the dangerous wound of the convalescent was now explained. But only partly so. The look that Peggy had surprised in Anastasie Galitzin's face meant something more than mere solicitude for the safety of one of Russia's banished Grand Dukes. It was the Princess who had been shocked at the information, but it was the woman who had showed pain. Was there—had there ever been—anything between Anastasie Galitzin and this—this Peter Nichols?

Facts about the early stages of her acquaintanceship with Anastasie Galitzin now loomed up with an unpleasant definiteness. She had been much flattered that so important a personage had shown her such distinguished marks of favor and had rejoiced in the celerity with which the intimacy had been established. The thought that the Princess Galitzin had known all the while that the Grand Duke was living incognito at Black Rock and had merely used Peggy as a means to bring about this visit was not a pleasant one to Peggy. But the fact was now quite obvious. She had been making a convenience of her. And what was now to be the result of this visit? The Princess did not yet know of the engagement of His Highness to the scullery maid. Who was to tell her?

The snobbish little heart of Peggy McGuire later gained some consolation, for Anastasie Galitzin emerged from her room refreshed and invigorated, and lent much grace to the dinner table, telling father and daughter something of the early life of the convalescent, exhibiting a warm friendship which could be satisfied with nothing less than a visit on the morrow to the sick-room. And His Highness now very much on the mend, sent word, with the doctor's permission, that he would be charmed to receive the Princess Galitzin at ten in the morning.

What happened in the room of the convalescent was never related to Peggy McGuire. But Anastasie emerged with her head erect, her pretty face wearing the fixed smile of the eternally bored. And then she told Peggy that she had decided to return to New York. So after packing her belongings, she got into Peggy's car and was driven much against the will of her hostess to the Bergen cottage. Peggy wouldn't get out of the car but Anastasie went to the door and knocked. Beth came out with her sleeves rolled above her elbows, her fingers covered with flour. The Princess Galitzin vanished inside and the door was closed. Her call lasted ten minutes while Peggy cooled her heels. But whether the visit had been prompted by goodness of heart or whether by a curiosity to study the lady of Peter's choice at close range, no one will ever know. Beth was very polite to her and though she identified her without difficulty as the heliotrope-envelope lady, she offered her some of the "cookies" that she had made for Peter, and expressed the warmest thanks for her kind wishes. She saw Anastasie Galitzin to the door, marking her heightened color and wondering what her fur coat had cost. Beth couldn't help thinking, whatever her motive in coming, that the Princess Galitzin was a very beautiful lady and that her manners had been lovely. But it was with a sigh of relief that she saw the red car vanish down the road in a cloud of dust.

His convalescence begun, Peter recovered rapidly and in three weeks more he was himself again. In those three weeks many interesting things had happened.

Jonathan K. McGuire had held a series of important conferences with Peter and Mrs. Bergen who seemed to have grown ten years younger. And one fine day after a protracted visit to New York with Mrs. Bergen, he returned laden with mysterious packages and boxes, and stopped at the door of the cottage, where Peter was taking a lunch of Beth's cooking.

It was a beautiful surprise. Mrs. Bergen whispered in Beth's ear and Beth followed her into the kitchen, where the contents of one or two of the boxes were exposed to Beth's astonished gaze. Peter, of course, being in the secret, kept aloof, awaiting the result of Mrs. Bergen's disclosures. But when Beth came back into the plush-covered parlor, he revealed his share in the conspiracy by producing, with the skill of a conjurer taking a rabbit from a silk hat, a minister and a marriage license, the former having been hidden in the house of a neighbor. And Jonathan K. McGuire, with something of an air, fully justified by the difficulties he had been at to secure it, produced a pasteboard box, which contained another box of beautiful white velvet, which he opened with pride, exhibiting its contents. On the soft satin lining was a brooch, containing a ruby as large as Beth's thumbnail.

With a gasp of joy, she gazed at it, for she knew just what it was, the family jewel that had been sold to the purser of the *Bermudian*. And then she threw her arms around McGuire's neck and kissed him.

Some weeks later Beth and Peter sat at dusk in the drawing-room of Black Rock House, for McGuire had turned the whole place over to them for the honeymoon. The night was chilly, a few flakes of snow had fallen during the afternoon, so a log fire burned in the fireplace. Peter sat at the piano playing the "Romance" of Sibelius, for which Beth had asked, but when it was finished, his fingers, impelled by a thought beyond his own control, began the opening rumble of the "Revolutionary Étude." The music was familiar to Beth and it stirred her always because it was this gorgeous plaint of hope and despair that had at the very first sounded depths in her own self the existence of which she had never even dreamed. But to-night Peter played it as she had never heard him play it before, with all his soul at his finger tips. And she watched his downcast profile as he stared at vacancy while he played. It was in moments like these that Beth felt herself groping in the dark after him, he was so far away. And yet she was not afraid, for she knew that out of the dreams and mysticism of the half of him that was Russian he would come back to her,—just Peter Nichols.

He did presently, when his hands fell upon the last chords and he sat with head still bowed until the last tremor had died. Then he rose and turned to her. She smiled at him and he joined her on the divan. Their fingers intertwined and they sat for a long moment looking into the fire. But Beth knew of what he was thinking and Peter knew that she knew. Their honeymoon was over. There was work to do in the world.

Milton Keynes UK
Ingram Content Group UK Ltd.
UKHW040831071024
449371UK00007B/732